W9-ADN-792

WITHDRAWN

Studies in English and American Literature,
Linguistics, and Culture:
Literary Criticism in Perspective

Studies in English and American Literature, Linguistics,
and Culture

Edited by
Benjamin Franklin V
(*South Carolina*)

Editorial Board

Literary Criticism in Perspective

James Hardin (*South Carolina*), General Editor

Benjamin Franklin V (*South Carolina*), American and
English Literature

Reingard M. Nischik (*Mainz*), Comparative Literature

About *Literary Criticism in Perspective*

Books in the series *Literary Criticism in Perspective,* a subseries of *Studies in German Literature, Linguistics, and Culture,* and *Studies in English and American Literature, Linguistics, and Culture,* trace literary scholarship and criticism on major and neglected writers alike, or on a single major work, a group of writers, a literary school or movement. In so doing the authors — authorities on the topic in question who are also well-versed in the principles and history of literary criticism — address a readership consisting of scholars, students of literature at the graduate and undergraduate level, and the general reader. One of the primary purposes of the series is to illuminate the nature of literary criticism itself, to gauge the influence of social and historic currents on aesthetic judgments once thought objective and normative.

A History of the Commentary on Selected Writings
of Samuel Johnson

Edward Tomarken

A HISTORY OF THE COMMENTARY ON SELECTED WRITINGS OF SAMUEL JOHNSON

CAMDEN HOUSE

Copyright © 1994 by
CAMDEN HOUSE, INC.

Published by Camden House, Inc.
Drawer 2025
Columbia, SC 29202 USA

Printed on acid-free paper.
Binding materials are chosen for strength and
durability.

ISBN:1-879751-94-1

Library of Congress Cataloging-in-Publication Data

Tomarken, Edward, 1938-
    A history of the commentary on selected writings of Samuel
    Johnson, 1738-1993 / Edward Tomarken.
              p.   cm.   -- (Studies in English and American literature.
    linguistics, and culture. Literary criticism in perspective)
              Includes bibliographical references and index.
              ISBN 1-879751-94-1 (alk. paper)
              1. Johnson, Samuel, 1709-1784--Criticism and interpretation-
    -History. I. Title. II. Series.
    PR3534.T659 1994
    828'.609--dc20
                                                                    94-1787
                                                                    CIP

Acknowledgments

I WISH TO THANK THE UNIVERSITY Press of Kentucky for allowing me to reprint portions of chapter 1 of my book, entitled *Johnson, 'Rasselas,' and the Choice of Criticism* (1989).

Ralph Cohen introduced me to Samuel Johnson's writings when I was an undergraduate: his influence, from a theory of genre to a belief in the importance of the history of criticism, is manifest throughout this study. Northrop Frye directed my graduate work on Johnson, and although my thesis was completed twenty-five years ago, I find that some of the entries in this bibliography were suggested by Frye, who characterized the Ph.D. reading list as, like the signs on wartime brandy bottles, "reinforced." Since the recent death of Northrop Frye, I have come to appreciate more deeply the tolerance of a great critic who valued love of literature over adherence to his own position.

At an early stage Michael Coyle and David Radcliffe read the entire manuscript. I wish to thank them for their constructive suggestions. At a somewhat later stage, the following scholars commented on various chapters of the book: John J. Burke, Jr., Robert Folkenflik, Gwin Kolb, Alan McKenzie, Lawrence Lipking, and Howard Weinbrot. Their prompt and helpful advice has been invaluable. I believe Johnson would have been pleased that this project about critical differences has also brought some critics together. My colleague David Mann volunteered to proofread the bibliography, a gesture typical of his kindness and helpfulness for the past two decades.

My research for this book was aided by two sabbaticals provided by the English department of Miami University and three grants, two summer research awards from the Miami University Research Committee and an American Society for Eighteenth-Century Studies grant to study at the William Andrews Clark Memorial Library in Los Angeles. I received valuable assistance from the librarians at both the U.C.L.A. and the Clark libraries, as well as at the British Library, the University of Kent at Canterbury Library, and particularly from William Wortman at the Miami University Library.

I had the good fortune to receive personal help from friends and family during the past twenty-five years of reading, writing, teaching and conversing about Samuel Johnson. Stephanie Wilds-Shea has continued to help our family under the most trying circumstances for herself and her family. Bernard and Monique Labbé have provided a tranquil seaside retreat, Le Moana, for writing. For twenty-eight years Pamela Porter has graciously put up with a foreigner in her house and garden and remained tolerant about scattered books and tree limbs. Martin and Elizabeth Porter have offered wonderful wine and food with suggestions for crossword puzzle solutions, while Christopher, James, and Anthony Porter have kept us amused and musically informed. Peter and Dana Tomarken welcomed me into their home during research trips to Los Angeles. Jason, Alexis, and Candace made gallant efforts to humanize a scholar. James Tomarken has patiently provided excellent medical advice. The dedication is an inadequate attempt to express my gratitude to my daughter for tolerating the physical clutter and mental distraction of an academic household and for caring enough to laugh at her parents. My greatest debt, as always, is to Annette Porter Tomarken, who has been at once the midwife to a Johnson book for the third time and a loving, nurturing, and caring wife.

Abbreviations

Boswell's *Life*: followed by volume and page number from *Boswell's Life of Johnson*, eds. George Birkbeck Hill and L. F. Powell. 6 vols. Oxford: Clarendon, 1934-64.

Dictionary: Samuel Johnson. *A Dictionary of the English Language*. 4th ed. 2 vols. London, 1773.

CH: followed by page number from *Johnson: The Critical Heritage*. ed. James T. Boulton. New York: Barnes and Noble, 1971.

For

Emma Sandford Tomarken

Preface

THIS STUDY IS A HISTORY of commentary on selected writings by Samuel Johnson dating from their first appearance to the present. Since this volume is one of the first in the *Literary Criticism in Perspective* series devoted to British authors, it seems appropriate to begin by asking why do we write histories of criticism? Because literary criticism is itself a genre, we shall better understand it and improve our critical comments by being familiar with previous commentary and earlier modes of approach. New interpretations cannot avoid using aspects of old ones, and innovative methods must to some extent combine elements of those from the past. But perhaps criticism is too vast and amorphous to be treated fruitfully as a genre. That is indeed a possibility, one that was palpable during the index-card phase of this project. The reader can judge this matter by deciding if this survey itself is adequately described in the *Conclusion*, where a generic approach forms the basis for a new kind of literary method that I call, borrowing a phrase from Ralph Cohen, a "New Humanism."

As an interpretive history not a chronicle, this study is necessarily selective. Some readers will expect to find a separate section devoted to the biographers of Johnson, particularly to James Boswell. Scholars and critics of the past thirty years have demonstrated that Johnson's writings are as important as his life and that they stand on their own apart from Johnson the man. Compelling evidence for valuing the writings in themselves is seen on almost every page of this study. Indeed, the controversy between Johnsonians and Boswellians is out of date: they pursue complementary subjects but toward different ends that warrant separate treatment. Limitations of space also prevent me from including those writings that are the subject of commentary that is not mainly literary critical in nature. Much important commentary has been written on Johnson as a prose stylist, political and economic polemicist, diarist and letter-writer. Most conspicuous by its absence is the *Dictionary*, which illustrates my principle of selection. Although a large amount of literary criticism has been devoted to the *Dictionary*, most of the commentary is technical, in this instance lexicographical. Inclusion of only those portions of the canon where the commentary is predominantly literary criticism is made in the recognition that much valuable material has unfortunately been excluded.

This book follows the chronology of the genres of Johnson's career employed by James Clifford and Donald Greene in their critical bibliography, *Samuel Johnson: A Survey and Bibliography of Critical Studies*, and by Donald Greene and John Vance in the updated version, *A Bibliography of Johnsonian Studies, 1970-1985*. It begins with the early biographies and concludes with *The Lives of the Poets*, written in the last four years of his life but representing a new and different kind of writing for him. My decision to proceed generically stems from my belief that a writer is best served by attending to his or her generic choices, that is, to the reasons why a work is presented by an author to the reader as an "imitation," a critical biography, an ode, or an oriental tale. It may turn out, as Johnson would remind us, that the writer has little choice in the matter and writes the kind of work that enables him or her to earn a living. Even granting that common occurrence, the conventions of genre convey privileges and constrictions to the writer and engender specific sorts of audience expectations.

Critics also make generic choices that may be different from those of the work subjected to their criticism. A biography may comment on Johnson's *Lives* without itself being a critical biography. Indeed, entire books have been written on Johnson's literary criticism although Johnson does not use the term in his own titles. Nevertheless, I believe that critics have as much right as other writers to their own decisions about genre. I give preference to Johnson's choices because it seems to me that an important initial task of criticism is to explain what Northrop Frye calls the writer's "radical of presentation," the choice of genre. My reasons for this position will be illustrated in the final remarks on the Shakespeare edition, *The Lives of the Poets*, and the Conclusion where neglect of precisely this matter is considered. But honoring Johnson's genres entails violating those of many of his commentators. Some will, I expect, be disappointed to find no section of this work devoted to Johnson's prose style or to his literary criticism, while others will look for topics like morality or religion that deliberately cross generic lines, to mention but a few of the possibilities. Instead of eliminating these valuable materials, I select portions from these kinds of works that are most pertinent to the topics of this study, bearing in mind that the generic categories are a means to my own interpretive goals.

Moreover, some of my remarks are methodological and theoretical in nature even though most Johnsonians steadfastly avoid this abstract realm. I point out in a number of sections that a price is paid for this evasion, and that in my view substantial progress will not be made until we face the theoretical implications of practical critical approaches.

Finally, the Works Cited section is chronologically arranged and contains only those works mentioned in the text.

Contents

1: The life of Savage and Other Early Biographies

AT THE BEGINNING OF HIS CAREER, Johnson wrote a number of brief biographies dating for the most part from 1738 to 1750. The majority of these narratives were printed in the *Gentleman's Magazine* or in Robert James's *Medicinal Dictionary* 1743-45. Since the Yale edition of these works has not yet appeared, the most readily available compendium is J. D. Fleeman's *Early Biographical Writings of Dr. Johnson* (1973). This volume contains thirty biographies, many of which when first published were unsigned but have since been attributed to Johnson by various scholars. For an account of the bibliographical history of each biography, see the Introduction to Fleeman's collection. The most famous of these early undertakings, the life of Savage (1744), is included, in a revised form, in the *Lives of the Poets*, 1779-1781, the familiar title for the work that was originally entitled *Prefaces Biographical and Critical to the Works of the English Poets*. The life of Savage has received far more critical commentary than the other early lives and will therefore be treated separately.

The Early Biographies Except for the life of Savage

The early biographies by Johnson remain neglected and unappreciated. Modern scholars have overcome the nineteenth-century prejudice against them as hack work, having demonstrated that they are full of valuable observations relating to Johnson's views of most topics, from religion to history. But as a genre in themselves they are still neglected, analyzed almost solely as precursors of the *Lives of the Poets*. One of the earliest reviews of these writings is by Samuel Palmer, who in 1775 makes reference to Johnson's life of Cheynel

(1751) in an edition of Edward Calamy's *The Nonconformist's Memorial; Being an Account of the Ministers Who Were Ejected or Silenced after the Restoration.* Palmer remarks that, given Johnson's religious principles, he is not surprised to find a "satyr both upon Dr. Cheynel and the times," but he recognizes that even if not without "blemishes," Cheynel is treated by Johnson as a "great character" (2, 467). The polemical nature of Johnsonian biography is taken for granted: the reader is left in no doubt about Johnson's approval or disapproval of his subject's behavior. But it is important to note that in the eighteenth century it was not assumed that a clear view of the subject of biography and of the historical events precluded fair-mindedness. However, not all of Johnson's contemporaries accept this position. In 1782 Vicesimus Knox faults Johnson as a biographer for offering an expression of his "spleen" instead of an "exact and authentic account of individuals" (2, 49-51).

During the eighteenth century, however, the fact that Johnson wrote polemical biographies for his livelihood did not mean that they could be dismissed as mere "hackwork." In 1787, Sir John Hawkins, in his *Life of Johnson*, explains the genesis of these lives:

> He had, so early as 1734, solicited employment of Cave; but Cave's correspondents were so numerous that he had little for him till the beginning of the year 1738, when Johnson conceived a thought of enriching the Magazine with a biographical article, and wrote for it the Life of Father Paul, an abridgment, as it seems to be, of that life of him which Johnson intended to have prefixed to his translation of the History of the Council of Trent. The motive to this and other exertions of the same talent in the lives of Boerhaave, Blake, Barretier, and other eminent persons, was his wants, which at one time were so pressing as to induce him in a letter to Cave ... to intimate to him that he wanted a dinner. (89)

The great respect for Johnson as a biographer in his own age is best expressed in the opening sentence of Boswell's *Life*: "To write the Life of him who excelled all mankind in writing the lives of others ... may be reckoned in me a presumptuous task" (1, 25).

During the nineteenth century, however, these early lives were neglected, presumably because as the products of necessity they were of little intrinsic import. Early in the twentieth century these materials began to be treated with more respect. In 1916, in a general study of English biography, Waldo Dunn credits Johnson with the "abolition of panegyric" (102). In the 1920s, Joseph Epes Brown and André Maurois reiterate Dunn's position and point out that manifest in these early lives are the principles that Johnson is later to spell out in *Rambler* 60 (1750) and *Idler* 84 (1759). In the 1930s after

Allen Hazen makes a case for attributing ten additional lives to Johnson in James's *Medical Dictionary*, some scholars examine these biograhies more carefully. Bergen Evans explains that Johnson gives more emphasis to the private and domestic than to the public and political without sacrificing the truth because for Johnson "truth is moral" (310). In 1935 Arthur Melville Clark notes that Johnson recommends autobiography because it is closer to the truth but would not have approved of Rousseau's *Confessions* because Johnson "wanted truth but not *all* the truth" (12). A year later Albert Britt declares that Johnson's lives are as much "landmarks" in biography as Shakespeare's plays are in drama (67). In 1943 Edward McAdam examines the sources for the lives of Sarpi, Blake, and Drake. He demonstrates that, while often relying heavily on a single predecessor, Johnson abbreviates some of the factual material in his sources in order to make room for "generalizations and interpretive comments" that distinguish these lives from the "ruck of journalism" and point toward the techniques of *The Lives of the Poets* (476). The discussion of the ethical aims of the early lives distances them from the stigma of hackwork, but the relationship between the truth and pleasurable elements is unclear.

In the next two decades Johnson's biographical art was treated with increasing respect and related to his religion, his sources, his contemporaries, and his theory of biography. Considering the prose style of the life of Browne, Mary and Philip Wagley suggest that Johnson is drawn to Browne's Christianity because it is based on "faith, hope and charity" and that Johnson is influenced in his own writing by Browne's "choice of words" (324-25). John Garraty asserts that Johnson is "surely the greatest figure in eighteenth-century biography" (84). John Abbott questions what he believes to be McAdam's assertion that Johnson's abbreviations of his source materials result in the distortion of history. Abbott maintains that, on the contrary, Johnson grasps the significance of his predecessors' position but uses it for his own moral and philosophical purposes. During this same period, however, John Butt calls into question the relationship between Johnson's theory and practice. The fundamental principles of Johnson's theory, according to Butt, are a strict adherence to the truth, as well as a preference for discriminating anecdotes and autobiographical or domestic facts. In practice, however, Butt finds that Johnson does not publish his own autobiographical writings, sometimes tells a tale "from sheer love of anecdote," and has a higher regard for truths that forward piety than for others. Butt concludes that what Johnson "said" is more impressive than what he "did" (32). F. V. Bernard examines the source material for the life of Frederick III of Prussia. Discovering that the predecessors for this life as well as those of this early period that are reprinted in the *Lives of the Poets* come from the *Gentleman's Magazine*, 1738-45, Bernard contends that during this period Johnson was engaged in one of the most intensive periods of historical research in his career. Careful analysis leads to reevaluation of nineteenth-century assumptions: even Butt shows a new respect for Johnson's theory of biography.

During this same period, James Clifford and Donald Greene each demonstrate that the genres of biography and autobiography take their modern form in the eighteenth century, not the romantic period, in large part because of Johnson's commitment to "truth." Clifford contends that the question for the modern biographer of how much to tell—weighing the right to privacy of the family and surviving relatives against the general reader's need for access to the facts—was the same for Johnson, who first articulated and faced the problem. Greene argues that biographers of Johnson need to follow Johnson's own practice and theory, which places most confidence in autobiography as a source of truth. But how Johnson's generic innovation is related to his interest in truth is not considered.

In 1974 Charles Batten's study of the sources for the life of Roscommon reinforces Abbott's contention: Johnson makes careful and respectful use of his source but is selective enough to advance his own position. A year later Richard Reynolds goes a step further in a similar direction in his study of the precursors for the life of Boerhaave. Neither "entirely derivative" of his predecessors nor completely subjective, Johnson's narration is "better organized, more steadily focused, and more honestly, yet feelingly, described." The result, Reynolds concludes, is an account that gives more "pleasure" than those of his contemporaries (129). Now some of the originality of Johnson's lives is attributed to "literary pleasure."

After the appearance of Fleeman's edition and Batten's study of the revisions and sources for the life of Roscommon, Richard Wendorf and O. M. Brack Jr. establish the bibliographic background for the lives of Collins and Drake respectively. In 1979 John Burke returns to the topic considered by Butt, the relationship between Johnson's theory and practice. Monitoring Johnson's progress through the early biographies in terms of subject, method, technique, and tone, Burke finds that in these writings Johnson gradually comes to practice what he later preaches in *Rambler* 60 and *Idler* 84 until there is a nearly perfect match between theory and practice in the life of Savage (1744). Nevertheless, for Burke, there is one striking exception to the match between theory and practice. Johnson's later theoretical statements fail to account for the importance of the "sympathetic imagination" in producing successful biography. Yet it is Johnson's large-hearted sympathy for his subjects, Burke insists, that stands out in his best biographies even when he must judge them harshly. That deeply felt sympathy is what makes his practice of the art of biography still so remarkable and still so compelling.

(30). Even for Johnson, the question of the relationship between literary pleasure and truth remains unanswered.

In the latter part of the 1980s Catherine Parke published an essay on Johnson's biographical thought process that became part of a chapter of her book, *Samuel Johnson and Biographical Thinking* (1991). Parke argues that the method of biography is for Johnson a "habit of mind," an approach that is to be found not only in the biographies but also in the remainder of the canon. A "conversation with history" is for Parke characteristic of Johnson's mind, to be seen in early works such as the preface to the *Preceptor* and *The Vision of Theodore*, the writings of the middle years, the *Dictionary* and *The Plays of William Shakespeare*, and finally and most overtly in the *Lives of the Poets*. The early lives that had to be rescued recently from Victorian neglect now become central to the Johnson canon, enabling us for the first time to understand why Johnson chose the biographical genres for some of his earliest writings. But analyses of these early biographies are rare because modern criticism has yet to unlock the dichotomy between historical truth and literary pleasure even though for Johnson the two are not mutually exclusive. Future researchers need to begin by explaining how in the eighteenth century literature serves the purposes of historical veracity.

The life of Savage (1744)

Commentary on the life of Savage is divided between the moral condemners and the psychological explainers; as a result, most commentary focuses upon Savage as a man. Johnson, however, included the life of Savage in the *Lives of the Poets*, the original title of which we recall is *Prefaces Biographical and Critical to the Works of the English Poets*. Most critics recognize that the *Lives* are both biographical and critical and that Johnson always suggests a relationship between these two sections. Yet in this particular respect, commentary on the life of Savage seems to me to have made very little progress. It is generally assumed that although Johnson recognized that Savage's writings are seriously flawed, he included him in the *Lives* because as young writers they struggled together for survival in London. Yet Johnson devoted considerable space to Savage's writings, indicating in clear terms their beauties and faults. In my view, Savage was of interest to Johnson because his failure as a poet as well as a person indicates something important about the life of the writer in the eighteenth century. The debate about the life of Savage that has persisted since its first appearance would be altered considerably if this factor were taken into consideration.

In 1787, Sir John Hawkins, in his *Life*, analyzes the relationship between Johnson and Savage.

It may be conjectured that Johnson was captivated by the address and demeanor of Savage, at his first approach; for it must be noted of him, that, though he was always an admirer of genteel manners, he at this time had not been accustomed to the conversation of gentlemen; and Savage, as to his exterior, was, to a remarkable degree, accomplished: he was a handsome, well-made man, and very courteous in the modes of salutation (29).

Later in his *Life* Hawkins turns to the life of Savage.

The manner in which Johnson has written this life is very judicious: it afforded no great actions to celebrate, no improvements in science to record, nor any variety of events to remark on ... But if the events of Savage's life are few, the reflections thereon are many ... It farther exhibits to view, a man of genius destitute of relations and friends, and with no one to direct his pursuits, becoming an author by necessity ... Interspersed in the course of the narrative are a great variety of moral sentiments, prudential maxims, and miscellaneous observations on men and things; but the sentiment that seems to pervade the whole is, that idleness, whether voluntary or necessitated, is productive of the greatest evils that human nature is exposed to (65-66).

Boswell, on the other hand, stresses the reader's fascination with Savage.

In Johnson's 'Life of Savage' ... a very useful lesson is inculcated, to guard men of warm passions from a too free indulgence of them; and the various incidents are related in so clear and animated a manner, and illuminated throughout with so much philosophy, that it is one of the most interesting narratives in the English language. Sir Joshua Reynolds told me, that upon his return from Italy he met with it in Devonshire, knowing nothing of its authour, and began to read it while he was standing with his arm leaning against a chimney-piece. It seized his attention so strongly, that, not being able to lay down the book till he had finished it, when he attempted to move, he found his arm totally benumbed. (1, 165-66)

Boswell also comments on the striking similarity between the narrator "Thales" of *London* and the character of Richard Savage, "but the fact is, that this poem was published some years before Johnson and Savage were acquainted" (1, 166). These remarks are followed by a "digression" on the question of whether Savage is, as he claimed, the child of Lady Macclesfield. Boswell admits that the preponderance of the evidence suggests that Savage was an impostor, but he still feels the matter remains in doubt. The two most famous eighteenth-century biographers of Johnson emphasize very different aspects of the life of Savage. Hawkins finds an austere warning against idleness. Boswell has some doubts about the historical accuracy of the narrative but applauds the wise moral reflections: the fascination of Savage as a character is furthered by Johnson's forcefully written narrative. In this distinction between Hawkins and Boswell we see the beginning of the critical difference between those who disapprove on moral grounds and those who give more weight to the affection and fascination for a friend. This controversy helps explain why the life of Savage is the only one of the *Lives* of interest to the Victorians, an age when sin and sympathy are equal ingredients of an important new form of theater, the melodrama.

In 1842 Charles Whitehead distinguishes between Boswell's and Johnson's attitudes toward Savage. Boswell, according to Whitehead, believed that Savage lacked the legal evidence of his parentage, but Johnson accepted Savage's claim. Whitehead goes on to cite "Mr. Galt," who in 1831 asserts that Johnson in his credulity concerning Savage's version of events undermined himself. Whitehead's remarks serve as part of a preface to a novel entitled *Richard Savage: A Romance of Real Life* that presents the "facts" of Johnson's account in a "romance." The intent of this work was to elaborate upon the details in Johnson's account in order to demonstrate that Johnson was fully warranted in accepting Savage's view of his life. Whitehead's book was reprinted throughout the nineteenth century and in 1896 was reissued "with Eighteen Etchings on Steel by John Leech." The double alteration of genre involved in the conversion of biography to romance and in the use of illustration suggests the desire to change the perspective on the familiar dichotomy: seeing Savage in a new light is designed to elicit less condemnation and more understanding.

However, the question of historical accuracy continued to be debated. In 1843 Robert Chambers concedes that Savage is a "type of a wretched man of letters" but accuses Johnson of being too indulgent toward his subject, as if Savage has been under "some moral prohibition [against working] honestly, as other men do, for his own bread" (66). Chambers concludes by admitting that the life of Savage appears to him "false and dangerous" in an age "superior to that of Johnson" (68). In 1858 an anonymous reviewer points out that while Johnson gives a "regular meaning" to Savage's life in a "masterly manner," he lacks pity for the countess whom Savage claims as his mother, a partiality that "bends the truth" (708-11). In the same year W. Moy Thomas contributed a series of articles in *Notes and Queries* to demonstrate that Savage's claim to aristocratic ancestry is false: he concludes "I have not, I confess, any doubt that Richard Savage was an impostor" (448).

Instead of continuing the Victorian debate about the "facts," twentieth-century critics turned to the romantic or fictive aspect of Savage. In 1901, a play, "Richard Savage," was performed at the Lyceum Theater in New York City. So far as I have been able to ascertain, the manuscript for this drama has not survived. But the program makes clear that Johnson's account is the source for the play: "For the facts upon which this play is founded the author is indebted chiefly to the biography of Richard Savage, as contained in Dr. Johnson's 'Lives of the Poets.'" The plot synopsis, also in the program, further suggests that the drama is structured in accord with Johnson's biography.

ACT I   The attic home of poet and player.
ACT II   Drawing-room in Colonel Brett's house.
ACT III   Lord Tyrconnell's home.
ACT IV   A Part of Old London near Temple Bar.
ACT V   A Corridor in Newgate Prison.

We note here a generic shift from narrative to drama, suggesting a change in focal point from factual content to dramatic spectacle. Within the same decade, Stanley Makower produced a biographical novel entitled *Richard Savage: A Mystery Biography*, with a Gravelot engraving, "The Representative" [Poet], that contains the following caption: "After a study of pictures like this of the poet as an ideal type and of Hogarth's pourtrayal [*sic*] of misery in 'The Distress'd Poet,' the life of Savage acquires an interest different in kind from any that a portrait of the poet himself would have provided. The features of the man have escaped posterity, but the ideas he represented are over all sharply accentuated" (vi). Makower explains that Johnson sees "Savage resplendent in a scarlet cloak embroidered with gold lace, his toes peeping through his shoes" (249). A novice in London, Johnson is shown the ropes by Savage; "Johnson did not stop first to consider if his new friend's distress was due to his own folly." Makower concludes that "even the fierce but inaccurate condemnation of her (Anne Brett's) cruelty which marred Samuel Johnson's noble biographical essay ... remained unchallenged" (385). Separating Johnson's ideas about the distressed poet from the facts in his account of Savage made it possible to represent the meaning of the life of Savage either as fiction or as drama. Makower converted the biography of Savage into a story of the life of the distressed poet, permitting reflection on the midnineteenth century's treatment of its writers.

It remained for Walter Raleigh to point out that Johnson's life of Savage makes a similar point.

Johnson had wandered the streets with [Savage] for whole nights together, when they could not pay for a lodging, and had taken delight in his rich and curious stores of information concerning high and low society ... Towards Savage he is all tenderness and generosity, yet he does not for an instant relax his allegiance to the virtues which formed no part of his friend's character. He tells the whole truth; yet his affection for Savage remains what he felt it to be, the most important truth of all. His morality is so entirely free from pedantry, his sense of the difficulty of virtue and the tragic force of circumstance is so keen, and his love of singularity of character is so great, that even while he points the moral of a wasted life he never comes near to the Vanity of condemnation (19).

This sympathetic portrait represents, according to Raleigh, an alternative to Boswell's image of Johnson "sitting on that throne of human felicity ... roaring down opposition" (20). At the end of his study Raleigh returns to the life of Savage in order to demonstrate that Johnson's "greatness" resides in the "generosity of his temper" (173). The bond between Savage and Johnson was their shared experiences as struggling authors in London during the 1730s and early 1740s, which Raleigh understood as cultural history.

But by 1935 Gwyn Jones used a wholly fictive structure, a novel, that unlike Makower's, did not use the term "biography" in the title, to recast Johnson's biography of Savage. The "class consciousness" accentuated in the Great Depression of the thirties made Savage's futile attempt to be recognized by the aristocracy a point of more pronounced interest. In a 607-page narrative, Jones frames the Johnson/Savage story as a "picture of the British class system" (11). Having been rejected by the aristocracy, Savage found consolation in the full life of being a writer because "anyone can be a poet" (595). The veil of fiction enables Jones to elude the question of whether this "class-consciousness" is more a twentieth- than an eighteenth-century phenomenon.

In 1939 Jack Lindsay reconsiders Savage's poetry. Although forgotten because third-rate, the poetry helps "shatter the Augustan stereotype" by way of its "rich new colouration" that anticipates the "light-effects" of Gainsborough, Constable, and Turner. According to Lindsay, Savage in his life as well as in his art was a "forerunner of the English romantics and of the great English landscape painters because he had that ceaseless consuming ache to regain his lost 'mother'" (386-93). How Johnson, who for Lindsay is clearly a promulgator of "the Augustan stereotype," could be moved to sympathize and write about Savage in preromantic terms is left unexplained. Once Savage is seen as a victim of marginalization, the romantic preoccupation with the isolated, neglected artist takes precedence over literary history.

In the next decade Edgar Johnson pursued the distinction between the biographical and critical aspects of the life of Savage. E. Johnson in general argues that the critical parts of Johnson's biographies are less effective than the biographical portions. The difference is particularly marked in the life of Savage, where honesty is difficult since Johnson felt attachment to his friend but nonetheless presents him as "an ingrate and a dissipated scoundrel" (149). A few years later an anonymous writer for the *Times Literary Supplement* points out that as a poet Savage scarcely exists for moderns, but as a man he is known because of Johnson. Joseph Wood Krutch takes Edgar Johnson's position considerably further by asserting that Johnson is "blinded by his own partiality" to the fact that Savage is "either self-deluded or an out-and-out impostor." Indeed, Krutch explains, Johnson's "intimacy" with Savage is the result of "his interest in character and his social tolerance as opposed to his theoretical intolerance" (77-79).

Yet within a few years the only modern biography of Savage appeared. In a study somewhat misleadingly entitled *The Artificial Bastard: A Biography of Richard Savage* (1953), Clarence Tracy states that the life of Savage is "Johnson's best study of character, and one of the best ever written by anyone. But factually it is unreliable" (vi). Setting out to separate facts from conjecture, Tracy finds with regard to Savage's claim to Lady Brett and Lord Rivers as parents, that he is not able "to settle it finally." Nevertheless, Tracy grants that Savage's claim to aristocratic parentage "may be genuine and that at least the claim against him has been overstated" (vii-viii). Tracy's volume is by far the most meticulously researched of the accounts of Savage's life: it is remarkable that after over two centuries Tracy sides with Johnson concerning the most controversial contention of the life of Savage. The widely held assumption that Johnson has distorted the historical record of his friend is now seen as unwarranted. Indeed, as one of the reviewers of Tracy's biography points out "in general his conception of Savage's character is the same as Johnson's" (294). Tracy, unlike Moy in the previous century, sets out to test the validity not of each fact of the life of Savage—essaying each tessera in the mosaic—but of Johnson's general perspective in the sense of a cohesive picture made up of factual fragments. The coherent narrative aspect of history takes precedence over the earlier focus on the chronicling of facts.

In a 1956 work, Benjamin Boyce contends that Johnson's biography of Savage was affected by two traditions: the factual lives by Savage himself as well as others, and the romance tradition represented by *Roxana* and other fictions about children rejected by their parents. Since Tracy has demonstrated that the accusations of historical inac-

curacy are exaggerated, it is necessary, according to Boyce, to emphasize that Johnson's life also has affinities with the fictive or novel
tradition. Indeed, Boyce asserts that Lady Brett is made "more consis-
tently a bitch by Johnson" than even by Savage himself (597). H. A.
Morgan goes on to point out that although the "reputation of Johnson as a writer has long been obscured by the reputation won for
him by Boswell as a personality," now some "reputable critics together with a small but increasing body of readers have come to realize that Johnson could write as well as talk well" (38). That the life of
Savage is pointed to as an example of Johnson's excellence as a
writer helps explain why Cyril Connelly places it among the *Great
English Short Novels.*

Nevertheless, historians did not relinquish their claim to the life
of Savage as biography. In a 1957 general study of biography, John
Garraty notes that Johnson was "surely the greatest figure in eighteenth-century biography" in that he "rejected panegyric," stressing
"practical values," and advancing the interest in the "individual,"
the "non-political, non-religious figures." "Beyond all else," Garraty
concludes, "Johnson exemplified the urge to understand," most no-
tably in the life of Savage, whose story is told without "disguising or
omitting his weakness" but with "compassion" (84-85). In another
general study of biography, Richard Altick claims that "Samuel
Johnson was the most fortunate event in English literary biography." Johnson was, "above all a moralist," according to Altick, the
first great advocate of "personal as opposed to public, biography" and
his lives are written in "Johnsonian prose," not "Johnsonese," that
is, marked, not by pomposity and pretentious language, but by clarity
and forthrightness. Finally, for Altick, Johnson's dedication to truth
is most notable in the life of Savage (46-52). Historical truth, which
in the Victorian period was tested in a specific and piecemeal fashion—rather as nuggets of stone are assessed for their gold content—
apart from the literary or narrative aspect of history, is now seen as
inextricably bound up in the radical of presentation; form and content cease to be readily distinguishable.

In the 1970s and 1980s the historical and literary elements were
treated as functions of one another. Donald Greene refers to the life
of Savage as "Johnson's masterpiece of biography," explaining that
"the power and feeling with which Johnson tells the story are closer
to the novelist's art than to that of most biographers." Greene, like
Krutch and many others, sees marked parallels between Savage and
Johnson himself, particularly when the two were both struggling authors. Greene suggests that part of the appeal of the life of Savage resides in the "pioneering application of psychological analysis to biography" (82-85). William Vesterman points out that Johnson learned
from his Parliamentary reporting to see both sides. In *Irene* he tries
to present both sides without his heart in it. He achieves this goal in

the life of Savage, the first example of the dialectical life of writing. John Dussinger characterizes this dialectic as a Greek tragedy that is determined by Savage's circular compulsion to put off his own benefactors. Johnson's concept of the "monster-woman" who attempts to undermine the patriarchal family, Dussinger continues, is a classical concept that is combined with a "deterministic pattern for the hero that serves to obviate the narrator's moralistic judgments concerning vanity and self-delusion." The result for Dussinger is a contradiction. "The commitment to objective truth that the biographer here ascribes to his culture may be normative in principle; but in the daily experience of anxiety, in the painful consciousness of the known and the belated sense of the unknown, compulsive drives, Savage's futile circularity, this narrative tells us, demonstrates the uniformity of discourse" (128-47). Dussinger's concept of discourse is designed to encompass the two contrary aspects of the life of Savage, the literary and the historical/psychological, a division Johnson subscribes to in theory but goes beyond in the life of Savage. Those who believe that in principle Johnson never loses his faith in the objective truth of biography are cautioned by Dussinger to examine the implications of his practice in the life of Savage. Discourse theory enables Dussinger to broaden the range of critical vocabulary, combining that of the method used by Johnson *in* with that of commentators *on* the life of Savage. Criticism here first shows awareness of the polarity between literary pleasure and truth, even if that dichotomy remains unresolved.

In 1974 Paul Alkon employs reader-response criticism to demonstrate how the old nuggets of truth can be maintained in a narrative structure. If we consider, Alkon suggests, the response to Savage after Johnson, we find that biographers treat him less sympathetically than had Johnson. In 1842, for instance, Whitehead alters the narrative to first person and changes some details of the narration in order to "regain some personal empathy." Alkon concludes that perhaps reader-response criticism needs to be tempered with the "old formalism" so that the facts of the narrative and the narrative techniques that evoke reader-response are seen in relation to one another (139-50). Walter Jackson Bate, on the other hand, focuses on the generic innovation of the life of Savage. Bate lists five generic elements: "high-minded Plutarchian" ideals, "human life and manners" of "the new realistic fiction," details like those in "criminal biography," reflections of the sort found in the "moral essay," and assessments of writings common in the "critical biography." Nothing like this biography, Bate maintains, had been attempted before. Previous biographers "had tended instead to list titles, as they appeared chronologically, with a few sentences of description. Here ... Johnson created the prototype of his own *Lives of the Poets*" (221-23). Since both reader-response and generic models can be applied to the life of

Savage, we are left to wonder why one is to be preferred over the other.

In 1978 Robert Folkenflik published the first full-length study of Johnson as a biographer. He justifies his subject matter by pointing out at the outset that Johnson's "career as a professional biographer was almost coterminous with his career as a professional writer" and that Johnson valued moral knowledge over all other kinds of knowledge except for religion (22-25). The object of biography for Johnson, according to Folkenflik, was to see the "subject as a man like other men and in distinguishing the subject from all other men" (56). The key issue for Folkenflik is in connecting "Art and Life": that relationship is seen as "problematical," one that Johnson always approached with caution (141). After describing the kind of "plain style" that Johnson used and recommended for biography, Folkenflik concludes his study with an examination of the life of Savage, which is selected because it best exemplifies the biographer "who eats, drinks, and lives with his subject." Adapting Walter J. Bate's concept of "satire manqué," which Bate applies to *The Vanity of Human Wishes*, Folkenflik describes Savage as a "tragic hero manqué" because he not only fails to realize his full promise but "never becomes aware enough of the meaning of his own actions." In this way Johnson is seen to balance the satirical and sentimental sides of his subject, and the failure to be truly tragic is the fault of Savage, not of Johnson" (212-13). In 1980, Frank Ellis suggests that since Savage and Johnson share failed tragedies it is not coincidental that Savage is seen by Johnson as a "failed tragic hero" (346). We are left, however, to wonder why Johnson chose to present Savage as a failed tragic hero. Does this failure reflect upon the man, his society, both, or something else altogether? Once the literary qualities of the life of Savage are recognized as separable from its historical import, it is subjected to careful formal analyses, but the themes that emerge do not sufficiently answer the historical questions raised by the life of Savage.

Ten years later Martin Maner suggests a dialectic similar to Folkenflik's but in reader-response terms: the final purpose of the "balancing of impulses" in the life of Savage is, Maner maintains, "to make the reader share Johnson's humane and compassionate recognition of the mixture of wisdom and folly, vice and virtue in every human soul" (73). Virginia Davidson revises Bate's generic view. The biography of Savage is seen as sui generis because history provides as sensational a tale as the novel invents: it therefore constitutes a "generic jump." "By taking biography beyond the merely commemorative (or defamatory) and demonstrating the complexity of his subject," Davidson concludes, "Johnson established the genre's significant mimetic relationship to actual human nature ... altering its course ... and proved that biography, like poetry, might aspire to be more philosophical ... than history" (72). But the displacement of this thematic balance from the text to the reader or human nature leads to the familiar question of whether the life of Savage is a reflection on Savage, his culture, or both.

These unanswered questions erupted in the 1980s with the reemergence of the familiar controversy about whether or not Johnson is defending Savage, demonstrating that formalist analysis has not laid this ghost to rest. For example, David Schwalm argues that Johnson successfully defends Savage. Opposing the concept of "conflicting strategies" that results from some seeing a "vindication" and others finding an "exposé," Schwalm contends that the biography is not disjointed because it shows moral condemnation is too "easy as opposed to sympathy or charity" (142). Thomas Kaminski attempts to demonstrate that Savage is not to be identified with Thales, the narrator of "London," which would further the case for those who see Johnson as an historian distancing himself from his friend. But Isobel Grundy accuses the narrator of bias that distinguishes the life of Savage from history. Arguing that the "gratuitous malignancy" in Johnson's portrait of Lady Macclesfield shows an absence of interest in character motivation, Grundy argues that "although appearing in biography," Lady Macclesfield "remains a fiction" (139).

Now that thematic balance is not considered a satisfactory resolution, the old dichotomy is revived. Donald Greene locates the excellence of Johnson's early biographies in "his shrewd psychological comments on the motivation of his subjects and those they interacted with" (15). In fact, Johnson does such a good job of establishing motivation in the life of Savage that Greene suggests that Johnson at times sounds "like a parody of a modern social worker." The question for Greene is whether Johnson in his effort to establish reader empathy for Savage has distorted the historical facts (23-30). William Epstein employs a Foucauldian model to demonstrate a historical shift from ancient religious institutions to modern secular ones. Epstein contends that this biography is an "adage of misery" because patronage at this time is on the wane, and Savage becomes a "child of the public" in an emerging "bourgeois commercialism." Johnson "reveals and conceals the individualizing tactic through which mid-eighteenth-century cultural discourse institutionalizes the shift from a sacred to a secular form of pastoral power" (154). Toni O'Shaughnessy, on the other hand, argues that Johnson is skeptical of any truth about the individual self. Sharing with Hume the assumption that identity is conventional and responding to the "indeterminacy of identity itself," Johnson, according to O'Shaughnessy, "builds Savage's self-fiction into his own text" (489). The critics of the 1980s were dissatisfied with the thematic equilibrium of the 1970s; Johnson was seen to come down finally on the side of Savage as an individual or as a representative of the subculture of the eighteenth-century writer. Literary themes were replaced by ideological positions: if the earlier formal analyses avoid conclusions, particularly those of historical significance, the ideological positions of the 1980s go too far in the other direction, arriving at large generalizations on the basis of one instance.

In *Samuel Johnson and Biographical Thinking* (1991), Catherine Parke makes the life of Savage a turning point in Johnson's career. She develops the thesis that Johnson comes towards the end of his life to realize what has always been implicit in his work: that biography is "our principal means of learning, of sizing up situations, of formulating and solving problems" (2). Specifically, for Parke biographical thinking involves a "conversation" between the present and the past. Johnson sees Savage, according to Parke, as deficient in this respect, constituting "a pervasive flaw in the way Savage thought and thus in the way he could relate accurately both to himself and to others" (112). Totally consumed with the immediate moment, "Savage was a man for whom the present world was the self: thus, he was not on speaking terms with the world" (113). Finally, the life of Savage itself indicates that the literary, psychological, and historical cannot be separated: thematic, generic, character and cultural analyses must be brought to bear upon one another. Once again, the familiar dichotomy between the individual's responsibility and his or her cultural restrictions reappeared, now in the form of the man who is unable to converse with the world, a formulation that itself expresses the present conflict between thematics and ideology. My belief is that this battle is not capable of resolution and that Johnson is interested in mediation not resolution. The laudable elements of a culture regularly destroy promising individuals, and the most undeserving of individuals use precisely that rationalization to blame the culture rather than face their own responsibility. Johnson makes Savage a fascinating failure to suggest the inadequacy of each extreme—individual and cultural, thematic and ideological—because ethical judgments expose the limitations of our concepts of individuality and of our ideologies.

The issues discussed in relation to the life of Savage have grown steadily broader over the two and a half centuries since its first publication, from the early investigations of Savage's birth to considerations of Johnson's view of history, his depiction of the life of the eighteenth-century writer, and his biographical method of thinking. The attempt to separate the historical dimension of the life of Savage from the other facets of the narrative was not successful. Commentary on Johnson's life of Savage leads to reconsiderations of Johnson's thought, culture, and historical method. Fruitful new research will need to explain why the life of Savage moves commentators to reconsider both Johnson as a biographer and the milieu of the eighteenth-century writer.

2: Nondramatic Poems

JOHNSON MAY BE THE ONLY POET whose reputation rests on the basis of one poem, *The Vanity of Human Wishes*. Even those who focus on *London* or "On the Death of Dr. Robert Levet" regularly refer to the *Vanity*. Johnson's nondramatic poems will therefore be treated as a single entity.

Johnson's reputation as a poet has suffered since the nineteenth century from the belief that he is a product of an age of prose and himself lacks the sensitivity and delicacy requisite for a poet. According to this view, the "neoclassicals" are only capable of satirical poetry. The *Vanity* is therefore attacked on two counts, for not being a satire and for lacking the lyrical qualities of nonsatirical poetry. The main defense against this position is that the poem is tragic and thus equidistant from satire and lyric poetry. But the problem then becomes how to reconcile the tragic aspect of the *Vanity* with the religious conclusion. My own view is that the *Vanity* is a kind of satire, different from that of Pope and Swift, in that its ridicule of vanity is based upon the awareness of less vain alternatives that are provided by the perspective of religion. Such a position requires a more flexible conception of satire as a genre and a critical method that permits literature to be applied to the extraliterary realm of conduct.

The most pertinent of Johnson's own comments on his poetry is his insistence, in a 1738 letter to Edward Cave, that the original sections of the imitated poem "be subjoined at the bottom of the page, part of the beauty of the performance (if any beauty be allowed it) consisting in adapting Juvenal's sentiments to modern facts and persons" (CH, 43). Johnson thus makes clear that the original passages being imitated are to be kept in mind by the readers of *London* (1738) and *The Vanity of Human Wishes* (1749).

In his *Life*, Boswell explains that the *Vanity* "has less of common life, but more of a philosophick dignity than ... 'London'" (1, 193). Although David Garrick preferred *London*, as a "lively and easy" depiction of "what was passing in life," to the *Vanity*, which is "hard as

Greek," Boswell recognizes that the latter "is, in the opinion of the best judges, as high an effort of ethic poetry as any language can shew," particularly the passages involving the young enthusiast and Charles of Sweden. The "noble conclusion" Boswell cites as deserving of our "grateful reverence" for "the assurance that happiness may be attained, if we 'apply our hearts' to piety" (1, 194-5). Illustrating the "deep and pathetic morality" of the *Vanity*, Boswell recounts an anecdote from Mrs. Piozzi of Johnson reading the section on the life of a scholar and bursting "into a passion of tears" (4, 45).

But William Shaw attacks Johnson as a poet: "His poetry, though not anywhere loaded with epithets, is destitute of animation. ... We are now and then struck with a fine thought, a fine line, or a fine passage, but little interested by the whole. ... After reading his best pieces once, few are desirous of reading them again" (71-72). And during the same period, Hawkins raises the question of whether or not Johnson had a "truly poetic faculty ... that power which is the result of a mind stored with beautiful images, and which exerts itself in creation and description." Hawkins goes on to respond in the negative, "of this Johnson was totally devoid" (CH, 303). In the eighteenth century, the issue was whether or not the poetry was too difficult or uninteresting for the reader to penetrate in order to get to the important message.

In the nineteenth century, on the other hand, questions were raised about the profundity of the poetry. In 1802 William Mudford uses Shaw's comments to discredit an anecdote in Boswell's *Life*, supposedly from Johnson himself, that Pope admired *London* and remarked that its author would soon be well-known. Mudford develops Hawkins's view to a position that was reiterated throughout the nineteenth century: Johnson "has been read, and praised, and imitated, as a philosopher, a moralist, and an elegant prose writer; but none yet ever did, or ever can, confer upon him the appellation of poet" (CH, 45). Although the *Vanity* is viewed as superior to *London*, both poems, in Mudford's opinion, are "too much given to reasoning and declamation ever to attain those heights of sublimity which astonish and delight." The problem is that Johnson's "disease," his "melancholy ... does not allow very vigorous or very frequent excursions to the intellect, his images are not much varied; and analogous ideas are generally excited by events the most dissimilar" (CH, 47-48). This psychological dimension, Johnson's melancholy, not nearly as prominent in Hawkins, becomes a mainstay of nineteenth-century critics.

John Aikin, on the other hand, was exceptional during this period in his praise of Johnson's poetry and his knowledge of its range. In 1804 Aikin refers to *London* and the *Vanity* as "perhaps, the most manly compositions of the kind in our language." The conclusion of the *Vanity* is characterized as "superior to that of the antient." Even more unusual, Aikin has high praise for Johnson's prologues, which are seen as "superior to the ordinary strain of these compositions." Finally, while Johnson's odes are criticized for their "frigid elegance," "On the Death of Dr. Robert Levet" receives high praise: "I know not the poem of equal length in which it would be so difficult to change a single line, or even word, for the better" (CH, 49-50). The implication that Johnson, who was supposedly devoid of beautiful images and deep feeling, has succeeded not only in 'moral verse' but also in odes and prologues, genres that feature imagery and self-expression, went unnoticed for a century.

The dualistic view of great prose moralist/prosaic poet was tacitly assumed by most romantic and Victorian critics. Of the high romantics, Scott, as one would expect, liked the *Vanity*, especially the "sublime strain of morality [that] closes" the poem (CH, 422), and Coleridge, equally predictably, disliked it, attacking the opening couplet as "mere bombast and tautology" (CH, 197). In 1831 Thomas Macaulay announces that "the reputation of these writings, which [Johnson] probably expected to be immortal, is every day fading" (CH, 431). In his entry on Johnson in the *Encyclopaedia Britannica* (1856), Macaulay admits that the *Vanity* is an "excellent imitation" but finds it difficult to decide whether "the palm belongs to the ancient or to the modern poet." Wolsey, in Macaulay's view, falls short of the original Sejanus, but Hannibal is surpassed by Swedish Charles, and "Johnson's vigorous and pathetic enumeration of the miseries of a literary life must be allowed to be superior to Juvenal's lamentation over the fate of Demosthenes and Cicero" (38-39).

But the negative opinion presumably prevailed, because of the paucity of commentary throughout the remainder of the nineteenth century and because—with the exception of the brief remarks of Byron and Scott—there was no positive critical commentary on Johnson's poetry until near the end of the nineteenth century. Even then the remarks were defensive. In 1878, Leslie Stephen characterizes Johnson as a poet in the following terms: "Johnson's best poetry is the versified expression of the tone of sentiment with which we are already familiar. *The Vanity of Human Wishes* is, perhaps, the finest poem written since Pope's time and in Pope's manner, with the exception of Goldsmith's still finer performances. Johnson, it need hardly be said, has not Goldsmith's exquisite fineness of touch and delicacy of sentiment. He is often ponderous and verbose, and one feels that the mode of expression is not that which is most congenial; and yet the vigor of thought makes itself felt through rather clumsy modes of utterance." Stephen concludes his study of Johnson with a brief introduction to the last lines of the *Vanity*: "The sentiment is less gloomy than is usual, but it gives the answer which he would have given in his calmer moods to the perplexed riddle of life; and, in some form or other, it is, perhaps, the best or the only answer that can be given" (193-5). Stephen was able for the first time in nearly a century to call attention to the profundity of the *Vanity* by admitting that it lacks delicacy and refinement.

In 1901 Harry Minchin imagines Boswell and Johnson brought back to life in the twentieth century. Johnson's poetry was better received than it was in the previous century. *London* has a "manly pity for suffering" although Garrick was wrong to place it above the greater poem, the *Vanity*, which is singled out for the "young enthusiast" passage and for its Christian conclusion (104-5). In 1905 William Courthope explains the basis for this new appeal. Experience of adversity is the foundation of Johnson's poetry. Thus, Thales, the speaker of *London*, is identified with Savage from whom Johnson learned about poverty and hunger in London. The chief characteristic of Johnson's "ethical poetry" is, for Courthope, the depth of feeling with which he illustrates universal truths. In the *Vanity* Johnson is "far more general" because his goal is to Christianize Juvenal, but even here the young enthusiast passage is markedly personal—particularly the change of the term "garret" to "patron" in response to his own experience with Chesterfield (203-6). The twentieth century ceases to assume that optimism is the norm. Johnson's focus upon adversity is now, not as in the nineteenth century a symptom of melancholia, but a clear view of the facts of life. In 1909, a reviewer of a new edition of Johnson's poetry remarks on "the great interest in Johnson at the moment" (330). Was the interest in Johnson as the poet of personal experience of hardship a manifestation of the pre-First World War attempt to avoid the public or political sphere about to erupt? In any event, at this point, it is difficult not to notice that historical forces beyond the range of literary criticism have an effect on the commentary on Johnson's poetry. Writers, both critical and creative, are not immune to the larger forces of history.

The next critique appeared at the end of the war, in 1918, when a term often used to describe Johnson psychologically was also applicable to this post-war period. In a study of the influence of Horace on Johnson, Caroline Goad finds that Johnson has "a strong and undeniable personal affection for Horace," an affinity for "Horace's observations upon the conduct of life, and sympathetic understanding of, though not acquiescence to, his fundamental melancholy" (269). Melancholy, we recall, was during the previous century a key term of disapprobation. In the same year William Hudson distinguishes between *London*, a mere imitation now out of style, and the *Vanity*, a reflection of Johnson's own experiences (34-42). The First World War, a new global historical experience, led to a new respect for the poetry of adversity, particularly when that experience was seen as producing melancholy.

In 1923 George Saintsbury points out that the heroic couplet in *London* is subtly but significantly different from that of the *Vanity*. Although, "the couplet, like other autocrats, cannot afford to transact with liberty in any way," the verses of the earlier poem are marked by "antithesis and balance" while those of the later one are "halved" or "folded" in anticipation of Goldsmith and Crabbe (461-63). A year later Thomas Quayle announces that eighteenth-century poetry is undergoing a "rehabilitation" from the traditional romantic antagonistic position popularized by Matthew Arnold. In fact, Quayle continues, *London* and the *Vanity* make less use of personification— one of the main targets of the old position—than of what he calls "Latin condensation" (140-41). Some latitude for personal expression is now seen in the heroic couplet, a form that was seen earlier as overly restrictive.

In 1925 Hugh Walker reiterates the view that *London* fails and the *Vanity* succeeds because only in the later poem does Johnson express his real feelings: while the earlier work contains a country ideal that is "inconsistent," the *Vanity* is remembered for little "romanticism but much deep morality" (229-31). In the following year S. C. Roberts introduces an anthology of Johnson's writings by pointing out that "*London* brought Johnson fame, but not a fortune, and he continued to 'write for bread.'" The *Vanity* is, in Roberts' view, "incomparably the finer" of the imitations because "it has a dignity and a sincerity which make it one of the best poems in the language for re-reading" (16, 29). Johnson's poetry was valued during this period not for abstract adversity but for conveying the personal experience of hardship.

But in 1929 Arthur Quiller-Couch asserts that in "On the Death of Dr. Robert Levet" Johnson, unlike Cowper or Gray whose elegies are marked by passion, was a "man of robust common sense who believed that instead of mourning old friends one should ever make new ones" (45). Not surprisingly Johnson's elegy remained neglected until it was recognized as being marked by feelings, however different from those of poets usually identified with preromanticism. On the other hand, in an introduction to a new edition of *London* and the *Vanity* (1930), T. S. Eliot places Johnson in the Augustan tradition of Pope before the change of idiom that demarcates the age of sensibility. Considered as examples of this kind, both imitations are among the "greatest verse Satires of the English or any other language," and even the originals by Juvenal are "no better." "A stern moralist" in the classical tradition, Johnson "hits the bull's eye." Of the *Vanity*, Eliot concludes, echoing Johnson, that if it be not poetry, "I do not know what it is" (308-10). In championing Johnson against the old guard, Eliot is also forwarding his own poetry and that of his contemporaries. The fact that Johnson is not a preromantic serves as a recommendation for Eliot, who sees his own poetry as deriving from a different and older tradition than that of romanticism.

In 1934 James Sutherland, expanding upon the suggestions of Saintsbury and Quayle, points out that the restrictions of the heroic couplet have been exaggerated. Using Johnson as an example, Sutherland admits that while the "balance or antithesis ... may interrupt the communication of experience ... inside the apparently rigid structure of the couplet there is room for more variety than has been admitted" (86-87). The craftsmanship of the poetry of this period, particularly the work of Pound and Eliot, was having an effect upon the commentary on Johnson's poetry. In fact, the relationship between poetry and criticism was reinforced. Poets defended in Johnson what was attacked in their own work, and their own poems manifested neglected aspects of Johnson's poetry.

In 1941 David Nichol Smith published the first scholarly modern edition, which is still considered, along with the Yale University Press edition, a reliable authority by specialists in the field. In his introduction, Smith explains that the "Feast of St. Simon and St. Jude," printed here for the first time, "has no parallel in the rest of Johnson" for "poetic fervour," and that it is probably because of this "enthusiasm" that Boswell passed it over. Johnson's greatest poem, the *Vanity*, is "a very great poem." But Smith believes that the greater poems "were wrung from this man of prose with an effort." Johnson, according to Smith, expressed his more private thoughts in verse—a side of Johnson not seen in Boswell's *Life*—particularly in his Latin poems. For instance, on completing the fourth edition of the *Dictionary* and on his deathbed, Johnson composed "romantic" poems in Latin, similar to the religious poems written shortly after his school days. Most of his verse in English, however, is "classical," with the possible exception of "On the Death of Dr. Robert Levet," which is characterized by Smith as a "generous and deeply felt elegy" (10-15). Smith advances the cause for Johnson as a poet in critical and bibliographical terms, but at the price of continuing to apply a romantic criterion for good poetry to Augustan verse, that of personal, deep feeling.

But this kind of scholarship was opposed by a practicing poet. In 1944, T. S. Eliot delivered a lecture (published in 1946) asserting that Johnson's claim as a major poet rests on the basis of the *Vanity*. In the same year Joseph Wood Krutch contends that the *Vanity* does not achieve what "Johnson himself declares are inevitably produced by the 'most engaging powers of an author.' Here are certainly no new things to be made familiar; and, to one reader at least, the 'familiar things are not made new'" (61-65). Eliot's attempt to explain his own innovative poetry led him to other criteria than sincerity and newness. Not until the 1980s was it recognized that "modern" poets share and respect the art of imitation, particularly as practiced by Johnson.

In 1947 Wallace Cable Brown continues the investigation of Johnson's use of the heroic couplet. In a detailed article, Brown examines first the minor poems, selecting the "Prologue to Comus" as the most advanced in technique. Then, turning to the major poems, he argues that the *Vanity* shows how Johnson's "poetical ear" serves to produce "pathos in isolation," an important and appropriate effect for "impersonal and didactic" kinds of poetry. Brown points out that despite the opposition of the romantics good poetry can be didactic and abstract: Johnson's didacticism is not coldly intellectual but "homogeneous" (53-61). In the same year Bertrand Bronson, in an essay on personification, analyzes "On the Death of Dr. Robert Levet." Bronson defends the opening image of the mine "because the ore which we hopefully extract never yields the expected return." The middle stanzas show that "Johnson loved Levet" by way of "personified abstraction." But for Bronson the two final stanzas fail: "it is regrettable that they fall steeply off in power; and noteworthy that they do so in the degree to which they descend from abstract statement to the biographical particulars" (226-28). Bronson thus attempts to demonstrate that Johnson's poetry is most moving when it is abstract and fails when it resorts to particulars, but it remains unclear whether this position constitutes a defense of Augustan abstraction or an attack upon its lack of particularity.

Three years later, the romantic position on Johnson's poetry is the focal point for John Robert Moore. After his death Johnson was, according to Moore, admired as a moralist, lexicographer, or conversationalist, but no one "understood him as a poet." The explanation for this neglect is that Boswell, Hazlitt, and Carlyle loved Johnson the conversationalist but "ignored the poet." The romantics were haunted by the spectre of Johnson that remained unrecognized by them: Moore demonstrates that having misrepresented Johnson as no poet because too set in his ways, the romantics nonetheless used his poetry and ignored his flexibility of mind, his attention to particulars. And while a few, like Hawthorne, Scott, and Byron, openly admired *London* and the *Vanity*, the others, were influenced by Johnson's verse in ways they never recognize (157-63). The implication that the romantics were influenced by the Augustans in ways that their own critical method precluded from consideration was ignored. Indeed, it still remains to be demonstrated how romantic poetry—in spite of the negative criticism by romantic poets—was influenced by the poetry of Johnson. This neglect of practice in favor of theory persists in the present.

In 1952 Donald Davie defends Johnson's poetic diction. The regular use of personification that previously was criticized is shown by Davie not to involve stale truisms but to result in "generalizations that are justifiable as they are 'worked for.'" For Davie, Johnson brings "a dead metaphor" to life in a "compelling and dignified idea." In the *Vanity*, Davie contends that Johnson achieves "purity of diction, a language at the center of all dialects and class differences." The doctrine that "poetry should have all the virtues of good prose" enables Davie to place Johnson in the tradition of Dante, Eliot and Pound (82-90). Clearly, modern poets like Pound and Eliot writing "unromantic poetry" helped to influence a reassessment of Johnson's poetry. In the same year, Ian Jack presents his view of the *Vanity* as a tragic satire. Reconsidering problems central to the Books of Job and Solomon, *Hudibras*, and *Rasselas*, the *Vanity* is for Jack a serious satire reminiscent, not of Horatian urbane irony, but of Juvenalian 'declamatory grandeur.' Since Johnson's form of abstraction is different from that of Donne or Keats, it is inappropriate, according to Jack, to condemn him for not doing what he was not trying to do. In Johnson's age "generalizations about human life" were considered "exciting," and this tragical satire suggests the limitations of the belief that the eighteenth century is an age of facile optimism (138-45). In this same year, F. R. Leavis places the *Vanity* in the tradition of "great poetry," an aspect of Johnson that Leavis believes is evaded by Boswell in his effort to produce an object for "middle brow complacency" (116-19). Now the "hardness" of the *Vanity* that put off Garrick recommends it to the critics who are rediscovering the Metaphysicals and defending Eliot and Pound.

But the tragic reading leaves some doubt about the nature of the religious consolation at the end of the poem. Francis Schoff suggests that in the *Vanity* Johnson goes beyond tragedy, turning "mordant mocking into abstract gloom" because "even if a man is not foolish in his desires he will suffer." The only remedy for this "melancholy imagination" is in the hereafter, but, according to Schoff, even that hope recedes" (293-96). Walter Jackson Bate, on the other hand, finds more resolution at the end of the *Vanity* in the following terms. *London*, Bate explains, "gives a personal genuineness to the stately heroic couplets as the poem dwells on the crime, the political corruption and squalor of the London metropolis, and as it works toward the climactic theme, 'slow rises worth, by poverty depressed.'" The *Vanity*, Bate continues, treats man's vain desires "with a courageous manliness and a rational stoicism joined with a strong religious fervor." The subject is "the enormous clutter of fitful desires and rival ambitions, of fears, projections, envy, and self-expectation that human feelings create in their confused impulse to assert themselves and find satisfaction. ... The premise—perhaps the principal premise of the poem ... is the 'treachery of the human heart,' which leads man to betray his own interests as he snatches, in his 'clouded maze,' at what he hopes will at last bring satisfaction" (18-20). But this treacherous human heart could be seen to serve tragedy or religious satire.

The following year, Chester Chapin continues the examination of Johnson's poetic language begun by Davie. Focusing upon personification, Chapin demonstrates that Johnson's poetry has gone up in the public estimation because now after Eliot and Hardy we are better able to appreciate how personification when skillfully employed renders the abstract as specific. Johnson is superior to his contemporaries in developing his abstractions toward metaphor: his "imagery lends weight to the idea, and the idea, in turn lends concrete facts to the imagery" (98-115). In 1957 Susie Tucker and Henry Gifford analyze the imagery of "On the Death of Dr. Robert Levet." The abstract notions of service and death are shown to be intimately connected to the concrete specifics of the imagery of the "mines and blasts" (9). Further investigation of Johnson's Latin as well as English poetry leads Tucker and Gifford to assert that the "pleasure of Johnson's poetry is mainly imparted by the images which give general truth a most moving personal ring" (248). And Christopher Ricks suggests that Johnson's portrait of Wolsey may be related to "attacks on Walpole," furthering the view that the concrete and general are united in Johnson's poetry.

But in 1959 John Butt distinguishes between Pope and Johnson as imitators on the basis that Pope is at ease with the concrete while Johnson is at his best when he aims at the "grandeur of generality" (19-38). Butt asserts that even though Johnson, unlike Pope, is in 1738 the more marginal figure he seldom uses political details, and when he does it is against the grain (19-31). In the same year, Mary Lascelles also assesses the imitations in relation to the originals. In her analysis of *London*, Lascelles differs from some of her predecessors in believing that Johnson takes the country ideal seriously: "Suffering from revulsion against his new surroundings ... Johnson might perhaps miss the irony in Juvenal's tale of country pleasures, yet find the denunciation of Rome ... heartily congenial. *London* has not the brilliance of its original," Lascelles concludes, "because it lacks the lightning flash of its irony." "A great tragic poem," the *Vanity* does not measure up to its original as satire. Lascelles's comparison of the Sejanus and Wolsey passages is exemplary: "Juvenal's approach to the fall of Sejanus is tactically unsurpassable. ... This it is ... to be an emperor's favorite; yet who would have the resolution to refuse. ... By comparison, Johnson's tale of Wolsey's fall is unimpressive: it proceeds as simple narration, in the single voice of the poet, and the tone of that voice is grave, compassionate, devoid of irony." Lascelles concludes: "this is not satiric irony ... it is tragic irony, learnt in the contemplation of life" (40-55). Notice that Butt and Lascelles assume that Johnson was attempting to do what Pope and Juvenal achieved. The most noticeable innovation of the *Van-*

ity, its religious conclusion, is viewed as a separate coda. The 1950s showed an increased interest in the details of Johnson's poetry—its diction, imagery, metrics and the generic possibilities as they are pursued in the imitation. The formal characteristics of the poetry came under new and more exact scrutiny and produced new questions. Does tragedy or satire prevail, and does the prevalence of one or the other constitute failure or success?

While Lascelles feels that Johnson's tragic irony derives from life weakens his satire, Vincent Buckley prefers the *Vanity* to *London* because the tone of the earlier poem is "unearned" and the later work gives particularity to its generalizations—especially in the passages on Wolsey, the young enthusiast, and old age (16-30). And Donald Greene characterizes *London* as an immature satire. "He eagerly seizes on the Walpolian iniquities and uses them as pegs on which to hang his own griefs: bribery and castrati and masquerades become projections and symbols of the Johnsonian dissatisfaction with the world" (91). In 1965 F. W. Hilles defends Johnson as a poet on the basis of the power of his perspective. The opening couplet of the *Vanity* is, according to Hilles, not redundant; it achieves the elevation necessary for viewing the exempla of vanity, but he is unable to explain how the new means lead to a new end. Although Johnson says nothing new he provides a "powerful manner of expression" for an orthodox Christian position (67-77). Yet Paul Alkon, comparing the *Vanity* to sermon XII, contends that "the reassuring conclusion of *The Vanity of Human Wishes* leaves us in more doubt insofar as it does not explicitly direct us to 'prosecute our business' as usual" (197-98). In the same year Arieh Sachs presents a secular reading, arguing that the phrase "extensive view" is the key to understanding the *Vanity*, "for the imagery of mental width and narrowness recurs throughout his writings—width inevitably connected with Reason and narrowness allied to Imagination. ... Whereas the narrow views which our obsessions impose upon us," Sachs explains, "make us time's fools, because we are so immersed in ultimately absurd earthly hopes and fears, the wide perspective of the general human condition should lead us to a rational other-worldliness" (77-79). The paradox in this last phrase suggests that the problem of explaining how the secular body of the poem is related to the religious conclusion remains unresolved.

But it was now beginning to become clear that Johnson in his imitations was interested in the relationship between an individual point of view and a larger context. In 1968 John Hardy replies to Greene's characterization of *London* as immature. The contrast between city and country, Hardy maintains, becomes "an extended metaphor of [Johnson's] essentially political theme." The plan of the poem is not "jejune," as Greene asserts, but serves the purpose of satirizing Orgilio who represents Walpole (253-67). Greene and

Hardy agree about the theme but differ about whether it should be applied to the speaker or the larger context.

In 1969 Howard Weinbrot published a study of Augustan imitation that contains a chapter on *London* and one on the *Vanity*. *London* is seen by Weinbrot as less successful than the *Vanity* because Thales's "ethos" has several flaws that weaken the force of the satire. Unlike Hardy, Weinbrot does not see a consistent view of the country; rather, the general view of a rural retreat is contradicted by the specific country scenes. Moreover, Thales' rage is characterized as "higher pitched" and "less convincing" because its overstatement "suggests its own weakness." Nor are we convinced of Thales' virtue since he seems so "arrogant in his pose at 'satiric superiority'" (165-191). On the *Vanity*, Weinbrot points out that many moderns view the poem as tragic because they neglect the consolation of the conclusion and are unaware of the "attack/praise" formula of Augustan verse satire. This pattern explains for Weinbrot why the body of the poem provides no examples of individuals "worthy of emulation," and the end points to "spiritual goods men may have, *on earth*, at *this moment*, [which do] not exist in the world of human wishes" (193-217). The precise nature of these spiritual goods and their bearing upon earthly desires is not clear. But Weinbrot was the first to recognize that the major issue in the *Vanity* is the relationship between the body of the poem and the conclusion.

The year 1970 was important. The seven positions selected represent the range of ideological views that began to emerge. Edward and Lillian Bloom study the relationship between Johnson and Juvenal in *London*. To the commonplace disparagement of Johnson for lacking the "fire and vehemence" of Juvenal, the Blooms counter that Johnson deliberately replaces the classical tone with that of a "rhetoric philosopher." Unlike Juvenal's speaker Umbricius, Thales is, according to the Blooms, "an intellectual" whose "erudition" provides evidence of his culture that has its roots "not only in wisdom but also in profound religion dedication" (107-44). William Kupersmith, remarking on the similarity between Johnson and Juvenal, points to the "ornate diction" and "disciplined versification" used to achieve a sublimity that parallels Juvenal's "Latin hexameter" and "declamatory grandeur" (71-72). And Sandford Budick approaches the *Vanity* in secular terms, as an instance of cultural demythologizing. One form of false wit, according to Budick, is a "hunger of imagination" that is not to be denied but "should review and reverse the object of hope and fear." In this respect, the *Vanity*, "more than a plea ... is a model of myth revision or demythology" (410-13).

Patrick O'Flaherty attacks the *Vanity* on the grounds that the religious consolation is undermined by secular gloom. Arguing that the philosophy of the poem "is nothing if not simple and dismal: its basic contention is that man by nature is condemned to indulge in hopes which will never be satisfied," O'Flaherty asserts that the satire is not a "mature expression of Johnson's version of life." Passages from the *Rambler* and *Rasselas* are cited that offer more "love and hope" than the dismal satire. Johnson's "pessimism," O'Flaherty concludes, "a projection of his gloomy intuition," takes its most intense and unrelieved form in the *Vanity* (517-27). Also during this prolific year, another essay reflects upon the methodology of reading an imitation. Raman Selden points out that the similarity between the original and the imitation may be superficial, since imitative conventions were often used to emphasize difference. The *Vanity*, Selden proposes, should be understood not only in the context of the individual satirists, Juvenal and Johnson, but also in terms of the tradition of the imitation. Viewing the *Vanity*, the "last major imitation in the history of formal satire," within this poetic historical continuum, Selden shows how Johnson uses and modifies the satirical verse conventions of his day to convert Juvenal's "grim detachment" into "tragic dignity" (293-301). Now that the individual nature of Johnson's imitation has been established, disagreements focus more pointedly on whether the result is tragic or religious.

Also in 1970, Donald Greene reformulates his position on *London*, as a satire that "purports to be a diatribe on the life of that city by one Thales, who it is hard not to suspect was modeled on Richard Savage." But the poem is very much a young man's poem, and its charm comes from the youthful exuberance and violence. ... A curious effect of the exuberance is that the reader's final impression may not be that life in London in 1738 is very depressing, as the poem ostensibly portrays it, but that, although exasperating from time to time, it is on the whole, great fun." The *Vanity*, on the other hand, Greene admits, is hard to read. The difficulty is the result of the Christian ethic, "a commonplace in [Johnson's] own time, [that] seems very hard for modern readers [to accept]. This teaching is that material self-seeking values—merely *human* wishes—are an unsatisfactory basis on which to build a life." This position, Greene maintains, is neither tragic nor pessimistic. "Happiness, then *is* possible, it *can* be 'made' (though not 'found'). ... The student of psychiatry will not be surprised at Johnson's insistence on 'mental health' and a 'calm mind,' or at his insight that happiness is not something one finds but something one makes" (34-38). It is not clear from Greene's analysis, however, how the satire on vanity is related to making happiness. So, in the same year, Walter Jackson Bate characterizes Johnson's *Vanity* as "satire manqué." Although Johnson's personality suited him to satire in many ways—his hot temper, an "unwillingness to be pleased," a propensity for "fidgety tart phrases," and the "prolonged outbursts of laughter"—"yet Johnson was not a satirist." In fact, "he had a hatred and fear of satire, which is what led him to be so antagonistic to Swift." The *Vanity* is chosen by Bate as the prototype for "satire *manqué*." The poem begins with "savage things," but then it changes: "Johnson starts to sympathize and to share," turning the poem into a form of "tragedy." In this sense, Bate explains, he agrees with O'Flaherty that the *Vanity* is a failure as a satire. What Johnson succeeded in doing in the *Vanity*, according to Bate, is taking satire beyond its traditional boundaries, a process that begins in the *Vanity* and ends in *Rasselas*. "If the method and intention of satire per se is a correction by ridicule, we have virtually none in *Rasselas*. In this sense especially, *Rasselas* marks a further stage in Johnson's wrestle with satire and deflection of it, already apparent in *The Vanity of Human Wishes*" (145-59). Once the focus shifts from means to ends, assessments of the conclusion vary, ranging from religious optimism to secular tragedy, which in turn affect whether the poem is regarded as successful or unsuccessful. This opposition between satire and tragedy, secular and religious, leads to the belief that religion and satire undermine one another: the problem is not that satire per se is antireligious but in delineating how satire and religion serve the same purpose.

    In 1971 A. D. Moody studies Johnson's revisions of *London* and the *Vanity*. Although he does not come to any momentous conclusions about these revisions, Moody's essay is a useful repository of the various stages in print of these two satires. The following year D. V. Boyd offers a reading of the two satires that replaces the ethical with the ontological, "not good versus evil but being versus nothingness," indicating the clear influence of Jean-Paul Sartre and the other existentialist philosophers. Boyd finds that *London* occupies an uneasy place between the works of Pope and Blake: Johnson "sees London as a mixture of human perversity and incurable physical evil." Thales is the "satirist as loser" whose sole concern is "personal failure," and his pastoral alternative is "unconvincing." Although the exempla in the *Vanity* are more convincing, they too fail "to conform to tragic expectation." O'Flaherty is right, according to Boyd, in seeing the predominance of despair except that "some types of action are clearly more perverse than others," while the Blooms are wrong to propose as an alternative "government of reason," for "man may wish in vain, but he will wish." In the end, the ethical decision of Hope and Fear is "deserted"; the satirist is "to renounce his quest for moral imagery and empirical discrimination" (395-403). The effect of Boyd's view is to locate a philosophical position for the imitation somewhere between satire and tragedy; differences between the *Vanity* and other similar Johnsonian works can be explained as the result of distinct genres. In 1973 Ian White turns to this issue by distinguishing between the *Vanity* and *Rasselas*. The narrative is concerned with "disappointed good intentions of wisdom and virtue"; the poem looks at "personal ambition and the af-

flictions of political, military, and intellectual prowess." This distinction in subject matter explains for White the difference in tone, the
story being "human" and the satire "cynical." Instead of the world of
"discord" in *Rasselas*, White believes that of the *Vanity* is
"profoundly political," revealing the "injustice of power and in-
famy" (115-25). Carey McIntosh compares the *Vanity* to the *Rambler*:
"Most of the lyrical moments in Johnson's prose celebrate one or
more of the various shades and successive stages of his experience
(or set of experiences); his powers of expressing emotion are more
fully exploited in *The Rambler* than in his poem *The Vanity of
Human Wishes*" (50).

During this same period, examinations of the generic elements of
"On the Death of Dr. Robert Levet" led to a deeper understanding of
Johnson's use of poetic conventions. Gayle Wilson points to the
epideictic elements of "On the Death of Dr. Robert Levet." Wilson
explains that Johnson attacks "Lycidas" in generic terms because, as
is pointed out in *Idler* No. 41, the poet's first task is to "stir Pity."
"Johnson's awareness as a poet of the necessity of observing decorum," Wilson concludes, "led him to select the epideictic oration as
the appropriate genre" (30-36). In 1974 Dustin Griffin reinforces the
findings of Gayle Wilson. "On the Death of Dr. Robert Levet" shows
that Johnson "was interested in generic criteria" but did not feel con-
strained by them. The elegy for Johnson is "simple but serious:"
"Lycidas" is too fussy and affected so Johnson combines elements of
the epitaph with the elegy, producing "sober praise and tender grief."
Thus Johnson offers Levet as an example to himself (191-208). A year
later Donald Mell clarifies his position on the elegy to Robert Levet.
Arguing for the connection in Johnson's view of the relation between "vigorous moral action and the creative role of mind and intelligence," Mell opposes René Wellek's view that such a connection
is "superfluous." For Mell, "On the Death of Dr. Robert Levet" is a
powerful "imaginative ordering of grief and praise" formed "into a
unique verbal structure that mediates between the idealization of art
and the facts of time and mortality inspiring it" (77-80). Careful analysis of this elegy demonstrates that Johnson understood generic
conventions and appropriated them for his own purposes. Problems
in the poetry cannot be attributed to Johnson's lack of generic sophis-
tication. Moreover, during the early 1970s the elegy on Levet received much attention as a religious poem about a man whom
Johnson witnessed putting Christianity into daily practice. This discovery serves as an antidote to the more abstract attacks on the conclusion of the *Vanity*. The elegy makes clear that Johnson's religion
was less a philosophical position than a commitment to quotidian
acts of charity.

In 1975 Paul McGlynn argues that the rhetorical form of the *Vanity* is the central metaphor or controlling structure. The poem is, as

Bate points out, a series of catalogs of crowds, and the general truths pass through the prisms of these exemplary crowds. "Preferment" is, according to McGlynn, the microcosm of all vanities: they "mount, shine, evaporate and fall." This repetitive movement is seen by McGlynn as "rhetoric as metaphor" that becomes "truth," the various ways in which human wishes are shown to be "specious." McGlynn concludes that this "catalogic rhetoric" proceeds, not from the structural constraints of the closed couplet, but from Johnson's moral view (477-82). But Johnson expresses his moral position in a variety of genres, the most notable being *Rasselas* and the *Rambler*. What the singular quality of the *Vanity* is remains a question.

In 1977 Walter Jackson Bate devotes a chapter in his biography of Johnson to the *Vanity*. Bate views the *Vanity* as the first of the writings that were to make Johnson "one of the supreme moralists of modern times—as one of the handful of writers who, in what they have to say of human life and destiny, have become a part of the conscience of mankind." Bate's high estimate of the *Vanity* deserves to be cited in its entirety:

> The result is a poem that (as was once said of Burke) dazzles the strong and educated intellect far more than the feeble, and sways intelligent and cultivated readers as a demagogue would a mob. Even in the Romantic period, when the condensed intellectual poetry it typifies was not in favor, Sir Walter Scott could praise the imaginative and moral depth of this poem, which "has often extracted tears from those whose eyes wander dry over pages profoundly sentimental."
>
> As the twentieth-century reconsideration of poetry began to mature and seek a new relation to the past, T. S. Eliot, on the basis largely of *The Vanity of Human Wishes*, eloquently argued Johnson's claim as a major, in some ways unique, poet. Within our own generation the poem has justly come to be regarded as a landmark. There is indeed nothing else like it in the English language, or indeed any other language. Johnson's own opinion of it could be expressed by the fact that when it was published (January 9, 1749), it was the first work in which he put his name on the title page. (278)

Bate points out that the *Vanity* more than any other work "reveals the image of reality that was fixed in" Johnson. "More essentially tragic than comic," this satire, according to Bate, adopts a double perspective, irony "in the author" and "in the world" that are both maintained until the end when the "Enquirer" is reminded that "religious love and faith have not been proved vain." Consequently, the poem traces two themes, man "athirst for wealth," "burning to be great," "Dogged by the envy and hate of rivals," and the "doom of

man" due "to inward and psychological causes." The final approach
to religion is therefore, according to Bate, "essentially by a negative
path." The two most common images of the poem are those of
"cloudiness and darkness" and of "rising and sinking" that render
"the clutch of human beings for permanence and security." Bate implies that this double perspective is unique to the poem: "In the first
case, we have adjectives that express what the person caught up in
the toils or strife feels ... In the second case, we have terms such as
treacherous, fancied, airy, which pronounce the judgment of an onlooker ... this combination ... is an essential part of Johnson's greatness as a moralist" (277-89).

But a year earlier, Lawrence Lipking suggests that a similar
"doubleness" in the religious tale, "The Vision of Theodore," helps
us understand how to read the *Vanity*. "The Vision," composed for
purposes of "education," specifically to teach us how to "master
habit," ends inconclusively, without our knowing whether or not
the narrator masters his habitual indolence. In the *Vanity* Johnson
most obviously writes of himself in the "young enthusiast," and
here again "the hope of making a choice fades" at the end when we
pause "on the brink of Christian mystery." Lipking believes that the
prose and poetic works share the notion that the self is a "prisoner of
Indolence," the remedy for which is to "look to your self," to learn to
read yourself (518-35). Bate's "double vision," on the other hand,
permits the critic to decide which side is more important, that of religious onlooker or of empirical moralist.

A number of critics now began debating whether or not interpretive factors can be resolved in the poem itself or require reference to
the larger historical context. Arthur Sherbo replies to Ian Donaldson's belief that the "falling houses" in *London* are generic conventions. Sherbo demonstrates from accounts in the *Gentleman's Magazine* and other works contemporary with *London* that falling
houses were in fact a danger of the time. Donaldson states that his
point is not to deny the literalness of the image but to assert that its
figurative aspect is more important (376-78). Howard Weinbrot considers the methodology of recent readings of *London*. Instead of pro-
jecting our reading of Juvenal upon the eighteenth century, we need
to know how Johnson read Juvenal. "The assumption that Johnson
read Juvenal as we do leads to inappropriate methodology and mis-
taken literary criticism." Specifically, there is no evidence that Johnson or his contemporaries responded to Juvenal's third satire ironically—an assumption, according to Weinbrot, shared by Lascelles,
Hardy, Kupersmith, and Donaldson. Weinbrot concludes that this
"undefended modern interpretation should not be foisted upon an
ancient poem," and that we cannot therefore use this argument to
explain the "diminished brilliance" of *London* (56-65). In 1977 John
Sitter applies a similar historical method to the *Vanity*. Sitter main-

tains that the "different voices" of the poem cannot be adequately explained in terms of Juvenal or Johnson. Rather, we need to be aware of the general developments taking place in the British poetry of the 1740s, the change from the age of Pope, when satire served as a "means of vexing" to the time of Johnson and his contemporaries when it became a "symptom of vexation." Sitter suggests that this knowledge of the changing poetic tradition leads to the realization that the conclusion of the *Vanity* is "ambiguous": "she," the agent who receives the final religious consolation, may refer to "mind" or to "wisdom," to the poet or to the reader (445-62).

At the same time, two critics argue for internal—as opposed to historical—evidence. Mary Murphy offers the results of her computer-assisted study of sight and sound words in the *Vanity*. She finds that these kinds of words are used on two levels: physically and symbolically to advance the theme of the "inadequacy of the senses to interpret reality and the limitations of human reason." Although Johnson uses sight words from the outset, such as "observation" "to invoke the reader to empirical investigation of objective reality ... the poem subverts the empirical process" (24-25). Raman Selden refines his position from 1972. Johnson differs from Pope in developing into his satire a tone of "pathos." In modernizing Juvenal, Johnson "introduces a new and independent poetic ordering of his model," adding a "subjective dimension." In place of Juvenal's "cool" and "detached" wit, Johnson maintains "formality" but adds "dignity" that is "tragic." This latter element is so pervasive in Johnson that even the religion at the end "doesn't detract from the tragedy in the body of the poem" (153-62). In the latter half of the 1970s, critics resorted to either internal/structural or external/historical evidence to bolster their positions. The familiar opposition persists: orthodox religionists versus those advancing a tragic reading. But the reemergence of an old and fruitless battle between formalists and historicists is short-lived.

In 1980 John Vance demonstrates that a historical passage in *London* refers at once to a historical figure from the past and one in the present: for Johnson's contemporaries such a connection is not unusual. Internal and external elements are now seen as controlled by Johnson. In the same year Howard Weinbrot subtly but significantly modifies his position on the *Vanity*. Weinbrot admits in a footnote that his position has changed concerning the British statesman (lines 73-90 of the *Vanity*): the attitude that he previously attributed to Johnson is now seen as that of the statesman (256, note 15). In addition, Weinbrot gives more emphasis to the element of "sympathy" in Johnson's satire as opposed to Juvenal's detachment. In the end Johnson's element of "love" produces reader implication: "We started the poem as uncommitted recipients of knowledge; we soon become agents of our own nastiness; we then become active or at least comprehending questioners and saddened viewers of the world we have made and inhabit" (252-61). Two historical critics here attest to the process of the poetic form being modified by history, by which historical allusions alter the poetic form, severely undermining the distinction between internal and external evidence.

But the procedure can also go in the opposite direction, from formal structure to history. In 1981 Geoffrey Finch attempts to understand the problem of *London* in terms other than those of "rhetoric" or "existential angst." Sincerity is the issue, Finch asserts, not in the sense of "true belief of the author" but "true to itself—it means what it says." The problem is that the Augustan poet is placed under inordinate hardship; at this time the "scars of poverty run deep in *London* even though it is Johnson's bid to make it." Finch decides that the dilemma is historical in nature. Since "writing involved alienation for Augustans ... making it," as Johnson finally does in the *Vanity*, is at the price of the "harmony he idealized" in *London* (254-62). Joel Weinsheimer uses *London* to question E. D. Hirsch's distinction between meaning and significance, for *London* is both at once, an imitation of Juvenal and an original poem, or, as Hans-Georg Gadamer had demonstrated, truth "submits itself to time and occasion" (320). The poetic form points to specifics of the period, to history.

But these methodological modifications were ignored. In 1982 Michael Cohen continues the tradition of viewing the *Vanity* as tragic. Aware that he is in accord with Lascelles and Damrosch and opposed by Greene, Boyd and O'Flaherty, Cohen makes overt what is implicit in the position of previous adherents by arguing that the kind of tragedy found in the *Vanity* cannot be accommodated to satire. "Like Johnson we can speak about a poem's effect even when formal explanations fail." The "sadness" of the *Vanity* is "profound and ... tragic in its dignity and inevitability" (410-17). Graham Cullum sees the tragic aspect of the *Vanity* as leading to ultimate, not merely formal, failure: it "abhors the folly of wishing at all." Centrally concerned with "fate," the satire fixes on what is "extrinsic and adventitious in life," and although Johnson tries to give moral coherence to the "portraits" he fails because "vanity is incoherence in experience." We are left, Cullum claims, with a "decidedly unbalanced poem in which man rolls 'darkling down the Torrent of his Fate'": the conclusion is based not on the "stability of truth but on the painful finality of its own unanswerable needs and desires" (310-16). The move from form to formal affect only produces the familiar differences, now formulated in terms of affective stylistics: the tragic affect in balance with or overpowered by religion.

During the mid-1980s Johnson's religion was reexamined in an attempt to find a new sort of orthodox resolution. In 1984 Chester Chapin takes up Charles Pierce's use of the end of the *Vanity* to exemplify Johnson's "spiritual anxiety." Johnson's Christianity, Chapin explains, is a process not a product, and it is in this respect that Johnson radically alters the Juvenal from beginning to end (72-74). Pierce, in *The Religious Life of Samuel Johnson*, points out that "nowhere did Johnson give a clearer indication of the role he wanted religion to play in human existence than at the end of the *Vanity of Human Wishes*." Unlike Juvenal whose conclusion emphasized man's independence," Johnson, according to Pierce, "chose to emphasize not self-reliance but rather man's profound dependence upon God for any possibility of happiness." Despite awareness of the weight of critical opinion against him, Pierce believes that the end of the *Vanity* is "an inadequate and unconvincing response." When Johnson asserts in the *Vanity*, "whate'er he gives, he gives the best," he is, according to Pierce, paying "more than lip service" to the "facile conception of divinity" that he attacked in Pope's *The Essay on Man* and Soame Jenyn's *A Free Inquiry*. Pierce admits that this position is at odds with Johnson's pronouncements elsewhere, and he attempts to explain this "tension." "Johnson was almost certainly inhibited by his desire to remain faithful to the spirit, if not the letter, of Juvenal's Stoic conclusion. ... [And], Johnson may well have possessed at this time some of the same reservations ... later recorded in the Life of Waller ... that he felt there was no way in which poetry could add to the force and truth of religious ideas" (112-16). Pierce argues that the literary constraints do not permit the full force of Johnson's religious affirmation. Reassessment of Johnson's religion still leaves open to question what happens to his credo when it enters the context of the *Vanity*.

Along with the assertion that the religion of the *Vanity* is not synonymous with Johnson's religion, commentators began to assess the historical import of the *Vanity* in terms of the history of poetry. Christopher Ricks, in a study of poetic language, turns to Johnson's "Battle of the Pygmies and the Cranes" to exemplify how his "feeling for context, together with his responsibility toward language, gives more force to his usage." Johnson's contribution to the history of the British poetic idiom is, Ricks contends, in the "metaphorical skill he would best display ... a revivification of dead metaphors into a disconcertingly relevant prominence, varying their dress and situation 'so as to give them fresh grace and more powerful attractions'" (85-88). A year later, David Perkins examines the influence of Johnson upon T. S. Eliot and other "modern poets." Specifically, Johnson is a part of the "compound ghost" of the *Four Quartets*, and generally "Augustan satire was at the heart of Modernism, and far more essentially than most people bear in mind," a point that is born out by our own analysis. For instance, Perkins points out that Pound cut from the first version of the "Fire Sermon" in *The Wasteland* heroic couplets, "Fresca in London," in imitation of Pope's *Rape of the*

Lock. The modern poets, according to Perkins, turn to the Augustans as part of their anti-romanticism, and Eliot becomes a sort of "Grand Cham in succession to Dr. Johnson." Eliot and other moderns who share his views are drawn, Perkins speculates, to the Augustan "prose tradition" in poetry that combines wit and satire in a structure that is alert and self-critical as opposed to "subjective afflatus." Perkins concludes that "Eliot identified more with Johnson than he did with any other English author" (304-12). Perkins's analysis suggests a topic he does not pursue: the secular and religious sections of the *Vanity* may be related in a way similar to those of *The Waste Land* and *Ash Wednesday.*

   In 1985 two critics present arguments for a satirical or tragic form of Christianity in the *Vanity*: they share the desire to account for the literary structure of religion in the poem. Michael Riley examines irony in *London* and the *Vanity* to argue that Johnson employs two kinds of irony, analytical and philosophical, the former predominating in *London* and the latter being more pervasive in the *Vanity*. The problem in *London* is that Johnson heightens analytic irony but cannot totally avoid philosophic irony. The result is a "deflation" of philosophic irony that we cannot be certain is intended by Johnson. In the *Vanity*, on the other hand, Johnson achieves a balance between these kinds of irony in order to demonstrate that the "human condition is not merely ironic in practice, as satirical hypothesis presumes, it is ironic in its foundation." Since "existence is dysfunctional in its very essence," Johnson concludes with the belief that "the sublime instability of faith can redeem the instability of human existence." "Faith" becomes "Johnson's proper irony" (108-29). William Kniskern examines the four longest exempla or portraits in the *Vanity* in order to demonstrate that they should be seen not as tragic but as satirical. Even Swedish Charles, whom Kniskern admits is "inevitably found to be 'tragic,'" exemplifies the "fall of pride" (635-44). But Riley does not explain what is ironical in Johnson's religion, and Kniskern does not make at all clear why tragedy and satire are mutually exclusive categories.

   In 1984 Thomas Jemielty attempts to show that the biographical evidence bolstering the argument that the *Vanity* is not a satire is one-sided. With regard to Swedish Charles, who is most often seen in tragic not satiric terms, biographical evidence shows, according to Jemielty, that Johnson "had little time for military ambition." And with regard to the "young enthusiast" section, which is thought by most to be autobiographical, Jemielty points out that the anecdote of Johnson in tears upon rereading it fails to mention that the passage also elicited his laughter. Biographical evidence points to a broader conception of satire than that of either Swift or Pope: "Johnson sees satire and charity as not necessarily incompatible" (227-37). But establishing that satire or tragedy, or a combination of the two, can exist side by side with religion still leaves unresolved the question of how these literary and generic restraints directly bear upon the religious conclusion of the *Vanity*.

In 1989 Edward Tomarken presents his position on *London* and the *Vanity* in separate chapters of his book, *Johnson, 'Rasselas,' and the Choice of Criticism*. *London* is understood as part of the process of trial and error that leads to Johnson's first satisfactory presentation in *The Vanity of Human Wishes*. Tomarken points out that since the early 1970s critics have been debating whether the organizing principle of *London* is London or Thales. This question is, according to Tomarken, never resolved. *London* raises a "question that it does not resolve. The romanticized image of the country estate directs the irony at the projection of an urbanite exiled to the country. But this satire destabilizes the poem, for the suggestion is that Thales's tale (all but thirty-four lines of *London*) is one of the satirical targets of *London*. ... The failure of *London* is a result of the penetration of its satire in implicating Thales, a self-exiled poet, in his own poem. For this reason, the reader of Johnson's poem feels that a profound picture of literary London has been rendered, one that in some respects goes beyond Juvenal's Rome" (126). Johnson first gains full control of this powerful satirical vehicle in the *Vanity*. Here the focal point is not the conclusion of the poem: "In my view, the study of religion in the *Vanity* has overemphasized the conclusion at the expense of the body of the poem. ... My interest is in the manner in which Johnson connects the concerns of this world with those of the hereafter. ... The *Vanity* ... implicates [its] own perspective on vanity in vanity ... [and] shows the reader how each human vanity points to a less vain alternative and leads to the celestial consolation at the end of the poem." An example of what Tomarken means by a less vain alternative is provided in his discussion of Swedish Charles: "The less vain alternative for Charles is to retire after Pultowa, a secular equivalent of the alternative Wolsey has at Cawood, the opportunity for a dignified instead of petty and dubious end." Tomarken concludes that "Johnson's religious faith drove him to pursue a process that commenced with the insight that the viewing of vanity is itself a form of human vanity. This response to vanity contextualized it, permitting another viewpoint that posited a less vain alternative" (128-49). Bate's "double vision" now serves to unite the secular and the religious. The less vain alternative is one available on earth, in history, but it is seen from above, from the religious perspective of vanity. In this respect the body of the poem is directly effected by the poetic coda.

In 1992 Gloria Sybil Gross offers a psychological description of *London* as "a belligerent poem about the corruption and vileness of the big city [that] conveys the impossibility of enjoying life under a manifest reign of terror." "For all its seeming partisan vigor," the poem for Gross "projects a fantasy of prodigious ruin" (42-43). The *Vanity*, on the other hand, "treats the subject of impetuous worldliness." "In the character of the straggler," Gross continues, "he identified with its tragic cast and restive conflict, now acutely to be owned." The body of the poem demonstrates how "desire is doomed to extinction," but at the end Johnson turns to the act of prayer that "may tame the wild excesses of nature and the scourge of Fate, as well as rescue man from chilling solitude. ... Thus inherent in 'celestial wisdom' Johnson finds vital links to the mental apparatus. ... He has not far to go in designating the function of the superego" (64-66). The dichotomy between the body of the poem and the conclusion, between the secular and the religious, that has prevailed throughout has reemerged now as a distinction between Johnson's psychological drives and his religious resolution. The task of future commentators would seem to be to understand why Johnson chose in the *Vanity* to combine secular choices with religious issues and to explain how the credo at the end bears upon the satire of vanity, how faith applies to the dilemma of Swedish Charles or the young enthusiast.

3: *Irene*

MOST CRITICS AGREE THAT *IRENE* FAILS as a drama. Two kinds of explanations are offered, one focusing upon style and the other upon stage spectacle. A number of the early critics make clear that the drama fails as a stage presentation; twentieth-century critics focus upon the language of the play. I believe that an analysis of the plot explains why the play fails for both eighteenth- and twentieth-century audiences. The stylistic problem is a symptom, not the root cause of failure: declamatory speeches are after all conventional at this time. The language intrudes for us not so much because of its dated style as because it is not integrated with the action of the drama.

At its first performance on the stage in 1749, *Irene* was not well received by reviewers. Of the two 1749 reviews I have found, both are negative, one somewhat flippant, the other more respectful and careful. Both are anonymous. The first reviewer expresses disappointment in *Irene*, then cites examples of the improbability of plot elements, such as two Greeks conversing in the Turkish Seraglio (18). The other reviewer is more even-handed. "Whatever beauty it may have, that of touching the passions is by no means allow'd it" because "the fate of Irene ... makes no impression on the audience." Although a "heap of splendid material, rather than a regular structure," *Irene*, the reviewer grants, promotes virtue and therefore "deserves applause" (16-34).

Boswell, in his *Life*, explains that Johnson began *Irene* in 1736 while an usher at Edial and completed it in 1737 in Lichfield (1, 108-9). By 1738 Johnson had announced in a letter to Edward Cave that he would be pleased to present him with a copy of the play. Not until eleven years later did it reach the stage and then only because his old friend David Garrick had become manager of the Drury Lane theater. But, Boswell explains, Garrick wanted changes made in the manuscript that Johnson resisted, and a quarrel ensued that had to be patched up by a third party. On the night of the first performance, Irene, who was to be strangled onstage, could not speak her lines because of cries from the audience of "Murder! Murder!" Thereafter, she was executed offstage. Even Boswell is hard-pressed to find the play a success: "Analyzed into parts, it will furnish a rich store of noble sentiments, fine imagery, and beautiful language; but it is deficient in pathos, in that delicate power of touching the human feelings, which is the principle end of the drama" (1, 196-98). Finally, Boswell reports that over thirty years later, in 1780, Johnson upon rereading *Irene* remarked, "Sir, I thought it had been better'"(4, 5).

Throughout the rest of the eighteenth century and most of the nineteenth century *Irene* was neglected by producers and critics. In 1894 George Radford points out that "Johnson is more popular than ever but it is his sayings from Boswell" that receive the most attention while "those who read Johnson's works are a small and, perhaps, a diminishing company." *Irene* is seen by Radford as typical of an "early difficult period in Johnson's life." The plot of the drama, according to Radford, demonstrates Johnson's labors, especially the last two acts where the difference between Irene and Aspasia over apostasy is complicated by Aspasia's love for Demetrius, a Greek, and Abdalla's love for Aspasia. The staging is seen as equally fraught: Radford reiterates Boswell's story of the quarrel between Garrick and Johnson, adding that the drama remained on the stage for nine nights because of Garrick's generous consideration for Johnson's financial needs (95-115).

In 1919 Arthur Walkley points out that although Johnson was a "playgoer for over 40 years," he had "strong reason" rather than "quick sensibility," which explains the failure of *Irene*. Johnson, Walkley explains, chose tragedy because "it was 'in the air' even though after he received his pension in 1763 nothing except friendship forced him to the theater." Walkley believes that Johnson ignores the "optics of the theatre," confusing judgment of reality with aesthetic judgment" (199-213). Up to this point, most of the twentieth-century commentary on *Irene* consisted of speculation about the elements of Johnson's disposition that prevented his succeeding at drama.

Detailed scholarship on *Irene* began with David Nichol Smith's essay of 1929 that, in modified form, served as the introduction to the play in the 1941 edition of the *Poems of Samuel Johnson*, which was revised and reissued in 1974. The nearly two centuries between the first staging of *Irene* and this scholarly landmark provided less than one hundred pages of commentary. Not surprisingly Nichol Smith's judgment is still generally accepted: "The mere number of performances is thus in itself no proof that *Irene* had not succeeded on the stage. A more important indication is that neither Garrick nor any other actor thought of reviving it during Johnson's lifetime. Nor, it would appear, has it ever been acted since, though when it was included in John Bell's *British Theatre* it was adorned with a frontispiece representing Miss Wallis as Aspasia—a part which she is not known to have played." Using the terms Johnson applies to Addison's *Cato*, Nichol Smith suggests that the failure of *Irene* resides in its use of "dialogue too declamatory, of unaffecting elegance, and chill philosophy" (267-77).

In 1944 Bertrand Bronson further pursues the problem of style in *Irene*, concluding that the language fails because it is divorced from the reality of everyday speech. In 1970 Donald Greene modifies this position by suggesting that the diction is not flawed but does put off twentieth-century readers: "the blank verse of *Irene* remains a barrier between the modern reader and what Johnson was trying to do in the play, which was well worth doing" (46). Greene's suggestion that eighteenth-century dramatic conventions impeded understanding of the significance of *Irene* leads to two kinds of defenses of the play. Shifting attention away from the didactic language and toward the organic structure, Marshall Waingrow in 1965 reminds us that the "heroine of *Irene* is Irene," the purveyor of the tragic theme (91). Building upon Roy Wolper's historical research, which demonstrates that Johnson understood and appreciated the theater of his day, Philip Clayton, in 1974, asserts that, when properly understood in terms of its period and genre, that of "neo-classical tragedy," *Irene* is "curiously successful" (122). Nevertheless, in a comprehensive study of 1976, James Gray, after considering the various close readings of the structure of *Irene* and the research on the history of its genre, concludes in terms reminiscent of Nichol Smith's judgment of over fifty years earlier: "It would be comforting after this extensive examination to record a verdict of great tragedy manqué, of 'great failure,' but we can only say with Johnson himself that we thought it had been better. The moralist gets in the way of the dramatist" (87).

In 1989 Edward Tomarken asserts that *Irene* is a historical tragedy and examines the plot, which he claims has been neglected. Focusing upon Abdalla, who is crucial as the mediator between the two camps of Aspasia and Irene, Tomarken points to an inconsistency: "Why do Hasan and Caraza murder their emperor's mistress on the word of Abdalla, a man they know to be a traitor, having themselves informed against him in the previous act?" Johnson, according to Tomarken, is determined that the audience know that Abdalla is "doomed from the beginning of the denouément," thereby undermining "Irene's argument for the political expedience of apostasy." By this means, Tomarken argues, Johnson attempts to show that "the question of apostasy is meant to be seen in its historical context, as a practical possibility for Irene in the Constantinople of 1453" (114-16). The implication is that the problem of *Irene* resides not in Johnson's disposition nor in the twentieth-century audience's unfamiliarity with eighteenth-century theater conventions or in the stilted language: *Irene* fails because of the imposition of a rigid religious presupposition upon a historical context that resists such didacticism. The future of *Irene* criticism therefore calls for a closer examination of the relationship between considerations of style and analyses of the action of eighteenth-century theater.

4: Periodical Essays

JOHNSON WAS KNOWN THROUGHOUT THE NINETEENTH and part of the twentieth-century as the Rambler, but there is little evidence to suggest that during this period his periodical papers were carefully analyzed. Rather, the essays are frequently referred to as repositories of moral and religious apothegms. When eighteenth-century periodicals are carefully examined, however, scholars soon find that the *Spectator* is also marked by religious and moral aims. This research gradually reveals that the Spectator is a different kind of speaker than the Rambler. Johnson's narrator is more high-minded, less chatty and sociable than that of Addison and Steele. But the reason that Johnson developed this modification of his predecessors' mode is not clear. I believe that an examination of the manner of unfolding of Johnson's periodicals reveals an interest in the thinking and judging procedure. Most commentators assume that the main interest is the product or truth, not the process. Nineteenth-century readers invested so much in the orthodox and established views of the *Rambler* that they neglected to notice the procedure of the essays that renders these conclusions provisional, or as Johnson formulated it in *Rasselas*, where he revises most of the concepts from his periodicals, a conclusion in which nothing is concluded.

Although it is generally assumed that the *Rambler* (1750-52), Johnson's first series of periodical essays, was less successful than the *Spectator*, the initial reviews were, in the main, very complimentary. In 1750 the *Daily Advertiser* refers to the author, the Rambler, as one whose "Learning and Wit have all their pow'rs combin'd." At different dates during the same year, the *Gentleman's Magazine* reproduced two positive comments from other publications: 1) The *Rambler* "exceeds any thing of the kind ever published in this kingdom, some of the Spectators excepted—if indeed they may be excepted" (465), 2) "A new writer, blessed with a vigorous imagina-

tion, under the restraint of a classical judgment, a master of all the
charms and graces of expression, [has] lately made his appearance to
the public under the stile and title of *The Rambler"* (CH, 63). And as
a testimony to the international audience of the *Rambler*, the *Gentleman's Magazine* reprinted a French review that first appeared in
France in 1752, then in The Hague in 1754, and in Berlin in 1755. The
following passage is a fair sample:

> Le style est élégant, mais tendre, composé, *surnaturel*, un peu
> dans le goût de votre beau *Télémaque*, que j'avoue à mon
> honte n'avoir jamais pu lire d'un bout à l'autre. D'excellentes
> réflexions, de froides plaisanteries, de la morale, de la critique,
> des caractères, des songes, des allégories encore. *Ah! M. John-
> son* ... donnez-moi la monnaie de vos fictions. C'est une
> chose assez commune dans vos écrivains mais inifiniment
> rare chez les nôtres, qu'un style net et concis, également pur et
> naturel (138).

The first female public comment on the *Rambler* appeared in
1761. Anne Penny transcribes the *Rambler* essay entitled "Anningait
and Ajutt: A Greenland Tale" into verse and presents her compliments to Johnson:

> O! Johnson, fam'd for Elegance and Sense,
> Whose works, Instruction and Delight dispense;
> Where nice Correction charms our wand'ring Eyes,
> And in whose Lines embellish'd Beauties rise;
> Say! will you deign this humble Verse to hear.
> Sprung by your Thoughts, and Nurtured by your Care:
> A Female Bard, unknown to Wit or Fame,
> To you inscribes what from your Genre came (4).

This same year an anonymous reviewer in the *Critical Review* is
generally favorable to the *Idler*, and admits that it is approved by the
public, but objects to its lack of humor, having finished it "without
feeling one impulse to risibility" (481). The following year Anna Seward prefers the *Rambler* style to that of the *Spectator*. Addison
"frequently finishes his sentence with insignificant words ... [which]
utterly precludes that roundness, that majestic sweep of sound in
which the Johnsonian periods so generally close: periods that my ear
finds of such full and satisfying harmony, as not to need either
rhyme or measure to add more sweetness. In truth, rhyme and measure are but the body of poetry not its spirit, and its spirit breathes
through all the pages of the *Rambler"* (CH, 23). In 1782 Vicesimus
Knox explains, however, that he prefers the *Spectator* to the *Rambler* because of Johnson's "pomposity" of style, which, however

much it improves the language, puts off readers. In this respect, the *Adventurer* in Knox's opinion is an improvement over the *Rambler*, but it lacks the "sweetness of Addison" (136-37). At this point it was a matter of dispute whether or not the *Rambler* was at first well received.

In 1791 Boswell suggests that both sides have a point. "As the Rambler was entirely the work of one man, there was, of course, such a uniformity in its texture, as very much to exclude the charm of variety; and the grave and often solemn cast of thinking, which distinguished it from other periodical papers, made it, for some time, not generally liked" (1, 208). But, Boswell continues, "the Rambler has increased in fame as in age." And he adds, "I profess myself to have ever entertained a profound veneration for the astonishing force and vivacity of mind, which the Rambler exhibits" (1, 212-13). Boswell also defends the humor and worldliness of the *Rambler*. "Though instruction be the predominant purpose of the Rambler, yet it is enlivened with a considerable portion of amusement. Nothing can be more erroneous than the notion which some persons have entertained, that Johnson was then a retired authour, ignorant of the world; and, of consequence, that he wrote only from his imagination when he described characters and manners" (1, 215). Some, Boswell admits, complain that the style is "involved and turgid, and abounding with antiquated and hard words. So ill-founded is the first part of this objection, that I will challenge all who may honour this book with a perusal, to point out any English writer whose language conveys his meaning with equal force and perspicuity"(1, 217). Boswell claims that by his day most of the objections to the style and humorlessness of the *Rambler* have been overcome. In short, Johnson has achieved fame as a writer in no small part due to the *Rambler*. But the defensiveness of these remarks suggests that the case for the greatness of Johnson's periodicals was still to be made.

The following year Arthur Murphy describes the *Rambler* as Johnson's "great work." "It was the basis of that high reputation which went on increasing to the end of his days. The circulation of those periodical essays was not, at first, equal to their merit. They had not, like the Spectators, the art of charming by variety. ... It must, however, be acknowledged, that a settled gloom hangs over the author's mind; and all the essays, except eight or ten, coming from the same fountain-head, no wonder that they have the raciness of the soil from which they sprang." Murphy admits that the Rambler often employs a "pomp of diction": "There is, it must be admitted, a swell of language, often out of all proportion to the sentiment; but there is, in general, a fullness of mind, and the thought seems to expand with the sound of the words." Murphy describes "the *Adventurer* as a continuation of the *Rambler*. The *Idler*, in order to be consistent with the assumed character, is written with abated vigour, in a style of ease and unlaboured elegance" (CH, 69-72). In the 1797 *Encyclopaedia Britannica* article on Johnson, George Gleig analyzes the *Rambler* style. Noting that the prose has been overly praised and excessively censored, Gleig points out that most of the censure results from repetition of rhetorical devices: "He who reads *half a volume* of the *Rambler* at a sitting, will feel his ear fatigued by the close of similar periods so frequently recurring; but he who reads only one paper in the day will experience nothing of this weariness." Instead of choosing Addison or Johnson as the better stylist, Gleig judiciously suggests that the reader can decide: "that style should be considered as best which most rouses the attention, and impresses deepest in the mind the sentiments of the author" (CH, 72-73). It should be kept in mind that Gleig's article was replaced by that of Macaulay in 1856. During the eighteenth century, objections to the Rambler's style were seen as initial and temporary; in the long run, the occasionally opaque writing did not detract from the ultimate wisdom of the *Rambler*. Throughout the eighteenth century, the prevalent assumption was that the periodical essays served to socialize a relatively unsophisticated new class of readers. Since Johnson's moral and religious position was usually taken to be above reproach, the only question was whether or not his style appealed to this kind of reader.

In 1802 William Mudford subtly but significantly alters the question by asserting that he respects the goal of the *Rambler* but has misgivings about the means to that end. "The great design of this work was to instruct mankind; to teach the happiness of virtue and religion ... A more noble and exalted undertaking could not employ the mind of man." But "Johnson naturally possessed a misanthropic way of thinking. ... A young mind rising from a perusal of the *Rambler* would conceive the most melancholy ideas of human nature and human events. Mankind would appear to him as an undistinguished mass of fraud, perfidy, and deceit" (CH 75-76). Almost imperceptibly, the focus has shifted from style to content.

In the same year, however, Alexander Chalmers has unreserved praise for the *Rambler*. Presumably unaware of Mudford's view, Chalmers announces confidently: "On the general merit of this work, it is now unnecessary to expatiate: the prejudices which were alarmed by a new style and manner have long subsided." The *Rambler* "has laboured to refine our language to grammatical purity; and to clear it from colloquial barbarisms, licentious idioms, and irregular combinations. Something he *certainly* has added to the elegance of its construction and something to the harmony of its cadence." Addison is not seen as better than Johnson because the Spectator excelled at "observation of manners" while the Rambler did not "descend to familiarities with tickets and commodes, with fans and hoop-petticoats." Nor would Chalmers allow that Johnson's essays are without humor: pointing to twenty-one examples, he asserts that if these are not instances of humor "it will be difficult to say where genuine humour is to be found." Chalmers concludes by pointing out that "the religious and moral tendency of the *Rambler* is, after all, its principal excellence, and what entitles it to a higher praise than can be earned by the powers of wit or of criticism" (CH, 81-84). But clearly Mudford does not agree. He begins a nineteenth-century concern about the tone of Johnson's religion: does the gloom apply only to worldly endeavors or does it also taint Johnson's Christianity?

In 1805 Hannah More, in her *Hints towards Forming the Character of a Young Princess*, devotes a chapter to the periodical essay. This genre, in More's view distinctly British because based upon its free press, is best exemplified by Addison and Johnson. In terms of "moral purity," Johnson stands first, but Addison is better on "characters and episodes." Johnson's characters are abstractions while Addison's are people. Addison is as acute a critic as Johnson but is more elegant. Johnson, the "moral traveler," is deeper but is less pleasing than Addison. The *Idler* is for More the most "engaging" of Johnson's series, while the eastern tales are in general the best of his individual essays (2, 149-68). In 1809, Sir Samuel Egerton Brydges judges, on the basis of Elizabeth Carter's correspondence to Miss Talbot, that the early reception of the *Rambler* was marked by "general coldness, discouragement, and even censure and ridicule." "Had Johnson, instead of dealing in general truths, executed his pen in temporary personal description of manners and characters he would have instantly engaged the attention of vulgar mists and procured present fame." In addition to being out of fashion in his choice of subject matter, Johnson also employs a style that is "heavy and laborious" leading him to be "coarser but solider than Addison" (10. 75-76). In the same year Nathan Drake points out that while the *Spectator* employs a variety of styles, the *Rambler* deliberately cultivates a "uniform style." Unfortunately, Drake continues, "this uniformity of texture [is] not well calculated to procure immediate popularity." Gradually, however, the *Rambler* gains ground with men of taste like Samuel Richardson, who recognize Johnson as one of the "early correct grammatical writers." Indeed, Drake points out that the style of Johnson's essays, particularly the *Rambler* (since he asserts that the *Adventurer* and the *Idler* are written in greater haste), is "greatly original, and greatly more correct, dignified and majestic, than any to which we had been accustomed." In short, the Rambler's prose style is Johnson's greatest contribution to his culture: "if Addison be excepted, no writer of the eighteenth century can be said to have contributed so highly, so copiously, and so permanently, to the improvement of our literature and our language, as

Johnson" (1, 483-87). At this point the debate about Johnson's religion could be evaded if the *Rambler* were recommended on the basis
of style. What in the eighteenth century was a means toward an end
now became an end in itself: the Rambler's style was useful to maintain the "purity" of the language. When the style was attacked, however, no justification remained for preventing the elimination of
the *Rambler* from libraries and classrooms.

In 1819 William Hazlitt places Addison and Johnson in the tradition of the great Renaissance essayists, Montaigne and Bacon. Hazlitt
prefers Addison to Johnson for the *Spectator* has a "dramatic and
conversational tone" and a "charm" "quite lost in the *Rambler* by
Dr. Johnson." The *Rambler*, a "collection of moral essays or scholas-
tic theses," a commonplace book of general topics, according to Hazlitt, lacks "original thought ... familiarity of illustration, knowledge
of character, or humor," and its style is uniform "pomp." Hazlitt
concludes that the best of Johnson is in Boswell's *Life*: "the man was
superior to the authour" (195-201).

Hazlitt's opinion seemed to prevail during the next period of our
history, for very little commentary was to be found until the end of
the Victorian period: the paucity of criticism suggests that during
this era Boswell dominated over Johnson and that the latter represented, what Johnson's *Dictionary* was expected to provide for Becky
Sharp, a repository of establishment politics and moral absolutes.
The predominant opinion is expressed by Thomas Babington
Macaulay, whose entry in the *Encyclopaedia Britannica* in 1856 replaced that of Gleig. Although "admired by a few eminent men," the
Rambler, according to Macaulay, "was at first very coldly received";
then it became popular as an example of proper writing style, and
"the author lived to see thirteen thousand copies spread over England alone." Macaulay admires "the acuteness of his observations on
morals and manners ... [but admits] that his diction was too
monotonous, too obviously artificial and now and then turgid even
to absurdity" (41-42). Hazlitt and Macaulay so baldly separate style
from content that their own method precludes their seeing any connection between them.

In an 1883 essay aptly entitled "Of a Neglected Book," George
Birkbeck Hill points out that Macaulay and others neglect the *Rambler*, which is, according to Hill, not as serious and sober as has been
supposed. In fact, it is exemplary of Johnson's "middle style," an appropriate means to "rouse" the reader to "what the Rambler has left
behind him" (418-23). And in 1886, Mowbray Morris remarks that
Johnson is "probably the most familiar to us of all dead men ... yet
[he] remains one of the Great Unread" (361). The separation of style
from content was a key factor in the nineteenth-century neglect of
Johnson's writings: aside from the manner of presentation, the assumption was that the content is a series of old saws. Hence in 1878

Leslie Stephen returns to a modified version of Macaulay's position. While a moralist is not expected to be original, Johnson, Stephen believes, "rather abuses the moralist's privilege of being commonplace. He descants not infrequently upon propositions so trite that even the most earnest enforcement can give them little interest." "These defects," Stephen explains, "have consigned the *Rambler* to the dustiest shelves of libraries" (175-76).

In 1902 Edwin Bowen articulates the historical concept of the periodical essay that has been implicit for some time. The periodical essay is, for Bowen, aptly defined by Johnson in the second definition of his *Dictionary:* "a loose sally of the mind; an irregular undigested piece; not a regular and orderly composition." Seen as derivative of the comedy of manners, the eighteenth-century periodical essay was employed by its inventors Addison and Steele to offer the "spice of scandal, and to exhibit foibles of the time with a humour that should not be impure." Johnson was the first major writer to imitate these two founders of the genre, but his "ponderosity" is far removed from Addison's "graceful elegance and lightness of touch." In Bowen's view, the *Rambler* only lasted two years because Johnson's "heavy wordy" style was not suited to the periodical essay (13-20). A similar point is made three years later by a writer signing himself as "Ranger," who states that Boswell is right in pointing out that the essayist must not be a "majestic teacher," particularly not in an "undeniably heavy" manner. At this point, a negative assessment of Johnson's style was sufficient to remove him from the curriculum, to relegate his work to the dustbin.

In the Leslie Stephen lecture of 1907 at Cambridge University (published in 1910), Walter Raleigh significantly changes Stephen's position. Admitting that Johnson refuses to attempt to surprise his readers, Raleigh asserts that "the pages of The Rambler ... are aglow with the earnestness of dear-bought conviction, and rich in conclusions gathered not from books but from life and suffering ... Almost every number of The Rambler contains reflections and thoughts which cease to be commonplace when the experiences that suggested them are remembered." Raleigh maintains that Johnson's essays are "more profound than Addison's" and his prose "will not suffer much by comparison with the best in the language" (12-17). Raleigh is fighting a rear-guard action against the general opinion that the *Rambler* is a heavy-handed imitation of the *Spectator.* For Raleigh, Johnson makes reference to experiences beyond the ken of Addison and Steele. However, it is significant that Raleigh introduces the criterion of experience, suggesting a substantial and unique goal for Johnson's style.

In 1924 O. F. Christie devotes the first full-length book to *Johnson the Essayist,* pointing out that although Johnson's conversations are read, his "Essays are neglected" in spite of the fact that "his real opin-

ions are to be found in his books." Christie's goal is to group Johnson's various essays not as a "system of philosophy ... but as a consistent and coherent whole." Although, Christie asserts, the *Rambler* is
popular in its own day, now "Johnson is scarcely visualized without
Boswell," and modern commentators reinforce this generally negative judgment. (It should be kept in mind that Christie, like others,
is making reference to the use made of certain of Boswell's phrases
taken out of context. As we have seen, Boswell's comments on the
Rambler in particular but also on others of Johnson's periodicals are
very positive.) On style, Christie maintains that Johnson excels at
"imagery," and at a picturesqueness of phrase that serves the purpose of "spiritual insight." Morality, we are informed, is for Johnson
the "civic duty of a writer," enabling him to relate his life as writer to
his writings, a notion reminiscent of Raleigh's point. Christie then
demonstrates that Johnson's essays are reflective of the history of his
age, ranging from city to country, from scholarship and education to
women and the domestic scene, from politics to religion. In representing the issues of his age, Johnson is compared by Christie to
Dickens (5-6, 58, 94). The notion of experience introduced by Raleigh
is now broadened to include the whole of Augustan culture.

   In 1927 Lawrence F. Powell produces evidence that, as had been
previously supposed, the *Adventurer* essays signed "T" are by Johnson and that the *Adventurer* as a whole had been a profitable ven-
ture. Within two years David Nichol Smith demonstrates that although Boswell implies that none of Johnson's prose works were
revised by Johnson, the *Rambler, Adventurer,* and *Idler* are all revised for stylistic purposes. In 1935 Mallie Murphy devotes a short
essay in *PMLA* to demonstrating that the term "trinkets" is "below
Mr. Rambler" and attempts to explain in historical terms why Johnson uses it (926-28). Clearly the use of the *Rambler* style as a cultural
touchstone, so prevalent during the period of Becky Sharp, continues well into the twentieth century.

   In 1938 Willis Pratt defends the *Rambler* against Leigh Hunt's attack on Johnson's "religious pessimism," his views on Spenser, Milton and Shakespeare, and his "artificial and pedantic" style. Pratt
replies that "Hunt's mind [is] not of sufficient station to see the great
humanity of Dr. Johnson" or to penetrate beyond the gloom of the
Rambler to "the wisdom" resulting from "bitter suffering" that
Hunt's "romantic temperament never allowed him to experience"
(70-78). Again, we see history in the largest sense affecting criticism:
the period of the Great Depression converted what the Victorians
saw as pessimism into realism.

   In 1939 Curtis Bradford reinforces the contentions of Chalmers
and Smith that Johnson made extensive stylistic revisions to his essays. Bradford is the first to establish that the fourth edition of the
Rambler contains the last authorized alterations. A year later Ellen

Leyburn examines the mottoes and quotations in the *Rambler*, along with the translations, and concludes that they constitute a "noble collection of English verse" (175). Bonamy Dobrée distinguishes between Addison and Johnson on the basis that Johnson "thumps" but does not talk down like Addison, who is lighter but less profound. The *Rambler's* "heavy artillery" is, however, "not without humour"; Addison's standard is "social" while Johnson's is "ethical" (22-24). The morality that for Hazlitt and Macaulay represented pomposity is here seen to serve a literary purpose.

In 1948 W. K. Wimsatt, Jr., devotes a chapter to the *Rambler* in *Philosophic Words*. Wimsatt points out that "the *Rambler* is, in the elaboration and complexity of its structures and in the weight of its vocabulary, the most concentrated, and in its length the most sustained example of the peculiarities which distinguish the prose of Johnson's maturity. To the end of his life Johnson remained the Rambler." Turning to the themes of the *Rambler*, Wimsatt maintains that "one of the most persistent themes ... is the lament for pedantic or fanatic science ... and even more important ... are those drawn from medicine and anatomy," which together provide clear evidence of Johnson's interest in the 'philosophic words' of his day. This kind of language, according to Wimsatt, soon becomes part of the very fabric of Johnson's style. "It was a way of writing which the Rambler had established as his own. ... Johnson's bent for philosophic imagery and diction was among the most permanent attachments of his mind" (54-69). Wimsatt establishes that Johnson's style is deliberate and singular, initiating critical analysis of the specificity of individual works.

In the 1950s Arthur Sherbo begins his scholarly investigation of Johnson's periodical essays: in six articles he analyzes the translations of the mottoes and quotations and the sources and revisions of the essays. During this same period, Edward Bloom categorizes Johnson's use of names, demonstrating that Johnson's purpose is "to evoke from his readers experiential responses, to recall through specific signs empirical general truths" (234). In 1953 W. H. Graham reiterates Raleigh's view that the *Rambler* deserves more readers than it currently has: this "splendid repository of wisdom and truth has ceased to attract readers because the 'didactic moral substance' lacks Addison's and Steele's lightness of touch" (50). Scholarship and criticism since Raleigh's time have established that Johnson carefully revised his periodical essays and that while employing the same genre as that of Addison and Steele his goals were different from those of the *Spectator*. But the precise nature of this difference remains to be clarified.

In a 1956 monograph on the periodicals and magazines from 1746 to 1820, Melvin Watson chooses Johnson, along with Addison and Steele, as the major influences of the period. "From the *Rambler* ...

the essay periodical received fresh inspiration and impetus" (16).
Similarly, later in the period, the reprints of Johnson's essays have a
significant effect: "In view of the potent influence of the Rambler
papers in book form it was inevitable that writers should attempt to
clothe Johnsonian thoughts and doctrines with Johnsonian phras-
ing. That no one succeeded was equally inevitable" (41). Understanding of the historical importance of the period essay brought
Johnson's essays new prominence. In the 1960s, A. T. Elder produced
two articles on Johnson's periodicals. The first demonstrates that
Johnson's use of humor is much more pervasive than had been
generally assumed. While crediting Stephen and Wimsatt with having located facets of Johnson's humor in the essays, Elder is the first
to categorize in a systematic way the many and various uses of humor—from "self mockery" and "plays on the gravity of Mr. Rambler" to "a direct satiric approach" and an "attack by means of irony,"
as well as the "subtle ironic affects" of a style directed at the
"disappointed hope" of a "fortune-hunter" and other vain pursuers.
This irony, Elder insists, is never "bitter" (58-70). In his second article, Elder categorizes the themes of Johnson periodicals. Dividing the
central concerns into six issues—humanitarianism, marriage, relation of parents/children, dependence on others, knowing oneself,
seeing the world as it is—Elder locates the "central theme of con-
tributing to society [as] the connective tissue of the essays" (630). Elder provides the thematic basis for distinguishing Johnson from
Addison and Steele, but the themes isolated do not explain how the
Spectator's humor and mode of socialization differ from those of the
Rambler.

In 1962 Robert Mayo published a study of the English novel in
the magazines of the period 1740-1815. Although the *Rambler* contains only one story of "novelette length," it is important "because of
its special emphasis on prose fiction, its pronouncements on the subject of the English novel, and its decisive influence upon the much
more popular *Adventurer*." Seen as central to the tradition of the
periodical essay, the *Rambler*, according to Mayo, is anomalous in its
highbrow demeanor, its avoidance of any mention of Mr. Spectator
at the outset, and in its focus upon the ethical position of the essayist
as opposed to more entertaining fictive genres. The one novelette of
the *Rambler*, "The History of Hymenaeus's Courtship," only qualifies as fiction because it is a series of four essays which are in most
respects, according to Mayo, indistinguishable from the other non-
fiction essays. Both the *Adventurer* and the *Idler* are only discussed
by Mayo as they serve as parts of larger entities that contribute to the
progress of the novel, but again Johnson's contribution is seen as
anomalous, almost outside the tradition of the English novel. The
reason for the Rambler's singular style, however, is not pursued.

During this same decade Bernard Kneiger attempts to characterize the morality of the "English Socrates" of the periodical essay in a way that is not systematic in philosophic terms. Kneiger concludes that "because of his complete grasp, based upon observation, of how people actually react in social situations and in relation to their estimation of themselves, because of the compassion underlying his understanding of human limitations, because of the nobility of his ethical aims, and because of his ability to penetrate into the heart of a situation ... Johnson's moral writings are universally valid" (367). But we are left to wonder whether the validity derives from unique precepts or old truisms.

In 1966 Rodman Rhodes focuses upon Johnson's epistemology on the basis of *Idler* No. 24. Johnson begins, according to Rhodes, by insisting "that philosophical accuracy is no substitute for intellectual endeavor." The mind, Rhodes continues, must fuse "Lockean wonder and Cartesian surprise, at the fact of thought with the act of thinking." So Johnson's empiricism "meant freedom," and Rhodes asserts that most mistakes about Johnson's epistemology emphasize either Locke or Descartes, judgment or invention, thought or thinking, instead of giving equal emphasis to both. For Rhodes, Johnson is both a rationalist and an empiricist; hence energy is defined in the *Dictionary* as "life." Rhodes concludes that "the mind thinking afforded conclusive evidence that man's dependence on matter guarantees his independence and is final proof that man's loss of intellectual stature but qualifies him the more to obtain it" (12-21). Here we begin to see Raleigh's concept of experience being used to distinguish Johnson from Addison and Steele. Johnson's balance between thought and thinking had become a new point of interest. The procedure of Johnson as essayist is being identified as a new point of interest.

Near the end of this decade R. M. Wiles demonstrates that the original distribution of the *Rambler* was more extensive than had been generally assumed. In the year of the first printing of the *Rambler* in London, numerous provincial newspapers printed excerpts and samples, so that by the time the first collected volumes appeared, "thousands of people ... knew what the essays were like in style and substance. He was more popular than he knew" (171). In the same year Jim Corder applies Aristotelian terminology to the rhetorical structure of *Rambler* No. 154. In *The Quarterly Journal of Speech*, Corder insists that the "ethical argument of *Rambler* No 154 begins with an attacking proposition that is sustained by the *confutatio* attacking vanity. Breaking his argument at paragraph eight with the recognition of natural (unlearned) capacities, Johnson moves into an expanding *confirmatio* attacking pride even as he acknowledges good in contrary positions. When he comes at last to the restated proposition in the last paragraph, it is a proposition enlarged and enriched by the convergence of views that seeks identification without conviction" (356). Not surprisingly it is generally assumed that Addison and Steele did not use such sophisticated rhetorical techniques, but we are left without any explanation of how the *Rambler* could be so popular when employing such sophisticated rhetorical devices.

In 1970 Donald Greene asserts that the *Rambler* "made Johnson's name," and "no more delightful or effective introduction to Johnson [is available] than the hundred or so *Idler* papers." After tentatively arranging the essays into categories, Greene concludes that "in many of these moral essays, especially in *The Rambler*, Johnson rises to generalizations of great thoughtfulness and beauty of language that reverberate in the reader's mind" (104-8). Leopold Damrosch, Jr., however, focuses on the manner of proceeding in the *Rambler*. Instead of treating the essays in the customary way as bits of wisdom, Damrosch points to two "rhetorical modes," the "dismantling" of commonplaces and "amplification" or meditation. Both are designed to reach the same audience as that of the *Spectator* but to encourage a "more rigorously critical kind of thinking. ... The heart of Johnson's mission," according to Damrosch, "is to make us stop parroting the precepts of moralists and start thinking for ourselves" (70-81). Damrosch helped explain why Johnson used more sophisticated techniques than other periodicalists.

Patrick O'Flaherty, however, attacks both Greene and Damrosch for giving undue emphasis to the means and neglecting the ends. "It is also difficult to accept Damrosch's opinion that Johnson strategically contrived reversals and conceived alternatives in order to force readers to think for themselves, to jar them towards the truth. When Johnson thought he knew the truth, he told the truth as directly as he could." O'Flaherty believes that the procedure of the *Rambler* results in "ambiguity and inconsistency." In fact, "the more deeply Johnson burrows into human motivations to expose for men the innumerable strategies and vanities which enable them to live with error, the keener this awareness becomes of the frailty of virtue and the closer he is drawn to an extreme fastidiousness." The result, O'Flaherty asserts, is not the "larger harmony" scholars are fond of isolating; "Johnson made no claim to having achieved such harmony and was apparently untroubled by the kind of inconsistency contained in [any] essay" (525-36). The *Idler*, O'Flaherty continues in another essay eight years later, adopts a different point of view. The *Rambler* sets out to create a "persona" whose gaze is inward and meditative; the *Idler* deliberately distances himself from the reader and society, adopting the stance of the satirist. But the perspective of the satirist is continually included in the satire: "Throughout the *Idler* observations which were offered in the *Rambler* as sober truths reappear in contexts which make them funny." Moving from the

Rambler to the *Idler*, Johnson turns to "satiric laughter" that is not "egotistical laughter," for it borders on "tragedy and contains the fullness of Johnson's love for mankind. ... Now, in the *Idler*," O'Flaherty concludes, Johnson "is moving towards and adopting the liberating stance which is definitively and richly assumed in *Rasselas*: humorous detachment without levity, pessimism without bitterness or gloom" (213-25). Now that Johnson has been clearly distinguished from Addison and Steele, O'Flaherty is free to focus upon the relationship between Johnson's periodicals and his other writings and to consider the development of his style from the *Rambler* and the *Adventurer* to the *Idler*. But he does not make clear how the increase of humor changes Johnson's goals.

During this same period the rhetorical tradition is continued in another essay in the *Quarterly Journal of Speech*. Michael Rewa locates a pattern in the "professedly serious" *Rambler* essays: "praise of sayer, tell why it was said, introduce context, then a comparison, and example, support with confirmatory testimony, conclude with a brief epilog." Rewa urges us to acknowledge Johnson's "sensitivity and debt to the conventions of rhetoric" (77-78). But he neglects to explain how rhetoric alters our understanding of the *Rambler*.

In 1974 Richard Schwartz argues for what he calls the "'eidolon' of Mr. Rambler," which is attacked as less successful than that of Addison in the *Spectator* because not sufficiently entertaining and detached from the self. But Schwartz affirms that Johnson, unlike Addison, does not claim "flawless virtue." Instead Johnson combines pride and humility derived from his concept of human vanity and his Christianity. Johnson is seen as changing the norm of the *Spectator*, merging the "gnomic genre of the Baconian essay with the compelling and inviting dimension of the personal essay" (196-202). Modification of the periodical persona, now seen as part of Johnson's goal, is further pursued by James Woodruff, who distinguishes the *Rambler* from contemporary competitors: "Johnson had an altogether more rigorous conception of the genre. At practically every point the *Rambler* seems sure of itself in a way that the *Tatler Revived* does not. While Johnson follows the *Spectator* in avoiding politics, the *Tatler Revived* from time to time exploits the subject. ... The *Tatler Revived* attempts everything that might sell copies: a well-tried editorial fiction is adopted; the natural interest in contemporary particulars is obviously exploited; instead of directing its appeal to an audience particularly interested in a certain subject— practical morality as the *Rambler* was to do—it attempted variety and a wide appeal by combining all of these. The *Rambler*, on the other hand, goes well beyond the ordinary notion of journalism with a much more unified conception of purpose and altogether subtler variety" (177). Four years later Woodruff compares *Idler* no. 40 on advertisements to its source in the *Spectator*: "Johnson's essay is much less pure mock criticism than Addison's; the schemata around which he structures it are more complex than the simple division of *utile* and *dulce* that shapes *Tatler* No. 224. Johnson is concerned with the rhetorical as well as moral implications of advertising, and in the course of developing his discussion introduces such currently fashionable topics as the sublime in a way which, though facetious, is also curiously serious. ... Although Johnson on advertisements is intricately involved with the ephemera of his time, he regularly balances among his sources of inspiration the literary and the actual. ... He sees the immediate and particular *sub specie aeternitatis* and enables and encourages us to bring universal truth to bear on our own present" (384-89).

In 1977 Charles Knight further develops the distinction between Johnson and Addison. According to Knight, Addison and Steele and their imitators share an "eidolon" whose "purpose is to reform society by reflecting in a conversational style upon its manners and patterns of behavior and by making generally accessible the wisdom found in the classical tradition. ... Almost none of these characteristics are present in Johnson's periodical essays. ... The Rambler introduced a startling departure from the traditional periodical format. ... During the period from 1712 to 1725, periodicals were published in a pamphlet form in order to take advantage of a loophole in the stamp tax that was then imposed upon periodicals, such as the *Review* and *Spectator*, which appeared in the costly newspaper format. The *Rambler* reverted to this 1712-1725 format: it had six pages, printed on a folio sheet and one half, with large type and often with an unfilled final page." The new format, Knight believes, "enhanced the dignity, seriousness and permanence of the medium," a part of the more general change "Johnson brought to the periodical essay as a genre." In addition to the format, Johnson used the first and last two essays as framing devices "to prepare the reader and to remind him of the centrality of the essay series as a commentary on human life." Working in a tradition that regarded the periodical essay as a fashionable form devoted to contemporary manners, Johnson insisted on "commonsense practicality ... discarding the traditional periodical eidolon for the more universal image of the writer as moral hero, struggling against the inner monsters of vanity, illusion, and frustrated ambition in order to achieve his social function as a moral teacher" (238-50). Here some specific differences were emerging between Mr. Rambler and Mr. Spectator as personae. But we still need to know what purpose is served by this new "eidolon" and other rhetorical devices.

In 1978 Peter Koper offers yet another rhetorical analysis of the *Rambler*. Koper defines a debate about Johnson's prose style going as far back as Chalmers, who, in 1803, was one of the first to defend the concrete element of Johnson's style as opposed to Wimsatt and most nineteenth-century commentators who characterized his prose as "philosophical" or "heavy" and "pedantic." In an attempt to combine both schools of thought, Koper employs rhetorical analysis to arrive at the concrete-universal of Johnson's prose style in the *Rambler*. "I find the governing feature of Johnson's style to be his handling of indefinite nouns and noun phrases and the pronoun references which they dictate. ... This pattern of noun usage, an indefinite noun used in its fullest distribution ... followed by a series of third person pronouns ... is the basis to a startling degree of Johnson's style of moralizing." In this way, Koper infers, with reference to Corder, Johnson is able to inspire "trust, in his moral truisms" (26-33). The critics of the 1970s focus upon the rhetoric of Johnson's periodicals in order to demonstrate that instead of following Addison and Steele, who welcome a new class of readers, Johnson points to a thinking process that serves a profounder ethical purpose. But since the profundity of that ethical purpose is not spelled out in specific terms, this assertion becomes merely rhetorical.

In 1980 William Edinger provides background for *Adventurer* No. 95. Selecting Voltaire and Dubos as representative of the poles of a prevailing critical controversy of the day between "neoclassicism" and empiricism, Edinger finds that Johnson integrates the two opposing positions: "We may suppose that the neo-Aristotelian tradition helped to keep Johnson's attention focused on the problem of general truth. But it was Johnson's firm grounding in the epistemology of Bacon and Locke, and probably too Dubos's demonstrations of how this epistemology might be applied to criticism, which enabled him to enliven and, as it were, expand the conceptualism of the *Poetics* by bringing it into more intimate contact with empirical reality" (37). And Alan McKenzie suggests that in the *Rambler* distribution and extent are paradoxically linked, much in the way that Aristotelian logic is related to his most famous student, Alexander, and his extensive conquests. "The care [Johnson] takes," McKenzie continues, "in distributing the abstractions whose extensions he has so carefully (and comparatively) established may make him a humanist and a writer who places great but manageable demands on his readers" (63). Here again we see more evidence of Johnson's deliberate use of rhetoric to serve his uniquely ethical end, although the nature of that end is not articulated.

During this same decade, Robert Olson publishes an essay and a full-length study on Johnson's mottoes for the *Rambler* and the *Adventurer*. The longer work is a useful reference tool for critics: each motto is carefully translated and placed in the context of Johnson's essay. In the introduction Olson suggests that, contrary to the widely held belief that most of the mottoes were afterthoughts, "Johnson sometimes sets his motto up first and uses it as a text for his essay" (xi). Olson's article also demonstrates that although Johnson says he avoids love as a subject, he makes considerable and deliberate use of Ovid, "and ten of these are from contexts that exude sexuality." Olson admits that Johnson's "dexterity in taking from the classical past one kind of material, in this case, bits of light-hearted amorous poetry, and transmuting such stuff into matter for his own serious literary and moral concerns, bespeaks a mind which knows what it is doing, even when it works in a spirit being gradually superseded, the spirit of the medieval monk cautiously treating a pagan text" (11-19). Olson's analysis raises the intriguing question of how the amorous and sexual allusions serve Johnson's ethical imperative.

In 1984 Hoyt Trowbridge presents an alternative to W. K. Wimsatt's approach to Johnson's language. Instead of avoiding concern about authorial intention, Trowbridge proposes to examine the *Rambler* from the point of view of the intentions of rhetoric, which he defines, in Aristotelian terms, as "the art or faculty of observing in any given case the available means of persuasion." Trowbridge grants that the eidolon of the *Rambler* is "a speaker to be respected and trusted, so that we are predisposed to believe what he says." But, Trowbridge insists, "the heart of my subject, because it is also the heart of Johnson's rhetoric is ... reasoned argument," a process that is defined in the terms of Greene and Schwartz as "always empirical." Hence Trowbridge focuses not like Wimsatt on "philosophic words" but upon the "language of logic," and even the fictional essays are seen to "operate as proofs" in the sense of "a highly probable, though not, of course, a demonstrative, proof." In fact, Johnson's reasoning on ethical questions, according to Trowbridge, "rests on similar assumptions about the limits of human understanding" and leads to the distinction between true and false rhetoric: "the language [Johnson] chooses is proportioned to the real moral worth or worthlessness of the person and actions he condemns or commends, and his arguments, though no more than probable, are as valid and strong as the condition of our existence and the imperfections of human understanding will allow" (200-216). Trowbridge's demonstration that the syntax of probability serves Johnson's morality is important, but we need to know how that insight alters our understanding of the periodicals from the view of Wimsatt.

In the same year, James Boyd White, a professor of classics, law, and English, includes a chapter on the *Rambler* in *When Words Lose Their Meaning: Constitutions and Reconstructions of Language, Character, and Community*, a study that relates English and the law because, as White explains, "in its hunger to connect the general and the particular, in its metaphorical movements, and in its constant and forced recognition of the limits of mind and language the law seemed to me a kind of poetry." White suggests that the significance of the *Rambler* is not merely "in the truth of a set of moral propositions and the validity of the arguments supporting them." Instead, Johnson "has a central interest in the place a particular statement holds in his own mind and experience as he utters it and in the place he can give it, by his writing, in the mind and experience of his reader, ... what distinguishes—to use his terms—'common-place' from 'principle.'" Johnson, according to White, makes precisely this transition from the beginning to the end of his essays: "Johnson's beginnings are thus a way of starting where the reader actually is, surrounded by truisms and clichés, in a condition of uncertainty or doubt, perhaps of essential thoughtlessness, from which he may be moved to a new position of clarity and truth. But the familiarity of the conclusions ... shows us something important about the condition initially addressed in the reader." The procedure of the essays is seen as a thought process: "The activities of mind by which these essays move thus comprise a steady pressure to correct and complicate; a constant openness to new facts or ideas; a repeated turning from system or theory to experience; and a hunger for balance, for the capaciousness of mind that can retain at once two opposing tendencies in their full force." The result is not "building blocks of a theoretical system. His conclusions are in this sense openended or presumptive in character, structurally tentative. Not that a particular conclusion is not firm, but it must be understood for what it is, as inextricably part of a larger system of expression. It is firm only in the context that gives it life and meaning and renders it a principle rather than a commonplace." A second result of this procedure produces a "moral language superior to our own," a process also used in the *Dictionary*, "a series of performances of proper meaning, demonstrations of the ways a word can be used well." Still another function of the language of the *Rambler* essays for White is "its integrative character. ... This language cannot be broken down into the modern categories of fact, reason, and value; ... the reader ... [is not seen] merely as one who now observes, now ratiocinates, now feels or prefers, but as one who does all these at once."

Finally White unites these two procedures: "I earlier said that the movement of these essays was from commonplace to principle; here I observe a movement from a kind of division of self and language to what I call integration, achieved in a moment of solitude or isolation. I hope it is clear that these are not two movements but one and the same; for his ending in solitude defines the condition out of which a language of principle can be made. The movement typical of the essays is a constant struggle through layers of feeling, patterns and habits of thought, and impulses of resistance to a kind of central awareness from which, and only from which truth and strength can flow." "Johnson's object," according to White, "is not to leave us with a wisdom that can be learned by imitation and repetition. His purpose is to teach us a method of contemplation and criticism, a kind of thought, by which we can remake our minds and lives by remaking our language and the culture it defines. ... What Johnson seeks to teach us is how to do it on our own; how to move out of our perpetually recreated condition of confusion, how to engage the mind and move it in the direction of truth" (138-61). The structural procedure of the essays is understood as pointing to a firm but provisional truth. White's analysis was the first to suggest in concrete terms how the rhetoric of Johnson's periodicals points to new ends, by crossing into the realm of the law. During the 1980s, Johnson's rhetoric—understood now in the broadest sense as structure as well as style—moved the reader beyond the realm of discourse to that of law, ethics, and human behavior in a general sense. It is not surprising, therefore, that the most recent entry was the first full-length study of the rhetoric of the *Rambler*.

In *Samuel Johnson after Deconstruction: Rhetoric and The Rambler* (1992), Steven Lynn explains why rhetoric is the appropriate method for this innovative endeavor. "How does a rhetorical analysis situated after deconstruction address the various obstructions to in-depth study of *The Rambler*? From such a perspective, Johnson himself is not a distraction from the text but a necessary construct for its analysis: the perception of structures and strategies and their effects stems from recognizing (inventing) Johnson's controlling intention" (18). The controlling intention for Lynn is religion: "But why if *The Rambler* is a religious work, is the Bible cited only 7 times in comparison to, say, 103 references to Horace or 37 to Juvenal? Partly because Johnson does not want to frighten off his largely secular audience. But mostly because his strategy in *The Rambler* involves the reader in a process of education that is not by any means a direct and confident route to salvation. ... His way to such a mazing grace in the *Rambler* essays involves such struggle and indirection because he perceives so clearly the forces ... that undermine and erode it. Such forces of skepticism and uncertainty, exposing the absence of any ultimately ordering Word, have arguably come together in our time most acutely in the project of deconstruction" (20).

What new light is thrown on the *Rambler* by a rhetoric of deconstruction, especially when Lynn himself has shown us that deconstruction in Johnson's own time suggests a different alternative than that of rhetoric? Deconstruction, Lynn explains, is not only appropriate for us but also for Johnson. "Johnson's view of language ... involves the recurrent deconstruction of a powerfully tempting and always returning myth of a pristine origin" (138). At this point Lynn turns to Wilbur Howell's distinction between old and new rhetoric. "The old rhetoric concentrates on persuasion, whereas the new rhetoric, partly in response to the needs of science, encompasses broader aims that include conveying information and investigating truth. ... The old rhetoric sees truth as equal to verbal consistency, and the new rhetoric recognizes a gap between words and things" (139). Johnson's use of the new rhetoric leads him, according to Lynn, "to the edge of a rhetorical cliff where he must either jump off, sit down, or walk back" (150). The Rambler is seen to jump: "but it is *The Rambler* that most powerfully and engagingly shows us how after deconstruction we may save the self, inevitably out of place here within language, by ceasing to believe in it and by believing in an Other elsewhere, creating our self-will by exercising it" (154).

If this "Other" sounds suspiciously like the "transcendental signifier," the anathema of deconstruction, Lynn confirms that suspicion by anticipating the opposition argument: "Motivated by my own desire to salvage and justify some sort of belief in a Transcendent Other, I have read that interest back into Johnson's *Rambler* to the exclusion of other concerns. I have read *The Rambler*, which appears to be concerned with many things, as a single-minded evangelical document, casting Johnson as a lay preacher out to win our souls for God" (157). The rhetoric of the *Rambler* becomes for Lynn the means to religion, leaving the reader to ponder how the periodical essay is to be distinguished from the sermon.

We seem almost to have come full circle. When they first appeared, the periodical essays, particularly the *Rambler*, were criticized for being too weighty, abstract, and pompous, lacking in the delicate touch of Addison and Steele. The defense of Johnson, in the eighteenth and again in the twentieth century, was that he used the essay for his own purposes, not social amelioration but a higher morality. Lynn implies that Johnson's morality was really his religion. But we should recall that in the nineteenth century it was pointed out that the *Spectator* is more religious than the *Rambler*. Indeed, one would be hard-pressed to find in all of Johnson's periodical essays anything as overtly Christian as Addison's "Vision of Mirza." The task of present criticism would seem then to be to explain how the ethical concerns of Johnson's periodical essays remain distinct from but not contradictory to his religion. Rhetoric, if it is to prove a useful tool in this endeavor, must be shown to serve the purpose of ethics, since an emphasis on morality is clearly what distinguishes Johnson's periodical essays from his overtly religious works, such as the sermons.

5: *Rasselas*

RASSELAS IS THE MOST WIDELY READ and continuously commented upon of all Johnson's writings. Since its publication in 1759
not a single year has gone by that has not produced a new edition of
or essay upon the text. Even during the nineteenth century, when
Johnson's own writings were overshadowed by Boswell's *Life*, *Rasselas* continued to be reissued and analyzed. In fact, because the Victorians value Johnson the man over his writings, *Rasselas* is the
only one of Johnson's literary works with a continuous critical history. As a *locus criticus*, *Rasselas* is the subject of a controversy that
began when it first appeared and that continues in the present. In
1759 one reviewer characterizes it as trite and threadbare, and in 1970
a critic describes it as marked by religious equivocation. But few critics are aware of this long and complex critical history. Ordinarily,
commentators distinguish their positions from those of their immediate predecessors and then present an innovative view that
combines, reuses, or slightly modifies approaches that have already
been disputed or discredited. For the *Rasselas* controversy is unique
in leading to the undermining not merely of interpretations but also
of methods of approach. A prism of critical methodology, *Rasselas*
has been subjected to every kind of approach: lack of awareness of
the history of *Rasselas* criticism is equivalent to methodological
naiveté.

    In the year of its first publication, *Rasselas* was reviewed, accord-
ing to Gwin Kolb in his essay of 1984, in at least fourteen different
periodicals (20-21). Most of the reviews are complimentary. The *Gentlemen's Magazine* praises the author for his "striking pictures of life
and nature" that served as happy illustrations "of most important
truths" (186). Similarly, the *London Magazine* points to the "most
important Truths" of the "moral Tale" as well as the "agreeable and
enchanting Manner" in which it is told (258). The *Critical Review*
applauds the choice of fiction as a means of moral instruction but
faults the lack of "plot, incident, character or contrivance" necessary
to "beguile the imagination." The tale is seen as a "beautiful epitome
of practical Ethics," but its author's talents are considered better
suited to the essay or dialogue than to fiction (372-73). Sharing this

negative assessment of the manner of presentation, Owen Ruffhead, in the *Monthly Review*, goes one step further to launch the first full-scale attack on the tale. This "romantic way of writing requires a sprightliness of imagination" that Johnson lacks. The style of *Rasselas* is labeled "tumid and pompous," and the characters are said to lack variety and a distinct manner of speaking. The narrative lacks "invention in the plan" and "utility in the design" because the topics are trite and threadbare, and the conclusion does not further any good end in society. The goal of Johnson's narrative, Ruffhead concludes, is to show that "discontent prevails among men of all ranks and conditions," a truth, he points out, that can be learned without traveling to Ethiopia (428-29).

Ruffhead is not questioning the truth of the message of *Rasselas*. Rather, he believes that the manner of presentation is so abstract and gloomy as to encourage in the young and impressionable reader despair. And most critics of the day, Johnson included, assume that fiction or romances are designed for such a reader (19-25). As we shall see, the question of the tone of the conclusion was contested throughout the nineteenth and into the twentieth century, but during this latter period the issue became whether or not the end is marked by a religious resolution. This alteration in the terms of the debate involves a shift in assumptions about the genre of *Rasselas*. It is generally assumed that the charge of gloom against *Rasselas* is synonymous with an attack on the religion of the narrative. But the eighteenth-century concept of the narrative and of the religious resolution appropriate to it was different from that of the Victorians and Moderns. The nature of this difference is made clear by considering an alternative to Ruffhead's position that was also published in 1759. An anonymous defender of *Rasselas* points out in the *Annual Register* that whereas most novels and romances of the day use superficial morality to lend a respectable appearance to an adventure story, Johnson employs the popular story form in order to convey important ethical doctrines in a pleasurable manner (477).

The point of contention for these first reviewers of *Rasselas* concerns not the religion of the text but whether or not the "beauties"—a term that can refer to aesthetic and formal properties as well as to moral strictures—of the story provide sufficient interest in and compensation for a gloomy, although accurate, picture of the futility of earthly endeavors. These critics share the assumption that the doctrine of Ecclesiastes, the vanity of human wishes, need not discourage one from savoring the limited licit pleasures of the mortal world. They disagree as to whether Johnson's "romance" leaves its young readers with as vivid an impression of the pleasures of everyday life as of the folly of man's grand designs. During the eighteenth century two attitudes toward the doctrine of Ecclesiastes were current, the more familiar one asserting that all earthly endeavors

are vain, and an alternative proposing that although all mortal
wishes are ultimately vain, some wishes are to be preferred to others.

The publication of at least six new editions of *Rasselas* between
1759 and 1810 provided some evidence against the early view that
the tale did not please or interest its readers. In the decade after the
death of Johnson, 1784-94, the flurry of lives of this most famous literary figure of the second half of the eighteenth century resulted in
both positions on *Rasselas* being presented in biographical terms.
One of the earliest of Johnson's biographers, Thomas Tyers, reaffirms that *Rasselas* is a "lamp of wisdom" (18), a judgment shared by
an anonymous editor who in 1787 feels confident enough of the appeal and wisdom of the book to recommend that young ladies imitate the Princess of Abyssinia, a "pattern and mirror of excellence"
(6). In 1787 Sir John Hawkins, however, disapproves of the tale because although "none of [Johnson's] compositions has been more
applauded than this," it is a "general satire" that exposes not only
follies but also "laudable affections and propensities." Hawkins is
generally credited with having begun the tradition of attacking *Rasselas* as a tale of despair and hopelessness. A careful look at his position, however, makes clear that he is carrying on the tradition of
Ruffhead, not accusing *Rasselas* of lack of a religious resolution.

> I wish I were not warranted in saying, that this elegant work is
> rendered, by its most obvious moral, of little benefit to the
> reader. We would not indeed wish to see the rising generation
> so unprofitably employed as the prince of Abyssinia; but it is
> equally impolitic to repress all hope, and he who should quit
> his father's house in search of a profession, and return un-
> provided, because he could not find any man pleased with his
> own, would need a better justification than that Johnson, after
> speculatively surveying various modes of life, had judged
> happiness unattainable, and choice useless. (371)

Hawkins concludes by warning those reading *Rasselas* "in the
spring of life" not to be "captivated by its author's eloquence, and
convinced by his perspicacious wisdom that human life and hopes
are such as he has depicted them," but to "remember that [Johnson]
saw through the medium of adversity" (366). Being now familiar
with the terms of Ruffhead's attack, we notice such phrases in
Hawkins as "the rising generation," readers in the "spring of life,"
and "he who should quit his father's house in search of a profession." Clearly, Hawkins has in mind the same young, impressionable reader who might be led astray by Johnson's austere, if accurate,
representation of life. Even a passing familiarity with the historical
tradition of *Rasselas* criticism suffices to call into question the gener-

ally accepted belief that Hawkins began the religious attack. That accusation did not arise until the nineteenth century. In fact, Hawkins'
confidence in Johnson's religious convictions is illustrated by the assertion in his biography that Johnson intended to write a sequel—an
intent that was never carried out— in which his hero was to marry
and conclude in a state of "permanent felicity."

Fate visited upon Hawkins the rare, if dubious, distinction of
converting speculation into fact, or nearly so. In 1790, Ellis Cornelia
Knight wrote a continuation of *Rasselas* that, as she explains in her
introduction, follows Hawkins's prescription. Entitled *Dinarbas*, this
story concludes with the double marriage of hero and heroine. The
tale is designed to show how Rasselas and his sister find what for
them constitutes the choice of life (92-94). Its chief critical interest resides in the fact that it has been neglected until recently. Even now,
Johnson scholars approach it as a work of historical interest, not as a
conclusion for the Johnsonian choice of life quest. That this sequel
has never been taken seriously as a commentary on *Rasselas*
demonstrates that the attempt to locate a particular choice of life is
mis-guided. Yet during the next two centuries critics continued to attack *Rasselas* for not providing a final choice of life for the prince,
unaware that *Dinarbas* exemplifies the inappropriateness of such a
resolution.

James Boswell, publishing a year later than Knight, considers
Rasselas on its own terms and devises a more successful reply to the
accusation of inordinate gloom. Despite his awe and respect for the
wisdom and "fund of thinking" of *Rasselas*, Boswell feels obliged to
comment on the author's "morbid melancholy":

> Notwithstanding my high admiration of Rasselas, I will not
> maintain that the "morbid melancholy" in Johnson's consti-
> tution may not, perhaps, have made life appear to him more
> insipid and unhappy than it generally is; for I am sure that he
> had less enjoyment from it than I have. Yet, whatever addi-
> tional shade his own particular sensations may have thrown
> on his representation of life, attentive observation and close
> inquiry have convinced me, that there is too much reality in
> the gloomy picture. (I, 343)

Boswell finds Johnson's picture of life not distorted but all too accurate. In response to Hawkins' attack, Boswell characterizes *Rasselas*
as a *Vanity of Human Wishes* in prose. But Boswell is not equating
the conclusions of the two works; his intention is to assert, in opposition to Hawkins, that the narrative no more encourages despair
than does the poem.

In 1802 William Mudford begins the process of turning the biographical defense of *Rasselas* against the text. That the tale was writ-

ten at a time when the author had to support a dying mother might excuse its "imperfect picture" of life but for the fact that the same pessimistic tone is found elsewhere in Johnson's writings, especially in the *Rambler*. This predominant melancholy is seen to produce a flawed view of reality. Mudford concludes that in illustrating his concept of the vanity of human wishes, Johnson produced "disquisitions" that have "few admirers" because they excite "no tumultuous sensations, nor awaken any sympathy" (80-105). Five years later Leigh Hunt takes Mudford's position one step further by asserting that the author's melancholy constitution results in some distortion of the truth. The author of *Rasselas* reminds Hunt of the astronomer who accurately perceives discrete facts but combines them into a whole that is fanciful (7). Here began the tradition, which continued throughout the nineteenth and into the twentieth century, of characterizing *Rasselas* as lacking in religious consolation because of the author's distorted view of reality. Coming to Johnson's defense, Anna Letitia Barbauld, in 1810, develops another aspect of Mudford's position, the abstract, almost unreal quality of *Rasselas*. The dominant motif of the tale, the search for a choice of life, is seen as artificial because most of us "will seldom hesitate upon a choice of life." Barbauld suggests that the proper, less trite moral to be drawn from the artificiality of the choice of life theme is a preference for what subsequent critics call, using the words of the princess, the "choice of eternity" (iii-iv). The melancholy that the reader experiences is, according to Barbauld, directed at the search for happiness in this world, not the next. The choice of eternity provides hope for the reader. The final result, Barbauld believes, is a balanced, not a distorted, position.

A subtle but significant alteration has occurred in the debate. In the eighteenth century commentators disagreed about whether or not the licit pleasures of this world receive sufficient emphasis. Nineteenth-century critics now began a debate concerning whether or not the gloom associated with the choice of life prevails over the consolation provided by the choice of eternity. This shift in critical position became most apparent in the difference of opinion between William Hazlitt and Sir Walter Scott. In 1819 Hazlitt refers to the tale as "the most melancholy and debilitating moral speculation that ever was put forth." "Doubtful of the faculties of his mind, Johnson trusted only to his feelings and fears"; he thus fell prey to his own "dangerous prevalence of the imagination" (201). Scott, on the other hand, defends *Rasselas*. Although manifesting the melancholy of the author, *Rasselas* puts forth a "friendly grave" philosophy that promises hope in the other world. The number of editions and translations of the narrative, Scott believes, attests to the fact that reading the tale is not a debilitating but an uplifting experience (5, xlv).

While Scott and Barbauld point to religious hope expressed in
the narrative itself, Elizabeth Pope Whately, in 1835, presents the
only other continuation of *Rasselas*, consisting of a Christian pilgrimage that ends with the choice of eternity. Imlac here is replaced
by a religious teacher named Everard, who leads the travelers from
nominal faith to Christian belief. Whately's sequel seems to have received even less attention than *Dinarbas*, for it was not discussed in
relation to *Rasselas* until an article by Robert Metzdorf appeared in
1950 (5-7). Metzdorf explains that Whately was not satisfied with
Rasselas because in concluding with marriage it leaves unresolved
the question of religious felicity. But Whately's tale does not, in fact,
succeed in advancing the religious question. In making explicit the
Christianity that is presumed to be implicit in the original, Whately
suggests that the religion of *Rasselas* is in need of further clarifica-
tion. We can conclude from the neglect of Whately's narrative as a
sequel to *Rasselas* that Christian conversion of the characters has
been regarded by both defenders and attackers as inappropriate. Yet
for over two centuries critics have claimed that *Rasselas* is designed
to arrive at an explicitly religious conclusion, unaware that Whately
provides the historian of literary criticism with a prima facie case
against such a position. The fact that these two sequels are conspicu-
ously absent from discussions of *Rasselas* is itself a form of literary
critical evidence, indicating that the forms of resolution in these
"sequels" have failed to satisfy critics.

Although the religious continuation of Johnson's tale was soon
forgotten, Boswell's biographical account continued to be employed
throughout the remainder of the nineteenth century. By the 1850s, it
became commonplace to preface editions of *Rasselas* with brief biographical essays that derived from Boswell. The scanty commentary
written between 1834 and 1860 is to be found in the introductory material to editions intended for the general public and for use in
schools. The London editions of 1823, 1838, and 1843 and the Edinburgh edition of 1824 recommend *Rasselas* for its firm moral strictures and its style. The anonymous 1823 edition proclaims that "the
moral, though not new, has, perhaps, never been before so ably, so
eloquently, inculcated" (vii). Its Scottish counterpart explains that
the "beautiful, useful tale" is one of Johnson's most "popular works"
(216). The 1838 and 1843 versions that I have seen, nearly identical
soft-bound, small books (measuring six by four inches), preface the
text with a three-page "Brief Notice" consisting of a very condensed
version of Boswell, introduced in the following terms: "to those
who look no further than this life the instruction of this sublime
tale will be of no avail" (iii). These inexpensive Victorian pocket
books were intended to present to the general public proper religious
and moral precepts in a fine literary style. Once the reader was
warned in the brief biographical sketch of the author's constitutional

melancholy and of the circumstances under which the book was written, the editors assumed that the tale would cease to be morally debilitating. Boswell was thus employed by Victorians to alter the view of *Rasselas*. The same argument that enables Boswell to explain how an accurate picture of reality points to Christianity was employed by many nineteenth-century editors to make allowance for the distortion of reality in what is otherwise an orthodox Christian tale. For this reason, the Reverend John Hunter, in his edition of 1860, warns his students about the "narrator's somewhat melancholy and desponding" tone but concludes that "if it darkens too deeply the scene of things temporal it at least causes thereby to shine more brightly the hope which emanates from things eternal" (xx).

The Reverend William West, on the other hand, points out, nine years later, that, although "tinged with his grief," *Rasselas* contains the religious optimism that Johnson expresses in a letter to Mrs. Thrale: "all is best as it has been, excepting the errors of our own free will." West is one of the first to attend to the exotic element of the happy valley, which he sees in relation to the *Arabian Nights*, *Paradise Lost*, Thomson's "Castle of Indolence," and Johnson's own translation of the Lobo-Legrand *Voyage to Abyssinia*. Johnson, he states, is fortunate in choosing this setting because it is "invested with all the romance of history and geography, religion and superstition." This most imaginative of Johnson's works, according to West, makes use of an exotic scene to unite genial pleasantry with a view of life "far from cheerful" (xxvii, xlii).

By the second half of the nineteenth century, when it was generally accepted that the somewhat despondent tone or slightly warped view of reality was compensated for by the Christian vision, commentators began to turn their attention to other aspects of *Rasselas*—the exotic and even the humorous. In his edition of 1879 Alfred Milnes is the first to assert that humor is a functional part, not simply an occasional ornament, in the story. For Milnes the end is still sad, although not as bitter as that of *Candide*, and the theme remains the vanity of human wishes. Nevertheless, the episodes containing the philosophy according to nature and the marriage debate are labeled comic "gems." Finally, Milnes points out that Johnson's tale "has been much more widely read than the far more vivacious work of Voltaire," a startling statement, however accurate or inaccurate, in an age when the man and his conversation are generally valued over his work (xxix-xxxii). The number of editions of *Rasselas* during this period suggests that, if not read more than *Candide*, it was at least one of the few of Johnson's works that was widely read. We know, for instance, of a law case occasioned by a pirated edition of 1883, a sure sign of public interest in a text (173-75); and in 1884 an anonymous reviewer in *Booklore* wrote that "although Samuel Johnson is generally known by his conversation and way of life as recorded by Boswell, one work [*Rasselas*] never lost its hold upon the popular mind" (5-11).

During the last quarter of the nineteenth century, when the religious question seemed settled by use of a distortion of Boswell, the exotic and comic elements were first carefully considered and *Rasselas* was first placed in the tradition of the novel. In 1894 Walter Raleigh includes *Rasselas* in his book entitled *The English Novel.* But while referring to *Rasselas* as a novel, Raleigh also is the first to call it an "apologue," another label still used today. In fact, Raleigh characterizes Johnson's achievement as the combining of these two genres: "the youth of the modern novel was a season of experiment, no rules of form had been determined, and a moral directly inculcated had never been disallowed" (204, 206).

By the end of the nineteenth century *Rasselas* had been defended against those in the early decades of the century, such as Mudford and Hunt, who asserted that the tale ends in despair. But the defense created new problems. As we have seen, hope in *Rasselas* is located in the choice of eternity theme. The question then becomes how the exotic and humorous elements relate to this other-worldly motif. Classifying *Rasselas* as a novel seems to offer a solution to this problem, but it necessitates including within that category the apologue, a term originally applied to beast fables and then by extension to moral allegories. The problem was that during the early twentieth century the novel was increasingly associated with realism and thus distinguished from moral allegory. Yet the term *apologue* was first applied to *Rasselas* in an attempt to include it within the tradition of the novel, while, as will soon become clear, most twentieth-century critics used the term to distinguish *Rasselas* from the novel.

Turning now to the twentieth century, we note the emergence of one issue that will be neglected for over a quarter of a century. In 1899 Oliver Emerson reminds his readers that his 1895 introduction to *Rasselas* used bibliographical evidence to question the universally accepted contention that Johnson wrote the tale in the evenings of one week to defray his mother's funeral expenses (499-509). When Emerson's argument was finally addressed, many of his conclusions were successfully refuted, but his position was not even contested until 1927. One reason for the neglect of Emerson's argument during this period is that the tradition of the gloomy, funereal tone of the choice of life motif in *Rasselas* remained unopposed: the question of whether or not the genesis of *Rasselas* involves a literal funeral was not considered important. Moreover, the assumption of a gloomy genesis served the prevailing position, since any religious difficulty could be attributed to the fact that the author was mourning the death of his mother.

Instead, critics were interested in generic explanations of the tone. C. S. Fearenside, for instance, further develops Raleigh's position.

Although a precursor of the novel. *Rasselas* contains more severe morality than most novels and fewer of the characteristics of narrative and story because it is an early and undeveloped example of the genre (vii-x). But Martha Conant, in *The Oriental Tale in England in the Eighteenth Century* (1908), places *Rasselas* in the philosophic, not the moral, category of oriental tales. What Fearenside sees as a moralistic novel, Conant characterizes as too general and abstract for the moral oriental tale. Johnson seems to Conant to be even more abstract than Voltaire, who at least considers happiness in *Candide* in such concrete terms as a "mistress" (144, 149).

The generic problem is thus a complicated one. Placed within the confines of the novel, *Rasselas* seems anomalous in its lack of fully developed characters, skeletal story line, and markedly open-ended conclusion. Treated as an oriental tale, *Rasselas* is typical in its philosophic quality and one-dimensional figures, but the oriental is, as Conant herself admits, of little intrinsic import. Because Conant and Fearenside conceive of literary history in restrictive generic terms, they remain within their distinct categories, seeing no relationship between their endeavors. Attempts to explain the tone of *Rasselas* in terms of a single generic tradition reveal that the tale contains elements of both the novel and the oriental tale but cannot be satisfactorily categorized as either the one or the other.

During the next few decades, a number of critics attempted to consider *Rasselas* as a novel bordering on either the philosophic oriental tale or the religious apologue. In 1910 A. J. F. Collins labels the tale "the philosophical novel or the novel with a purpose where the story is often a mere excuse for a theory of life" (xv). And in 1913 George Saintsbury describes *Rasselas* as "the most remarkable example, in English, of a novel, which is to a great extent deprived of the *agremens* of its kind," while leaving behind the "carcass of a very tolerable novel." Without interest in story, characters, or dialogue, *Rasselas*, according to Saintsbury, is a moral apologue: "Johnson used the popular form of the novel to communicate his thoughts to the general reading public" (34-35). Here Raleigh's notion that Johnson combines apologue and novel becomes more explicit. In particular, Saintsbury explains the unique quality of *Rasselas* by describing it as a religious allegory that uses the outward trappings of the novel.

But if the "novel" is merely an "envelope" used by Johnson to reach the people, W. D. Howells replies that audiences in the United States need "the truth clothed in more realism." For Howells, Johnson's irony is too subtle for the novel. Therefore, the categorization is questioned: "I call it a novel," states the sage conversing with Howells in his Editor's Easy Chair, "but I suppose you would stickle for the term heroic romance" (310). Howells's opposition to labeling the tale a novel serves as a reminder to us that, at this time, the motive for including it in this popular genre was an attempt to account for how the reader was moved by the doctrine of the apologue, the choice of eternity. But these two genres were gradually seen to point in opposite directions, the novel being realistic and secular and the apologue being allegorical and religious.

Instead of attempting to define *Rasselas* in generic terms, Percy Houston, in 1923, focuses on the basis of its moral and religious doctrine: "the pessimism of this little homily does not strike at the roots of religion and morality, but the fact of human misery was stated as something to be faced without questioning God's ultimate purposes." Johnson's avoidance of sentimentality, Houston hastens to add, "was not unfeeling" (196). *Rasselas* is thus placed at a considerable distance from the realistic novel; indeed, so much is the tale relegated to the realm of the fantastic that Russell Markland and Percy Armstrong point to similarities between *Rasselas* and the writings of Shelley and Emerson (368, 167). In 1924 Chauncey Tinker advances Houston's position by comparing *Rasselas* to the Bible and asserting that the exotic is a "mere trapping" for the moral (99). Here we see an important difference between the nineteenth and twentieth centuries. In the former the demonstration that *Rasselas* contains the hope inherent in the choice of eternity accounts for its appeal. In the present century, however, when Tinker advances a similar argument, Lawrence F. Powell reminds his fellow critics that *Rasselas* is still the most widely printed and most generally read of Johnson's literary works (124). For Powell the religious doctrine no longer provides a satisfactory explanation for the literary appeal of *Rasselas*.

At the beginning of the twentieth century, *Rasselas* was, for the first time, defended by being described as a novel. Although some, like Howells, rejected this argument, most commentators now sought a formal or generic explanation of the reasons *Rasselas* has earned its place among the classics of English literature. The explanation, that *Rasselas* is a hybrid of apologue and novel, was not widely accepted because it left undecided whether the conclusion is religious or secular, whether the tale ends with this-worldly realism or other-worldly faith. In the second quarter of the twentieth century, the genre and religious questions continued in the forefront of discussion, but the conclusions differed from those of the past. The fundamental problem, however, remained how to account for *Rasselas* not as a religious text but as literature.

In 1927 Ernest Palser, in a commentary designed for school and university students, suggests that *Rasselas* is a kind of novel that soon passed out of history. Viewed in terms of its Elizabethan, seventeenth- and eighteenth-century ancestors, *Rasselas*, according to Palser, has some of the euphuistic style of Lyly and some of the elements of realism, plot, and character found in Fielding. The progress of the novel ceases temporarily after the middle of the eighteenth century, which explains why Johnson's story contains less in the way of plot, characters, and real life than *Tom Jones*. A momentary aberration, a soon-to-be-extinct species, *Rasselas*, according to Palser, employs the euphuistic style to develop a spiritual novel that is didactic, not bitter. But the novel as a genre continues to move inexorably toward increasing realism because a picture of the unhappy side of existence can only avoid the accusation of a melancholy bias if it presents a realistic world. Palser explains that *Rasselas* appeared at a moment in history when it was possible to present a spiritual novel (17-18).

Rasselas was now seen as an aberrant form of the novel—a novel, in a sense, at war with the novel. In 1932 Norman Collins suggests that as a moral genius, Johnson wrote without any sense of the novel as a form: the idea of "Dr. Johnson telling a story is rather like that of an elephant herding sheep: something much smaller could do it far better." Infusing philosophic sadness into the novel, John-son "taught the English novel to be intellectual, a lesson that for natural reasons has rarely been applied since" (83-84). That Johnson maintained his intellectual integrity, refusing to bow down to the idols of the marketplace, was the reply to those like Howells who complained that *Rasselas* violates the principles of the novel, realism and the development of character. But the price paid for describing *Rasselas* as a spiritual or philosophical novel was to minimize the structural or novelistic qualities of the narrative.

For this reason Ernest Baker, in *The History of the English Novel* (1934), defends *Rasselas* by suggesting it is a singular kind of novel because of its use of the Orient. Johnson dresses up his sad philosophy in exotic ornament, approximating the novel: "thus the vogue of the pseudo-Oriental tale was bound to be transient and to leave no indelible mark upon the history of fiction" (5, 56). *Rasselas* is for Baker a masterpiece, but because no one can duplicate Johnson's delicate oriental presentation of ideas—maintaining a balance between abstract ideas and concrete ornament—the exotic does not long remain a significant factor in the history of the English novel. Historians of the novel continued to account for the unrealistic quality by pointing to the superficial exotic ornaments, which paradoxically result in a more careful and scholarly treatment of the oriental aspect of the narrative. Beginning this serious investigation, Harold Jenkins, in 1940, discovers that a number of details in the happy valley do not correspond to those in Johnson's translation of Lobo's *Voyage d'Abyssinie*, the work generally assumed to be the source for Johnson's exotica. Jenkins finds that the happy valley contains features from a number of Ethiopian travel books available in Johnson's day (13).

The increased prominence accorded to the oriental was directly related to Joseph Wood Krutch's new reading of *Rasselas*, first published in 1944. Describing the book as an example of the "pseudo-oriental tale ... familiar to [Johnson's] contemporaries as a vehicle for moral instruction," Krutch points out that the main theme emerges in the pyramid incident, which exemplifies the hunger of the imagination that preys on all human minds. The story concludes not with "vulgar" pessimism but with Johnson's "tragic sense of life." Specifically, Krutch asserts that although the travelers at the end of the tale return to the happy valley, the choice of eternity is "only the formal rather than the effective moral." Instead of representing opposition to the search for happiness, the return to the happy valley offers relief from the "secondary causes of distress and [possesses] in the largest measure the palliatives of security and pleasure" (174, 176, 183). Krutch emphasizes that *Rasselas* differs at once from an apologue in not finally ascending to the choice of eternity and from a romance by avoiding its traditional optimistic conclusion. A masterpiece, *Rasselas* squarely faces the dilemma of man on earth.

This turning point, the first secular reading of *Rasselas*, resulted from paying due attention to the literary qualities of the narrative, specifically the oriental setting and the humor. Krutch's careful research on the exotica led to the realization that the eighteenth-century oriental tale can no more be assumed to be religious than to be romantic or fanciful. Moreover, the increase in references to the comic moments in the narrative led Krutch to characterize it not as gloomy but as tragic, because tragedy can sustain within its scope humor (viii). By the middle of this century, *Rasselas* was for the first time defended in terms that distinguish the structure of the narrative from that of *The Vanity of Human Wishes*. Krutch's methodological innovation, however, went unrecognized for some time; his position was at first inserted into the old religious controversy as if his secular reading was merely another attack on *Rasselas* for lack of religious resolution. But within a decade his influence began to be seen in the increasing interest in the formal properties of *Rasselas*.

Strangely enough, Krutch's secular reading had less effect on the religious position than on that of a group of critics who, during the next two decades, the 1950s and 1960s, avoided entirely the question of whether *Rasselas* concludes in religious or secular terms. Here again, the generally accepted notion of the critical tradition was different from the tradition itself. For over a century the dichotomy between the choice of life and the choice of eternity had been repeated and was now widely accepted as the central problem in *Rasselas*. By the middle of the twentieth century, Krutch notwithstanding, critics continued to assume that the choice of life ends in futility and that the choice of eternity provides a counterbalance against hopelessness and despair. That this dichotomy did not obtain in the eighteenth century is still to be discovered. The twentieth-century critics inherited the nineteenth-century assumptions that result in the following problem for them: although the choice-of-eternity coda restores hope at the end of the text, almost all of *Rasselas* is devoted to the choice-of-life motif, which is regarded as gloomy. Since the tale remains popular, critics have to account for the appeal of the body of the tale. Many mid-twentieth-century critics try to demonstrate that the form or structure of *Rasselas* provides an aesthetic pleasure to counterbalance the gloom of the main theme. Krutch's position brings these choice-of-life features into new prominence.

In the 1950s the comedy of *Rasselas* was for the first time pointed to not, as in the past, as a sign of Christian hope but as a principle of literary structure. This view of structure as serving the purpose of comedy added a new dimension to the controversy. In 1950 Robert Metzdorf unearthed Whately's happy and distinctly religious continuation of *Rasselas*. Clarence Tracy claims that the need to alter or add to Johnson's conclusion is founded on a false view derived from Boswell. "Not a grim invective against life," *Rasselas* is, for Tracy, the "most sustained and most characteristic of [Johnson's] humorous compositions." Opposing Krutch's description of the tale, the prince, according to Tracy, "is a fool [who] never learns his lesson," an addict of "pure reason" who returns to a fool's paradise (303, 306, 308). Although, as we have seen, some earlier critics showed sensitivity to the comedy of the tale, Tracy was the first to present a complete position based on the humor of the narrative. His formulation reveals a misunderstanding of the critical tradition. Boswell, as we know, defends *Rasselas* against the need for a continuation on the basis of exactly the same literary theme as that of Tracy, namely, the vanity of human wishes. What, one may well ask, is the function of comedy for Tracy if it results in a notion identical to the somber view of Boswell? It is instructive that Tracy was attacked in just these terms by his contemporaries who, in various ways, unconsciously played the part of a critical ghost.

In 1951 Mary Lascelles and Gwin Kolb each oppose Tracy's position, but in different terms. For Lascelles, the humor of *Rasselas*, definitely an important factor, is of a delicate sort; the satire applies to those whom the main characters visit on their travels, not to the main characters themselves. At the end of their journey, the travelers are, according to Lascelles, not fools but people who, as a result of their lengthy journey, develop "a kind of philosophic love" that evokes our empathy (51). Kolb, on the other hand, accuses Tracy of treating *Rasselas* as if it were a string of *Rambler* essays; as an alternative, he puts forward a religious reading that he maintains to the present day. The tale is seen to have a distinct structure, one that serves not a comic but a serious purpose, namely, that all searches for permanent happiness on earth are doomed to failure. Having decided to write a narrative on the theme of *The Vanity of Human Wishes*, Johnson, according to Kolb, devised a vehicle for the "paucity of happiness" notion, which is considered under three headings: those who, like the inhabitants of the happy valley, have all material goods; those who, like the young men of spirit and gaiety, follow particular schemes; and those who, like the Bassa, occupy positions of power (702). Tracy is opposed in two different ways. Kolb accepts Tracy's theme, the vanity of human wishes, but characterizes it, like Boswell, as somber, not comic. Lascelles accepts the comedy but does not agree that the choice-of-life search is a puerile endeavor.

The old terms now came to serve a new purpose. Gloom that in the past was key for those attacking *Rasselas* for its lack of hope was now used by Kolb to advance a religious reading. Comedy that in the past was pointed to as a sign of the hope present in the narrative was now used to characterize literary structure in terms neither distinctly religious nor secular. It should now be clear that formalist arguments permitted for the first time assimilation of the full range of tone, from comedy to tragedy, but the debate continued for another twenty years until gradually the two sides came to a compromise.

Meanwhile, the generic discussion continued, but now with a more direct bearing upon the question of literary structure. In 1952 Frank R. Leavis claims that the tragic theme of *Rasselas* accounts for its "moral centrality and profound common sense, (115)" and, in the same year, John Robert Moore points out that although "generally regarded as a philosophical romance so devoid of action ... that one who read it for the story would hang himself" (36-42), *Rasselas* provides some elements of plot construction for Conan Doyle. Viewing *Rasselas* as a novel now meant that the gloom is seen as invested in a tragic or realistic literary form that was not designed to produce in the reader either despair or hopelessness.

While these generic, structural, and tonal questions continued to be debated, a psychological question was raised, one that is not exclusively biographical. In 1954 Richard Hovey examines the relationship between Johnson and the astronomer. But unlike previous commentators, Hovey characterizes not merely Johnson or his age but the kind of neurosis exemplified by the astronomer/author: "the mental illness" of the astronomer suggests "our own age rather than the Age of Reason." Like the astronomer's anxiety, Johnson's guilt combines with melancholy to take the form of self-mutilation and aggression against the self. Using biographical evidence from Boswell and Katherine Balderston, Hovey suggests that Johnson felt guilt with regard to his mother, and that he recovered, like the astronomer, by way of the company of other people (321-35). Maintaining that such a view of *Rasselas* is not Freudian but Burtonian, Hovey nonetheless claims that his reading reveals the modernity of Johnson's story. Psychological readings of this kind were completely ignored by those debating matters of genre, structure, and tone, so much so that thirty years later, as we shall see, this position is, in a number of respects, repeated without any acknowledgment of Hovey. The nature of this modern psychological position will become clearer when we examine Kathleen Grange's essay, a fuller formulation that appeared in 1962. At this point it should be noted that during this period Boswell's psychological explanation is as neglected as that of Hovey. Most critics in the 1950s believed that the problems of *Rasselas* could be resolved by recourse to a more careful study of the form of the tale. When this project failed, it again became permissible to consider psychological questions.

In 1956 Alvin Whitley, aware of the objections to Tracy's position, modifies the comic view into a reading that avoids commitment on the religious question. Whitley's point of departure is that both Tracy and Kolb have been too negative in characterizing *Rasselas* as a prose version of *The Vanity of Human Wishes*. Instead, the narrative comically satirizes "the illusioned view of life." In the first two thirds of the story, naive pilgrims examine foolish choices of life; although the last third of the book, comprising the visits to the astronomer and the old man, does "skirt tragedy," the manner remains comic. In the end, the travelers "return to the Happy Valley," a conclusion that gives the text its circular form (51, 65, 70). Whitley's comic circle shows the illusion inherent in the choice-of-life quest. Since the tale ends with the characters coming to an awareness of this fact, it is not necessary to consider an alternative, such as the choice of eternity.

Whitley was nevertheless attacked by those who opposed the attempt to use the comedy of *Rasselas* to avoid the religious issues of *The Vanity of Human Wishes*. William Kenney, in 1957, argues that the comic reading neglects the tragic aspect of the tale. Admitting that he derives this notion from Krutch, Kenney adapts it to a Christian reading (94-95). Two years later Agostino Lombardo extends this view by asserting that the hero of *Rasselas* is not Rasselas but Imlac. By virtue of his sober, pious bearing and his tale about his disillusionment with the world outside of the happy valley, the latter clearly exemplifies a tragic Christian position (47, 49). This formulation, however, raised a new problem: Imlac retires from the world to the happy valley while the prince travels in the opposite direction. Kenney, in a second article, points out that both characters eventually end in the happy valley and explains how the valley provides a resolution for both quests. Once the prince discovers what Imlac has previously recognized, that the choice of life can never be found, then he and his mentor both return to the happy valley, which offers the next best alternative. Kenney calls this option "diversification," and Bertrand Bronson characterizes it as the prince's equivalent of what "London was to Johnson. Though London is not the Happy Valley, it is the best available surrogate" (xvi).

Now we come to one of the most important moments in this history. In a three-paragraph reply to Kenney's essay, George Sherburn points out that the travelers cannot and do not return to the happy valley. This single structural fact alters most future interpretations of the tale. In spite of his future impact, Sherburn devotes less than a single printed page to his discovery. Sherburn objects to the optimism suggested by Kenney's view that the travelers return to the diversification of the happy valley. "One may regret Dr. Johnson's pessimism," he cautions, "but must face it." Furthermore, Sherburn continues, Imlac's return to disappointment in Abyssinia prepares us for the prince's attitude at the end of his journey: "the work ends in complete frustration. The travelers are now in the condition in which Imlac had formerly found himself before he achieved the Happy Valley, now closed to him and his companions" (383-84). By this means, Sherburn reaffirms the nineteenth-century position that *Rasselas* is exemplary of its historical period; the travelers' prevention from returning to the happy valley is viewed as consistent with the pessimism of Johnson and his era. Such a notion, for Sherburn, was not innovative and can hardly be said to constitute a textual discovery. Nevertheless, Sherburn's essay had a profound effect upon the commentary of the 1960s and 1970s, for it altered the conception of the structure of the text. Both the religion and tone debaters had to reformulate their positions. Imlac and his history present a problem. The sage, seen by some critics as the spokesman for the religious point of view, now narrates a tale, his history, having a different structure from that of the prince. Imlac ends his story with his decision to enter the happy valley, but Rasselas cannot return to the vale. How does one account for this difference? For those who focus on tone, the conclusion raises a new question: "The conclusion, in which nothing is concluded" cannot be neatly folded into the beginning. Abyssinia is not synonymous with the happy valley, so the tale can no longer be viewed as circular in structure. But because Sherburn presented his position in traditional terms, it took some time before the ramifications of his discovery were fully recognized.

In 1961 John Aden advances the secular element in the comic view. Comparing *The Vanity of Human Wishes* to *Rasselas*, Aden suggests that the poem delineates the "instinctive determinants" to self-deception, that is, hope, fear, or hate, while the prose work presents the "self-imposed or psychological determinants," such as fancy and eagerness, foibles which, unlike those in the poem, are "avoidable by a healthy and sound mind." One can learn how to overcome the limitations caused by credulity or naïveté in *Rasselas* but not those of fate in *The Vanity of Human Wishes*. The fatalism of the poem explains its distinct tone; its sobriety contrasts with the wry, ironic, playful attitude of the tale. Indeed, the terms "Christian" and "stoic" apply to the poem but not to the tale. The "choice of eternity," Nekayah's one passing reference to Christian doctrine, is a brief remark not identified as Johnson's final point. Moreover, the conclusion of the tale—and here Aden, presumably unaware of Sherburn, assumes a return to the happy valley—is "as pathetic as it is tragic," returning its spiritually weary characters to an infantile paradise. In so doing, *Rasselas* "seems rather a repudiation of the pessimistic and melancholy doctrine of the poem" (298, 300, 303).

Robert Voitle shares Aden's doubts about the Christian message; when Nekayah remarks on the choice of eternity, "we are more struck by the opportunity Johnson missed to dwell on the *de contemptu mundi* theme than by his passing reference to it" (40). Aden and Voitle move toward the application of the philosophic notion of *l'absurde* that was first presented explicitly by Ellen Leyburn. Comparing *Rasselas* to Albert Camus's *La Peste*, Leyburn asserts that both works advance the belief that although life is largely misery, commitment to an active life helps combat suffering. The main difference between the two tales, according to Leyburn, is that Camus uses an allegorical structure and particularized individuals while Johnson employs oriental trappings appropriate to grand generalizations. Leyburn insists that Johnson's narrative not be seen as a "doleful book" because, like Camus's narrative, it encourages activity, not passive despair. Indeed, Camus's atheism is not considered as alien to Johnson, for whom religion provides not comfort but dread of annihilation and damnation. Finding Johnson's position in *Rasselas* comparable to Camus's atheism, Leyburn makes obvious the threat posed to the religious position by the satiric secular interpretation, even though her own strategy is not to deny the religion of *Rasselas* but to highlight the similarity between it and *La Peste* (205, 209).

During this same period Kathleen Grange continues the psychoanalytic reading of *Rasselas* begun eight years earlier by Richard Hovey. Without mentioning her predecessor, Grange, like Hovey, focuses on the astronomer, characterizing him as schizoid and emphasizing that the travelers show varying degrees of understanding of this mental disease. Johnson is applauded for realizing that fulfilling the astronomer's needs—"desire for friendship, usefulness and ego-satisfaction"—is a more effective therapy than rational explanation (166). At this point, the psychological tradition divided into two separate but related strands. Hovey explains the astronomer in terms of the relationship between Johnson and his mother. Grange restricts herself to the text, focusing on the manner in which the scientist regains his sanity. I shall have occasion to return to this distinction between the textual and the biographical aspects of the psychological tradition. Here it is important to note that the other textual critics ignored Grange as they had Hovey. Psychological criticism was at this time almost completely neglected only to erupt, as Freud would have predicted, in the next generation.

The centrality of structural considerations is evidenced by Donald Lockhart's *PMLA* essay of 1963, which remains the most comprehensive study of the exotic background material for the happy valley. The previous scholarship in this field is divided by Lockhart into two categories: the literary school, favoring such traditional unrealistic sources as Milton's "suppos'd true paradise"; and the historical school, emphasizing Johnson's translation of Lobo and other travelers' accounts of Ethiopia. But Lockhart finds specific elements of the happy valley that cannot be accounted for by either of these two kinds of sources. He therefore turns to works available to Johnson that combine the paradise-on-earth convention with actual accounts of the exotic retreat set up for the children of the emperor of Abyssinia (42-58). Lockhart concludes that Johnson had done careful research for his happy valley well before the death of his mother, an assertion that prompted William K. Wimsatt to refer to this article as the "PMLAization of Johnson's working habits" (134). Nevertheless, Lockhart succeeds in documenting the fact that both historical and literary materials are pertinent to the happy valley.

That the secular and religious critics shared a commitment to the importance of form and were thus beginning to influence one another is attested by F. W. Hilles' attempt to mediate between them in 1965. In place of Kolb's two-part structure, Hilles offers a triune form, the result of subdividing the world beyond the mountains that Kolb considers as one unit. The abduction of Pekuah marks the beginning of a new section because, according to Hilles, the travelers who up to this point have been only observers are now participants. Having restructured the tale, Hilles characterizes the tone of the story as that of a "sad smile ... modern commentators ... overstress the comic elements ... as orthodox critics have dwelt overmuch on the tragic." But the words and structure "suggest a balance" (119). Hilles offers this alternative organic structure in an attempt to encompass both comedy and tragedy, the religious and the secular. Although beneath surface similarities, ultimate and irreconcilable contradictions remain, Hilles demonstrates that the abduction of Pekuah marks a new stage in the tale. The pyramid episode is seen as an event because it involves action, not merely conversation. And subsequent commentators felt obliged to come to terms with this structural phenomenon.

In 1967 Emrys Jones modifies Hilles's structure by extending the first part through chapter 16 and treating the last chapter as a separate "coda." In his conception of the conclusion, however, Jones was the first to develop the full implications of Sherburn's discovery. The last chapter functions, according to Jones, like the end of *Love's Labour's Lost*, to remind us that life is a critique of art, that is, the artistic form itself is "broken because the flow of life cannot be checked" (401). A part of the structure, the coda is seen to undermine artistic structuring; *Rasselas* is for Jones a form designed to break

open its own form. This important insight is, however, not adequately explained. The truism that life does not obey the laws of art
explains little about why a carefully structured work of art concludes
with reference to this fact. Nonetheless, Jones was the first critic to
suggest that the inability to reenter the happy valley indicates that
the humor at the end of *Rasselas* is directed at the form of all human
wishes and therefore applies to the form of *Rasselas* as well.

In 1968 Wimsatt gives two reasons for his doubt as to the significance of structure in *Rasselas*. First, the tale was written in haste, a
fact indicated by Johnson's "absentmindedness, his slight inconsis-
tencies of time and setting which suggest additions." For instance, in
the first edition, Pekuah is not referred to by name until chapter 30;
in the second edition, her name is added in chapter 16. Wimsatt
surmises that Johnson introduces the abduction of Pekuah in the
middle of the tale to increase the action and in revising the text hur-
riedly patched up the earlier section. Although not "serious aesthetic
deficiencies," these lapses produce a "lumpy, bumpy structure." Second, the divisions suggested by Kolb and Hilles can be as suitably realized in an essay as in a narrative. After tentatively proposing his
own six-part division, Wimsatt admits that all such divisions are of
"little aesthetic moment" because, lacking the structure of a novel by
Fielding or Austen, *Rasselas* has only the form necessary to meet its
modest requirements—"a quasi-dramatic narrative—not a beginning, middle and end but one of accumulation." Yet *Rasselas* is not
considered to be an oriental tale in any profound sense: "the deliberate simplification, even complacent ignorance about the actual col-
ors of life in the supposed locale of Johnson's story, is a kind of
counterpart and symbol of the general human truth he would be get-
ting at."

Nonetheless, Wimsatt does discuss the function of the exotic.
"What are we to make of the fact that the obvious element of morality is cast in the shape of an oriental tale?" Having given up on any
attempt at finding an "organistic" structure, Wimsatt turns to style.
The "moderate exoticism" of the style of the *Rambler* "does not find
its ideal setting until Johnson writes *Rasselas*." Producing a "sad
grim smile"—here Wimsatt, like Hilles, combines the somber
school of Kolb and that of comedy articulated by Whitley—the style
of *Rasselas* enables Johnson to conclude with a view of absurdity
suggestive of that of Samuel Beckett but at a higher level, where the
choice of eternity still means something, where eloquence remains—"an eloquence profound and moving" (115, 116-17, 124, 126,
128, 130). Wimsatt implies that Johnson's moderately exotic style enables him to look down into but remain above the abyss of absurdity.
The perception of structure evoked by *Rasselas* is the result of Johnson's style, an achievement, for Wimsatt, more important than the
fact that one cannot find an "objective correlative" for this structure

in the text. Hence, form becomes less significant than the perception of it, or the perspective that permits such a perception. Accounting for the rupture in the textual circle discovered by Jones, Wimsatt suggests that the structure is completed by the reader, who is guided by what one of Wimsatt's students, Stanley Fish, calls "affective stylistics."

The difficulty involved in the sundering of organic form to bolster a religious reading of *Rasselas* is evidenced in the position of John Hardy, who combines the views of Wimsatt and Jones. In the introduction to his 1968 edition of *Rasselas*, Hardy applies Jones's final insight, that life breaks open the circle of art, to indicate that Johnson's story is an eastern tale and a romance "in appearance only." The arbitrary and uncertain elements of life are used by Johnson, according to Hardy, to satirize "happiness-ever-after" assumptions inherent in the romance and the oriental tale. A *Vanity of Human Wishes* in prose, the narrative has for Hardy as its central irony that "in setting out to observe life, one risks letting life slip through one's fingers." The conclusion, he continues, is not pessimistic because the prince, "Johnson's hero," has "the last word," expressing his hopes. Furthermore, that the travelers do not return to the happy valley gives the story the configuration of a "parabola" rather than a circle, "for experience tempers but does not nullify naïveté" (xii, xvi, xxiv).

But if, as Hardy believes, *Rasselas* takes the form of a parabola that concludes outside of the happy valley and this side of the realm of eternity, how can the tale be a *Vanity of Human Wishes* in prose when the poem clearly concludes with the consolation of Christianity? Moreover, if the central irony of *Rasselas* is that "in seeking a choice of life you neglect to live," how does the irony apply to Imlac, especially when he utters this phrase? Hardy's attempt to demonstrate that the satirical puncturing of all human hopes and aspirations serves a religious purpose means that Imlac, the prophet of the tale, has unaccountably to be excluded from the satire. Yet Hardy makes clear that, for him, the prince, not Imlac, is the hero of the story.

In 1969, when Kolb's religious form had been questioned, Thomas Preston makes an important contribution toward a religious reading. Studying the two schools of interpretation of the Book of Ecclesiastes, one cautioning us to despise this world and the other encouraging a limited enjoyment of earthly pleasures, Preston applies the less austere one to *Rasselas*. This interpretation of Ecclesiastes maintains that although the only realm of total bliss is eternity, this life, where the prince pursues the choice of life, offers the possibility of partial contentment. As interpreted by Bishops Lowth and Patrick in the eighteenth century, this view insists that some modes of life offer less unhappiness than others and that one of man's duties is to search for such a state of limited but lawful pleasure. *Rasselas* is thus seen as a religious apologue with a commitment to life as well as to eternity. Not surprisingly Preston's historical findings reinforce the literary-critical research articulated in the present survey: as pointed out earlier, a number of eighteenth-century critics assume that the vanity of human wishes theme does not preclude the possibility of some licit mortal pleasure (274-81). It has taken Johnsonians two centuries to rediscover this fact because of their tacit assumption that literary criticism and historical scholarship need not be concerned with the history of literary criticism.

Nevertheless, as in the eighteenth so too in the twentieth century, this notion did not resolve the religious question. Commentators still disagreed as to whether in the end *Rasselas* recommends the pursuit of some vain endeavors or concludes that all such quests are equally futile. But the 1960s marked an important achievement. The tone debate came to an end. The comic secularists admitted to an element of gloom related to the notion of *l'absurde*. And those favoring a somber religious reading recognized an element of humor in the story. The larger differences between the religious and secular readers remained, but tone ceases to be referred to as evidence for one or the other position because most commentators now recognized the presence of either comedy and tragedy or laughter and irony. New problems, however, arose. Careful formal analysis reveals that Pekuah's adventure is unique and that the final chapter is aptly entitled "The conclusion, in which nothing is concluded."

In 1970 the religious debate was continued by Patrick O'Flaherty, who attacks *Rasselas* in an article entitled "Dr. Johnson as Equivocator: The Meaning of *Rasselas*." For O'Flaherty, the irony of *Rasselas* is all-pervasive; in opposition to Lascelles, he argues that the satire applies to the pilgrims as well as to those whom they visit. In addition to the specific episodes poking fun at one or another main character, the journey itself satirizes the pursuit of a choice of life. Moreover, "the world as depicted in *Rasselas* is bleak and forbidding," for the religion of the narrative offers no comfort, no resolution. Lascelles's concept of hope is rejected because the search encourages neither despair nor hope but is a "species of folly," and hope itself is presented as a neutral drive, neither good nor bad, simply persistent. Kenney's notion that comfort is provided by diversification is questioned because Imlac remains unhappy, as evidenced in his escape with the pilgrims from the happy valley. Insisting that religion is present in *Rasselas* even though there are references to chance, O'Flaherty returns to what he characterizes as Boswell's belief that the "paradox of *Rasselas* is that in it an absurdist view ... is not irreconcilable with the idea of a supervising Divinity." Since Christianity "does not teach utter absurdity and futility," O'Flaherty agrees with the Victorians who are "disturbed" by the religion of *Rasselas*, which does not finally ascend above absurdity but remains on the same level in a state of contradiction to it. Johnson presents us with "two fundamentally opposite interpretations of human existence lying side by side as if there was no reason for conflict." His religion, according to O'Flaherty, comes to be marked more by fear than by faith, and in *Rasselas* we have a kind of "catharsis; a purgation of sorrow in absurd comedy, and of doubt in a grimly deterministic philosophy of life which is revealed, on close analysis, as equivocation" (203, 205, 207, 208).

Although following in the tradition of the Victorian religious attack on *Rasselas*, O'Flaherty also appropriates the modern existentialist doctrine of *l'absurde* articulated, in very different ways, by both Leyburn and Wimsatt. Johnson is accused of equivocation because the notion of absurdity present in *Rasselas*, cannot be recon-ciled with the doctrine of Christianity in the story. These two doc-trines, according to O'Flaherty, negate one another. Here we con-front a new stage in the religious debate. The notion of *l'absurde* that has been rejected as secular by most of those advancing a religious reading is here accepted but seen to result in equivocation. Furthermore, O'Flaherty uses Boswell in an attempt to counter the suggestion by Wimsatt that *Rasselas* provides a religious perspective upon life's absurdity. But Boswell, as we know, does not accuse Johnson of equivocation. On the contrary, he asserts that *Rasselas* faces reality fully and that those who experience a questioning of faith in the tale are unable to face Johnson's unflinching view of the truth. O'Flaherty sees equivocation because he recognizes that the satire in *Rasselas* undermines all attempts at formal closure; the choice of eternity, like the choice of life, is never achieved. Because the religious question is raised but never answered, O'Flaherty believes that *Rasselas* ends with equivocation, not resolution.

Mary Lascelles, in a second article on *Rasselas*, pursues an alternative inference from O'Flaherty's argument, namely, that the religious question remains unanswered because Johnson is interested in a secular problem. For Lascelles, the question is "whether *Rasselas* is a profound essay in moral philosophy or a satire on the moralist's search for a clue to the riddle of life." Favoring the latter view, Lascelles believes that the religious reading must dismiss the oriental aspects of the tale as mere ornaments. She proposes a four-part structure, incorporating Jones's coda within the astronomer incident. Labeled as "dreadful," chapter 45, the conversation with the old man, is dismissed as a later addition and certainly out of place. "So everything turns on our reading of the final episode [the astronomer] and its central character." Denying Raleigh's assertion that this incident supplies "the picture with a shade darker than death itself," Lascelles sees hope here because the astronomer, unlike other exemplars of folly visited by the travelers, is cured of his delusion. The episode also has formal significance in transcending "the limitations of contemporary allegory and drawing on an older and greater tradition." As the astronomer develops from an allegorical character into one who comes to life, is cured, and joins the traveling party, *Rasselas* moves beyond the oriental allegory common in the periodical essays to develop the final theme of "the function, not in art but in life, of the imagination" (121-29). But since life, as Lascelles herself admits, does not enter until the end of the story, this notion leaves out of account most of the narrative, where imagination presumably can only operate in the context of art. In the same year as that of Lascelles's essay, Donald Greene also proposes a four-part structure, but one that ends in ambiguity. The conclusion of *Rasselas* is seen as similar to that of *Candide;* the larger issues remain unresolved, and one simply returns to one's garden (130-31). Influenced by Jones's innovative idea of a coda, Lascelles and Greene both advance readings that seek to avoid the religious question, yet they arrive at diametrically opposite conceptions of the reader's final response.

Harold Pagliaro attempts to incorporate this polarity within a dialectical reading of *Rasselas.* Employing a notion of time and timelessness that Geoffrey Tillotson first advanced in 1959 (97-103), Pagliaro approaches *Rasselas* as a novel. Ironically this essay appeared in 1971, the same year that Tillotson published an introduction to the tale that omits any reference to his own previous ideas on time. While Tillotson now believes that there is no important difference in form between *Rasselas* and a religious or moral essay, Pagliaro uses Tillotson's earlier notion to forward his case for the story as a novel. But the problem of how to include timelessness within the fabric of the novel is to prove a formidable one. The prince and Imlac are, according to Pagliaro, poles in a dialectic representing youth and age that finally become interfused; their opposition and eventual linking "define the fictional world" of *Rasselas.* By the end of the tale the two points of view become one; the "Imlac-Rasselas axis is an eternal one, yet changing, as Rasselas journeys toward Imlac." The reader, however, "identifies wholly with neither" of the characters. At the end, the Imlac-Rasselas axis is transformed into the choice-of-life/choice-of-eternity or time versus eternity axis: "the reader, unlike the characters who turn heavenward, may turn to the novel—its collection of mediated pairs of forces—both their antagonism and their interpenetration, in perpetuity" (243). The characters turn to heaven, and the reader is left with the form of the novel. Pagliaro has accepted O'Flaherty's belief that the religious and secular quests are irreconcilable; he differs from O'Flaherty in urging the reader to focus upon the secular novelistic structure. But that structure can no longer claim wholeness if it leaves out of account the characters' final decisions.

In the 1970s the brief respite from attack that *Rasselas* enjoyed during the 1950s and 1960s ended. The attempt to avoid the religious question by disclosing the holistic form of the choice-of-life journey was doomed to failure once it was seen that the narrative is not circular in design. Those favoring the religious reading could thus either attack the structure of the tale, as does O'Flaherty, or, like Wimsatt, argue that the lack of closure for the choice-of-life motif is itself a means of pointing to the choice of eternity. The early 1970s also produced a dramatic development concerning the difference between the end of the prince's journey and that of the history of Imlac. Now seen as a part of the larger context, Imlac is no longer assumed to be Johnson's spokesman, and his views are discussed in relation to those of the other characters in the tale. For example, in 1971, only five years after Tillotson and Kallich assumed that Imlac's poetic principles were synonymous with those of Johnson, Howard Weinbrot documents the function of the irony directed against Imlac in his "dissertation upon poetry." He demonstrates that some of the poetic principles in this chapter do and others do not coincide with Johnson's own beliefs (57-71).

The debate that followed the appearance of Weinbrot's article concerns the extent and kind of modification of the poetic doctrines implied by the satire: most participants, however, accept the fact that humor is present and functions in part to distinguish Imlac's poetics from those of Johnson. Paradoxically, the recognition that *Rasselas* is not an organic whole highlights the limitations of the circular aspect of Imlac's history, which was now seen as inscribed within a larger but open-ended kind of structure.

In 1973 Ian White argues that *Rasselas* can be seen to have as its final goal education. A "novel in miniature in which each chapter break and title has a function," *Rasselas*, according to White, catches the reader up in the story from the first sentence because Johnson writes "beyond his usual statements, in a kind of sublime which calls new powers into being." This sublime style distances the reader so that the characters and locations of the story can be perceived as "intellectual types" going through the stages of an educational process (24-30). But the same process that White finds to be contained in a novelistic form, Thomas Curley, also writing in 1973, describes as allegorical: *Pilgrim's Progress* provides "a thematic blue-print for the creation of *Rasselas*" that arrives at the choice of eternity (147-82). The question that remains unanswered is whether the educational procedure is secular or religious.

Carey McIntosh suggests that the two need not be viewed as mutually exclusive. Developing the notion of a paradox between the gloom of the choice-of-life motif and the hope inherent in the choice of eternity, McIntosh speculates about how the travelers, after making the choice of eternity, can continue seeking the choice of life

(193). But this all-embracing formulation raises a question about the nature of the relationship between the two quests. How is the choice-of-life quest altered after the choice of eternity has been made?

The nature of the problem now facing criticism is aptly illustrated by William Holtz's tribute, in 1974, to Joseph Wood Krutch. Explaining that Krutch recalls "discovering an identity of mood between *The Modern Temper* and the somber note of Johnson's work particularly his *Rasselas*," Holtz points out that "the story of Rasselas has no religious component and the prince's question hangs over this purely sublunary narrative unanswered." But, according to Holtz, Krutch differs from Johnson in being unable to maintain the balance between secular and theological. "Krutch's study is consistent" with the modern emphasis on Johnson's skepticism "in all matters but religious ones ... and his conflict between religion and experience." In his own life Krutch finally opposes the "radical discontent" of *Rasselas*. We have already seen, in our earlier discussion, that in 1944, when Krutch advances his "tragic" secular reading of *Rasselas* he does not express his personal dissatisfaction with such a notion. Holtz draws this inference from an admission Krutch makes in his autobiography. But the dilemma that Holtz locates in Krutch's personal life becomes a literary-critical one, that is, has a bearing on the *Rasselas* commentary of the mid-1970s. Once the structural configuration is seen to reside in the reader, not the text, the attitude of an important reader such as Krutch has critical significance. For the question now becomes what sort of critical posture is appropriate for the reader of *Rasselas*.

In 1975 Earl Wasserman responds to this question by attempting to demonstrate that the text itself directs the reader to an "implicit context." Specifically, the choice of Prodicus and the tablet of Cebes, archetypal stories known to schoolboys of the eighteenth century, are the models for the structure of *Rasselas*. The former is molded into the choice-of-life motif, and the latter becomes the basis for the journey or quest theme. Both, however, are markedly transformed by Johnson; the choice of life is never found, and the journey ends inconclusively. The consequence is "formal absurdity," which explains the "quiet" comedy and final functional ambiguity (5, 25). Although for Wasserman the formal subversion operates against the choice of life in favor of the choice of eternity, it is not clear from his argument why another reader cannot perceive it operating in the opposite direction. In fact, because of his emphasis on the subversive element in *Rasselas*, Wasserman is placed in the company of doubters by a critic forwarding an orthodox Christian position. Arguing that *Rasselas* is a proof for the immortality of the soul, Robert Walker describes Wasserman's view that the choice of eternity is only "the implicit theme of the book" as a position that "sounds like" the secular reading of Joseph Wood Krutch (153).

Here we see more explicitly what has been implicit throughout this survey: *Rasselas* evokes the deeply personal spiritual beliefs of critics, their assumptions about what in the story constitutes a religious or secular position. This survey of these views suggests that in avoiding explicit final commitment on the religious issue, *Rasselas* encompasses the various aspects of its own controversy.

But the battle within continued. A new stage in our history, however, is signaled by the fact that the religious position based upon reader response was now seen by a more traditional critic as equally suited to a secular reading. Also, it now ceases to be customary to refer to *Rasselas* as a *Vanity of Human Wishes* in prose because, on the one hand, religion, if seen to be present in the narrative, is characterized as less overtly present than in the poem and, on the other hand, the comic and exotic elements of the tale are clearly accepted as unique to it. In short, the religious debate now concern a narrower issue and is placed in sharper focus.

An instance of this modified focus is provided by the difference between William Vesterman and Walter Jackson Bate, both writing on Johnson the man. For Vesterman, the style of *Rasselas* gradually changes from that of the early chapters, which are marked by a detached and admonitory view of imagination—"ye who listen with credulity"—to that of the conclusion, where the characters are allowed the pleasure of creating imagined worlds, knowing that they cannot be "fixed": "so different is the last chapter from the first that the only hope finally deluded is the author's intention. As he deals artistically with the implications of the intentions, the imaginative effort involved brings out Johnson's greatest power, and the result for us is the history of a week in the life of the imagination" (104). Vesterman believes that Johnson begins with the intention of judging the travels from a religious perspective, but his artistic integrity leads him to conclude in a sublunary context. Bate, on the other hand, after admitting to the presence of many secular literary "archetypal forms," including the fairy story, the eastern tale, the pilgrimage idea, satire manqué, and the Bildungsroman, finds an implicit religious conclusion, which is never made explicit because of "Johnson's own inner taboo ... against specific religious discussion on his own part in his writing" (338). The difference here concerns only the final impression left on the reader; both agree that the body of the text contains religious and secular elements as well as comic and tragic moments.

But perhaps the best illustration that the debate about tone, a seminal term for the "New Criticism," has passed out of history while the religious question remains can be seen from the summary of *Rasselas* offered by the 1979 installment of that stalwart of standard opinion, the *Oxford History of English Literature:* compared now not to *The Vanity of Human Wishes* but to the *Rambler, Rasse-*

las is distinguished from the latter by virtue of its "fresh perspective," "intensity and compendiousness." The end of the tale, although "exceedingly austere," is seen as "far from despairing" (36-37). Thus, the religious question remained unresolved while the tone was characterized by combining the schools of gloom and grim smiles. The tone debate was thus brought to an end.

During the latter part of the eighteenth century, throughout the nineteenth century, and in the first part of the twentieth century, tone was discussed in direct relationship to religion, the shared assumption being that Christianity contains in its essence some form of hope. For a few decades in the middle of the twentieth century, a number of critics argued that the tone of *Rasselas* is a function of its literary structure, not of theological commitment. But when many recognized that the form of *Rasselas* is deliberately open-ended, religion was displaced from the text to the reader. Tone at that point ceased to be a decisive factor because the attitude inherent in one's religious convictions was seen to be individual and highly subjective. The tone debate was not resolved but abandoned because new critical assumptions rendered the entire matter moot.

Turning now to the 1980s, we can understand the critical concerns of the present decade by analyzing a few representative essays that adopt contrasting approaches to *Rasselas*. In 1981 Irvin Ehrenpreis returns to the structure of *Rasselas*. In a section of the essay entitled "Theory," Ehrenpreis explains that structure can only be of use if it refers to "a design conceptually prior to the completion of the work under examination, and established in such a way that both the author and the reader may know it." "In this sense," he continues, "structure is inseparable from literary genre." In the following section of the essay, Ehrenpreis defines the genre of *Rasselas*. He first explains that it is not a novel but a "proto-novel," then classifies it as a "philosophical romance" before deciding that it is an "oriental tale." Yet his concluding paragraph contains the following sentence: "A critic might notice that the features I have been examining appear in works by Johnson which in no way refer to oriental tales" (108-17). Ehrenpreis's struggle with the generic problem makes evident that Johnson includes elements from most of the narrative genres available to him but does not permit the reader to rest with one prevailing genre. In the same year Leonard Orr employs Walter Raleigh's view that the astronomer is the climax of the tale to advance a reading of *Rasselas* as a story about the abuse of power. When the travelers cure the astronomer, Orr argues, they also bring themselves "down to earth," to share desires no different in kind from those of the astronomer. In bringing the scientist down from the clouds, the travelers also recover from the "imaginative desires for power" (17). Orr thus adds still another generic possibility to the various ones posited by Ehrenpreis.

While these critics debated genre, or Johnson's means for achieving his goal in *Rasselas*, others considered the nature of the goal. In 1984, Bertrand Bronson suggests that in *Rasselas* Johnson can be identified with both the prince and Imlac in that like the young man he journeys outside the happy valley but like the older seer he realizes that the search for a choice of life is futile. However, later in his life when writing *A Journey to the Western Islands of Scotland*, Johnson has "not lost his zest for experience," but he now "fuses with Imlac" (163-86). A year later R. D. Stock attempts to set the balance against Bronson's view of "Johnson Agonistes," a position he admits has served its original purpose of modifying Boswell but now itself needs revision. What has been neglected, according to Stock, is the Solomonic wisdom of Johnson that is epitomized in *Rasselas*. This narrative, like the *Vanity*, is for Stock in "the generic tradition of Ecclesiastes." Johnson should be understood as a "religious existentialist"; not only a "Samson of Agonistes," Johnson is also a "Solomon of wisdom" (15-23). The religious resolution that Bronson finds at the end Johnson's life Stock locates at the end of *Rasselas*.

Alan Liu, on the other hand, avoids the entire question of genre by use of discourse analysis and psychoanalytic theory. One result of the move from text to reader, it should be noted, was the rise to legitimacy of psychological criticism. Furthermore, Liu's use of terminology derived from the works of Jacques Derrida and Jacques Lacan indicates that *Rasselas* has not lost its ability to attract new methods. Writing in 1984, Liu begins with O'Flaherty's notion of the equivocation between the choice of life and the choice of eternity. But instead of concluding, like O'Flaherty, that the religion of *Rasselas* is therefore flawed, Liu adopts a deconstructive strategy, focusing upon the equivocation. "The 'moral' of Johnson's first paragraph which tells us not to wish, is undermined by its own hidden wistfulness," that is, we are directed simultaneously to wish and not to wish. The result for Liu is a sort of hollow desire that produces the "embalmed signifier," the catacombs. Since the reader is here seen as at once the observer of the embalming process and that which is embalmed, instead of selecting either a religious choice of eternity or a secular choice of life, we are taken by Liu on a Lacanian journey in search of the psychological significance of the embalmed signifier. The "missing link" is Johnson's mother, a discovery that, according to Liu, gives added resonance to the term used in the catacombs episode, "mummy." Johnson's "guilt" about his mother is found buried in the text of *Rasselas*; Liu concludes that this "embalmed signifier, compelling such a complex wake of public denial and private hunger, is the central structure of Johnson's thought" (202-5).

But Steven Lynn employs deconstruction to arrive at the opposite conclusion. Lynn focuses on gender difference in the marriage debate, which, he believes, ends with Nekayah asserting that we must make an arbitrary choice and live with it. Hence *Rasselas* is seen to end in "undecideability," a state that for Lynn is fundamental to Johnson who situates himself between male and female. Johnson, like most deconstructors, according to Lynn, ends with the status quo, the choice of eternity, the only viable alternative to continual ambivalence. Catherine Parke makes a similar point in secular terms, demonstrating how Nekayah subverts Rasselas's male mastery stand. Here we see that deconstruction arrives at three different conclusions, one psychological, another religious and still another social. Deconstruction, as Derrida makes clear at the outset, is a radical strategy for subversion, and subverters are themselves not immune to deconstruction. But deconstruction that is here applied to selected interpretations has yet to be applied to methodologies.

At the end of this decade Edward Tomarken published the first book to base a new methodology on the history of *Rasselas* criticism. Tomarken infers from his history of *Rasselas* commentary covering the period from 1759 to 1986 that each method has a valid point. "First and most important, the religious question cannot be resolved ... [but] is a driving force. Second, in addition to being like most literary words, a mixture of genres ... *Rasselas* makes clear that it cannot be positively labeled or generically essentialized. Critics ... make decisions about which genres prevail on the basis of their interpretation. ... Third, although not circular in structure, *Rasselas* has functional formal properties. The abduction of Pekuah differs in kind from the conversational nature of episodes previous to it. And the astronomer incident is unique in a number of respects, not the least of which is the fact that the astronomer is cured and becomes a member of the traveling party." Tomarken goes on to point out that these three points correspond to the three ages of criticism in the historical survey. He therefore suggests that the methodologies from these three ages "be combined. The mimetic critics of the eighteenth century recognized that Johnson was not attempting to resolve the religious question but to represent it. ... The nineteenth-century commentators realized that *Rasselas* stretched generic conventions to their limits. ... The twentieth century ... has demonstrated that the literary quality of *Rasselas* is bound up with its structural properties." The combination that Tomarken devises leads him to demonstrate how "literary analysis can have extraliterary application" and to contend that *Rasselas* concludes "not with the choice of life but with the process of making a choice of life," a literary process that is shown not to be restricted to literature, "a procedure used in life, especially in choice-of-life situations, where we frame or contextualize elements from the flux of experience in order to interpret them" (36-7; 102-3).

My conclusion about the future of *Rasselas* criticism is that it cannot make significant advances until it faces its own history, particularly since *Rasselas* is the only one of Johnson's writings to have a continuous history of critical commentary. The problems that emerge from ignoring that history are apparent in some of the most recent commentaries. In 1988 Mark Temmer assumes that Robert Walker's argument that *Rasselas* is written to prove the immutability of the soul is widely accepted. And in 1989 Philip Davis takes for granted that Imlac is Johnson's spokesman. The reader of this selective survey will immediately recognize that such assumptions are questioned by the history of *Rasselas* commentary. But the problem is made most overt in four essays that appeared in 1990. All assume an orthodox religious reading of *Rasselas*. R. B. Gill compares *Rasselas* to *Vathek*. Johnson's tale is wisdom literature concerned with truths of the Bible, while Beckford "does not respond to the invasion of mature reflection." Charles Campbell and Richard Braverman come to nearly identical conclusions by examining water imagery and architectural sites respectively. For Campbell the secular journey is a self-consuming artifact leaving only the choice of eternity. For Braverman the catacombs make clear the futility of the journey that is apparent from the description of the palace in the happy valley. Lastly Nicholas Hudson suggests that Johnson's narrative is structured in accordance with the principles of Richard Hooker. Although Hudson admits that religion is a "peripheral concern" in *Rasselas*, he claims that we are left with Hooker's principles of religion.

None of these critics seems aware that the question of religion in *Rasselas* has remained a topic of debate for the past two and one-half centuries. Moreover, so much in these most recent positions is derivative and unacknowledged from the past that their innovations are obscured. My point is that *Rasselas* criticism is so active, so alive, that a critic's very survival depends upon knowledge of the history of commentary and awareness of the kinds of methods that have already been applied to *Rasselas*. Evasion of the history of criticism, of its methodological and theoretical implications, obscures originality and helps the Leviathan of the past, the abyss of history, swallow individuality. Evasion of the metacritical and theoretical issues related to *Rasselas* facilitates deconstruction of new readings. Significant contributions to the field will have to begin by recognizing that *Rasselas* exposes the limitations of present critical approaches.

6: Shakespeare Criticism

DURING THE EIGHTEENTH CENTURY THE QUESTION was whether Johnson does justice to Shakespeare as the greatest British playwright and whether the commentators on Johnson's Shakespeare do justice to Johnson as a critic. By the nineteenth century, both Shakespeare and Johnson were established as institutions. The romantics, therefore, were able to attack Johnson in order to alter the way in which we appreciate Shakespeare. Instead of the erratic, untutored man of the Renaissance theater, Shakespeare becomes the imaginative bard. Johnson's approach to Shakespeare was seen as outmoded because institutionalized and reified. For the next two centuries the romantic view of Shakespeare dominated criticism, so that even defenders of Johnson accepted the view that his eighteenth-century commonsense approach cannot do justice to the imaginative world of Shakespeare. Present-day evaluation of Johnson on Shakespeare continues to suffer from a tacit acceptance of romantic methodology. We need to employ aspects from Johnson's Shakespeare to form new views of the plays and alternatives to postromantic approaches.

George Colman, one of the first reviewers of the Shakespeare edition, is positively disposed and adopts a friendly tone. Concerning subscribers' complaints of the edition appearing later than originally promised, Colman comments: "But granting our Editor to be naturally indolent—and naturally indolent we believe him to be—we cannot help wondering at the Number, Vastness, and Excellence of his Production. A Dictionary of our Language; a Series of admirable Essays in the *Rambler*, as well as, if we are not misinformed, several excellent ones in the *Adventurer*; an Edition of Shakespeare; besides some less considerable Works, all in the Space of no very great Number of Years! and all these the Productions of a mere Idler!" Turning then to the *Preface* in a more serious tone, Colman suggests that Johnson is being too hard on Theobald and too easy on Hanmer and Warburton, but that these are minor concerns: "On the whole, this *Preface*, as it is an elaborate, so it is also a fine Piece of Writing. It possesses all the Virtues and Vices of the peculiar Stile of its Author.

It speaks, perhaps, of Shakespeare's Beauties too sparingly, and of his Faults too hardly; but it contains, nevertheless, much Truth, good Sense, and just Criticism" (CH, 162-63).

Two other reviews in 1765 are negative, if not outright hostile. The unsigned review (attributed to William Kenrick) in the *Monthly Review* blames the author for producing his edition considerably later than promised, refers to Johnson's opening remarks in the *Preface* as "trite" and "pompous," and remarks of the defense of the intermingling of comedy and tragedy that "we do not see the force of his reasoning." Even the famous defense of Shakespeare for breaking the three unities is questioned. Johnson argues that the audience does not mistake stage action for actual occurrences. The reviewer replies that credibility and the unities may be necessary to produce "apparent probability." Once in the theater, the reviewer continues, the spectator loses sight of the fact that he is not in Rome; this deception works on the audience's "passions," not its "understanding." Johnson's belief that the spectator compares the action onstage to actual experience is flatly contradicted: because his or her passions are engaged, the spectator is the "least capable of comparing the drama and life" (CH, 164-80). The anonymous reviewer in the *Critical Review* has high expectations that Johnson will surpass his predecessors—Rowe, Pope, Warburton, Hamner, and Theobald—but is disappointed, having expected Johnson to understand that Shakespeare is the sort of genius to be judged by "feeling," not "taste." In general, this reviewer applauds Johnson's positive comments and objects only when he criticizes Shakespeare. Accordingly, Johnson's position against the unities receives high praise (321-32). We notice here in the middle of the eighteenth century a number of aspects that resemble the romantic position, particularly the emphasis on the passions and the concept of dramatic delusion. But the motive at this time is different. Coleridge, as we shall see, wishes to modify the terms of our appreciation of Shakespeare. These earlier critics are anxious that Shakespeare be appreciated, not denigrated, by criticism, a position that is reinforced by the two pertinent books that appeared in 1765.

Benjamin Heath's *A Revisal of Shakespear's Text* makes only passing reference to Johnson, pointing out that the public is "under real and considerable obligation" to Theobald, has a somewhat less considerable debt to Pope, and that Warburton's "pretensions are pompous and solemn" (vii). William Kenrick's *A Review of Doctor Johnson's New Edition of Shakespere* is a heated attack upon Johnson. A sample vituperation should be sufficient. Concerning Johnson's comments on Warburton's notes, Kenrick cites the following from *Macbeth*, "An Eagle tow'ring in his pride of place, Was, by a mousing owl, hawk'd and kill'd," and remarks, "Dr. Johnson having neither preferment in the church, nor post in the state, the word

place may seem to want that strict propriety the critics require; yet, if
we reflect how nearly *places* and *pensions* are allied, there is not one
of Shakespeare's commentators who would make any scruple of
substituting one word for the other." (CH, 181-87). Johnson himself
never replies to Kenrick, but others do. One writer in the *Critical
Review* points out that the main objection to Johnson is to the pension that Kenrick would have been pleased to receive. Another writing in the *Monthly Review,* refers to Kenrick as the "Orlando Fu-
rioso" of criticism and advises him to lay by his "tomahawk" (457-
59). More germane than the counter-attacks on Kenrick is James Barclay's defense of Johnson. Barclay declares that Johnson's Shakespeare has aroused some disappointment from those who expected a
"compleat commentary." But Barclay sees Kenrick's critique in
broader terms: "IT IS A DOWNRIGHT AFFRONT TO NATIONAL
APPROBATION, TO STIGMATISE THAT MAN WITH IGNO-
RANCE, WHO HAS BEEN SELECTED FROM THE COLLECTIVE
LEARNED AS PECULIARLY DESERVING THEIR FAVOURS." Barclay points out that "the critic and scholar everywhere plead" in
Johnson's favor and that Kenrick should recall that "IT IS A RE-
CEIVED AXIOMATICAL TRUTH, THAT DULNESS AND ABUSE
SELDOM MAKE THEIR APPEARANCE BUT IN THE ABSENCE OF
REASON AND ARGUMENTATION" (CH, 189-91). Johnson's reputation as a critic was now of an importance equal to that of Shakespeare as an artist. As Pope noted earlier in the century, criticism that
arises as the handmaiden of the arts is now its competitor. Only
when criticism has established itself as a discipline is it possible for
the romantics to argue that its method needs to be modified.

But before turning to the nineteenth century, we need to understand that Johnson was not as typical of his age as is assumed. In 1770
Voltaire replies to a reference to him in the *Preface.* Regarding those
who complain of the indecorous behavior of Shakespeare's Romans
and kings, Johnson asserts that "these are the petty cavils of petty
minds." Voltaire replies:

I cast my eyes over an edition of Shakespeare produced by Mr.
Samuel Johnson. I found that he describes as "petty minds"
those foreigners who are astonished to find in plays by the
great Shakespeare that "a Roman senator should play the buf-
foon and a king should appear drunk on the stage." Far be it
from me to suspect that Mr. Johnson is given to clumsy jokes
or is over-addicted to wine; but I find it rather extraordinary
that he would include buffoonery and drunkenness among
the beauties of the tragic theatre; the reason he gives for doing
so is not less remarkable. "The poet," he says, "overlooks the
casual distinction of condition and country, as a painter who,
satisfied with having painted the figure, neglects the drapery."

The comparison would have been more accurate if he had been speaking of a painter who introduced ridiculous clowns into a noble subject, or portrayed Alexander the Great mounted on an ass at the battle of Arbela and the wife of Darius drinking with the rabble in a common tavern. (CH, 194)

Voltaire accuses Johnson of neglecting what is often taken to be a mainstay of eighteenth-century criticism, the concept of decorum. In addition, Johnson is criticized by eighteenth-century commentators for his textual position. In 1783 Joseph Ritson comments on the revision of the Shakespeare edition that Johnson finished with the aid of George Steevens in 1778. To Johnson's claim that he has collated the copies of the dramas available to him, Ritson asserts that Johnson and Steevens "never collated any of the folios" and concludes that this edition leaves the text in the "same state of corruption as was in the time of Rome" (iii-vi). In 1785 John Monck Mason reviews Edmund Malone's edition and mentions his dissatisfaction with all extant texts, "even that of Johnson" (ix). We now know that these assessments are inaccurate: Johnson did some collating and emended many corruptions of the text. But because in the next century he was used as the exemplar of the limitations of the "neoclassical" approach to Shakespeare, it is important to understand that Johnson's critical and textual position was not regarded by his contemporaries as typical of the age. On the contrary, Johnson's edition of Shakespeare was seen as so singular in his own day that it contributed both to the reputation of Shakespeare and to the stature of the discipline of criticism.

Turning to the romantic position, we need to consider three important critics. Employing Johnson's anecdote of the man who carries a brick in attempting to sell his house, Auguste Wilhelm von Schlegel attacks the Shakespeare criticism. "And yet how little, and how very unsatisfactorily does he himself speak of the pieces considered as a whole! Let any man, for instance, bring together the short characters which he gives at the close of each play, and see if the aggregate will amount to that sum of admiration which he himself, at his outset, has stated as the correct standard for the appreciation of the poet." In addition to objecting to the fragmentary nature of Johnson's commentary, Schlegel also disagrees with Johnson's opinion that Shakespeare's "pathos is not always natural and free from affectation. There are, it is true, passages, though comparatively speaking very few, where his poetry exceeds the bounds of actual dialogue, where a too soaring imagination, a too luxuriant wit, rendered a complete dramatic forgetfulness of himself impossible. ... But energetical passions electrify all the mental powers, and will consequently, in highly-flavoured natures, give utterance to themselves in ingenious and figurative expressions" (CH, 195-96). In the period

1811-16 Coleridge makes miscellaneous references to Johnson's *Preface* and *Notes to Shakespeare*. Defending Shakespeare's puns, Coleridge alleges that "puns often arise out of a mingled sense of injury, and contempt of the person inflicting it, and, as it seems to me, it is a natural way of expressing that mixed feeling." Coleridge also opposes Johnson's condemnation of Hamlet's refusal to murder his uncle when praying. "This conduct, and this sentiment, Dr. Johnson has pronounced to be so atrocious and horrible, as to be unfit to be put into the mouth of a human being. The fact, however, is that Dr. Johnson did not understand the character of Hamlet, and censured accordingly: the determination to allow the guilty king to escape at such a moment is only part of the indecision and irresoluteness of the hero." And, most important, Coleridge presents his conception of stage illusion as contrary to that of Johnson: "the true theory of stage illusion, [that] ... images and thoughts possess a power in and of themselves, independent of that act of the judgment or understanding by which we affirm or deny the existence of a reality correspondent to them ... [is] equally distant from the absurd notion of the French critics, who ground their principles on the principle of an absolute delusion, and of Dr. Johnson who would persuade us that our judgments are as broad awake during the most masterly representation of the deepest scenes of *Othello*, as a philosopher would be during the exhibition of a magic lanthorn with Punch and Joan" (CH, 197-99).

In 1817 William Hazlitt completes the romantic critique by suggesting that Johnson as a critic is wholly unsuitable for understanding the genius of Shakespeare. After citing Schlegel with approval, Hazlitt explains that he has to cite a foreigner because Johnson is not favorable to Shakespeare. But Johnson is "neither a poet nor a judge of poetry," and his *Preface* "is a laborious attempt to bury the characteristic merit of [Shakespeare] under a load of cumbrous phraseology—Johnson's power of reasoning overlaid his critical susceptibility." The problem is, for Hazlitt, that Johnson, the man of common sense, lowers "Shakespeare's genius to the standard of commonplace invention, [making] it easy to shew that his faults were as great as his beauties" (CH, 199-202). The romantics set out to disqualify Johnson as a critic of Shakespeare, and their success can be measured by the fact that Johnson's edition of Shakespeare remained without critical comment throughout the Victorian period. We see here the major tenets of romantic criticism: the defense of the textured nature of literary language, of illusion in the theater and of character as the major source of audience empathy, as well as the belief that genius is inspired by passion not reason. The resuscitation of Johnson on Shakespeare in the twentieth century clearly required that the critic adopt premises that are different from those of the romantic commentators. But this methodological point is not recognized until near the end of our century.

In 1903 David Nichol Smith points out what our survey of the nineteenth century has made manifest: "Johnson's *Preface* in particular was remembered only to be despised. It is not rash to say that at the present time the majority of those who chance to speak of it pronounce it a discreditable performance." Smith is one of the first since Johnson's day to set out to reverse this judgment. Concerning Johnson's position on the unities, Smith explains: "It was only after long reflection, and with much hesitation, that Johnson had disavowed what had almost come to be considered the very substance of the classical faith. ... His sturdy common sense and independence of judgment led him to anticipate much of what has been supposed to be the discovery of the romantic school. His *Preface* has received scant justice." Smith also defends Johnson's scholarship: "It is especially remarkable that Johnson, who is not considered to have been strong in research, should be the first to state that Shakespeare used North's translation of Plutarch. He is the first also to point out that there was an English translation of the play on which the *Comedy of Errors* was founded, and the first to show that it was not necessary to go back to the *Tale of Gamelyn* for the story of *As You Like It*." Smith assesses Johnson's textual criticism in the following terms: "Johnson's collation may not have been thorough but no modern editor can say that he proceeded on a wrong method. ... Johnson has included in his *Preface* an account of the work of earlier editors, and it is the first attempt of the kind which is impartial. ... Those who have worked with [Johnson's Notes] know the force of Johnson's claim that not a single passage in the whole work had appeared to him corrupt which he had not attempted to restore, or obscure which he had not endeavoured to illustrate. We may neglect the earlier eighteenth-century editions of Shakespeare, but if we neglect Johnson's we run a serious risk" (xvi-xxxi). Smith sends out the challenge to look again at Johnson's edition, but few choose that arduous path.

Three years later Beverly Warner refers to Johnson as "the great Leviathan of English letters," who makes his greatest contribution in his *Preface*, "which is, perhaps the most famous contribution of a like character. His textual criticism did not much add to his reputation" (110). In 1909 Charles F. Johnson, in a history of Shakespeare criticism, gives some attention to the *Notes* as well as the *Preface*. "Doctor Johnson" is a man of "powerful intellect and good sense" whose commentary can be relied on for common sense, "but when some necessary question of the play is to be considered, especially anything depending on the vital nature of the characters, this robust intellect is helpless." "A Classical scholar who knew little of Elizabethan literature," Johnson produced an edition that "was a disappointment, even in his own day. His criticism was vitiated by the pernicious idea that poetry must convey some definite lesson in morals. ... Johnson had not the slightest idea of the significance of the plays." Turning to the *Notes*, Charles Johnson asserts that we "cannot stand for Viola as an 'excellent schemer,'" and that Dr. Johnson "gives the preference to Tate's version of Lear." Even the position taken on the unities is seen as that of a "conservative classicist." In conclusion, Charles Johnson explains that "Dr. Johnson illustrates the prosaic and literal tendency of the eighteenth century" (113-24). Here begins the miscellaneous attitude to the *Notes*. Johnson's remarks are extracted from their context, which includes not only the remainder of his own remarks on the play but also those of other critics that he includes in his edition and comments upon.

In 1910 Walter Raleigh presents one of the first wholly positive assessments of Johnson's *Preface* and *Notes*. Raleigh stresses that Johnson's critical insights are to be preferred to scholarly pedantry: "Johnson's strong grasp of the main thread of the discourse, his sound sense, and his wide knowledge of humanity, enable him ... to go straight to Shakespeare's meaning, while the philological and antiquarian commentators kill one another in the dark." Of the negative portions of the *Preface*, Raleigh points out that "the detailed analysis of the faults is a fine piece of criticism, and has never been seriously challenged." Raleigh is the first to notice that the notes suggest an alternative to Boswell's view of Johnson: "Even those who love Johnson fall too easily into Boswell's attitude. ... The best of his notes on Shakespeare, like the best of his spoken remarks, invite discussion and quicken thought" (82-96). But the negative romantic view persists. The problem is that the able practical critic, like Raleigh, who examines Johnson's Shakespeare immediately confronts the limitations of the romantic position, but few actually consult the edition with care because romantic theory declares Johnson unsuitable as a critic of Shakespeare.

In 1917 Henry Wheatley is the first to point out that Johnson's Shakespeare is "practically the founder of the Variorum editions," for Johnson uses not only other editors but also the observations of members of "The Club." Nevertheless, Wheatley remains within the fold by maintaining that the great feature is "the noble preface," thus denigrating the *Notes* (164). In 1927 Thomas Raysor contests Nichol Smith's assertion that Johnson deals the final blow to the unities. "Johnson ... brought forward no new arguments; and indeed Dr. Johnson seems to imply a disbelief not only in literal delusion but also in any kind of dramatic illusion whatsoever." Raysor concludes that the English do not rid themselves of the unities until they read the German romantics (1-8). Raysor takes for granted that the romantic assumption of audience empathy as consisting in "delusion" is the only viable one. Coleridge's view of Johnson on

Shakespeare prevailed well into the twentieth century because of the lack of an alternative theory of audience empathy.

The depression of the 1930s set off a reaction to the romantics and a renewed appreciation for Johnson. Herbert Robinson respects the *Preface* as the "first attempt to arrive at a judicial estimate of Shakespeare's greatness." Unlike Coleridge, Johnson, according to Robinson, does not approach Shakespeare "with reverence," but more like present-day "rationalists" as opposed to "romantics." Some of Johnson's faults are that he is too moral or didactic, that he favors Tate's *Lear*, and that his argument on the tragedies is not sound. The notes "are superior to those of any other author" (125-40). In 1935 David Lovett argues that realism is a concept that leads to romanticism and the breaking down of the classical rules. Johnson's common sense is really a "sense of the realities of life." Johnson is confused when he refers to Shakespeare's characters as "species" not "individuals," but the concept of "species" begins to "fade" in the eighteenth century with the rise of realism (272-84). Lovett's confusion stems from his attempt to incorporate mimetic concepts within the method illuminated by the romantic lamp, for as Johnson well knew, the idea of the species, like all other ideas, can only arise with reference to reality.

Between 1948 and 1950, Arthur Eastman is the first to attend meticulously to Johnson's textual policy. First, Eastman determines precisely when Johnson worked on each of the original eight volumes and when he used the works of his contemporaries. Second, he establishes that the assumption that Johnson always uses Warburton as his copy text is not accurate: Johnson is eclectic, often using Warburton but occasionally resorting to Theobald and others. Thirdly, he demonstrates that Johnson's edition is unjustly relegated "to the limbo of unscholarly editions." In fact, Johnson adds between 14,000 and 15,000 textual changes, almost all in favor of "clarity" (1114). The increasing amount of scholarly attention to Johnson's edition of Shakespeare during this period suggests the need for a critical method that could account for this interest. But criticism is nearly a generation behind scholarship.

In 1951 Arthur Sherbo is the first to compare the *Miscellaneous Notes on Macbeth* of 1747, a sample of the work that was prepared for subscribers, with the notes to *Macbeth* in the finished version of 1765. Sherbo finds that Shakespeare is the author most quoted in the *Dictionary* (1755) making clear why most of the new notes use the *Dictionary* as their authority. Also, Johnson rejects eleven of his own early textual changes, showing his wariness of "over-zealous emendation." Sherbo concludes, however, that there is "little evidence of heightened aesthetic or critical insight" or "real Shakespearean criticism in the notes to the plays. For that one must go to the *Preface*" (44-47). In 1953 T. J. Monaghan is the first to record systematically the changes Johnson made in the revised edition of 1773. Although it was then believed that the only changes made were a sentence in the *Preface* and the note to the first appendix, Monaghan records a "large number of notes, most of them textual and explanatory" (235). In 1956 Arthur Sherbo published the first complete twentieth-century version of Johnson's *Notes to Shakespeare* as well as a monograph, *Samuel Johnson, Editor of Shakespeare*. In the latter he reverses his earlier pronouncement, pointing out that Johnson's greatest contribution to Shakespeare criticism resides not in the *Preface* but in the *Notes*. It seems likely that Sherbo's immersion in the *Notes* as a result of his edition altered his opinion. But neither Sherbo nor any other critic explains the spell the *Notes* cast upon its few attentive readers.

In 1960 the continuing prevalence of nineteenth-century assumptions is illustrated by Jacob Adler's analysis of the key phrase in Johnson's argument concerning the unities, "he that imagines this may imagine more." This position, Adler maintains, bases the response to literature not on the imagination but upon rationality. Although, Adler admits, Johnson does assert in *Rambler* no. 156 that "some delusion must be admitted," Johnson nevertheless takes a position "almost totally unempathetic" (226-28). Criticism had to wait for another generation for an explanation of how rationality can be related to audience empathy.

The division between bibliography and criticism was again manifest in the 1960s. In 1962 Donald Eddy modifies some of Sherbo's bibliographic findings. Eddy demonstrates that there are some significant alterations in the first two volumes of the 1765 edition and that one of the notes to *As You Like It* was changed (436). Two years later Paul Siegel labels Johnson a "liberal neo-classical critic" who often touches "the heart of the matter or raises fundamental questions" but whose remarks on character are "less germane for later detailed character analysis." This limitation is attributed to the fact that Shakespeare's characters are not "neo-classical mouthpieces" but "real" (7-9). The fact that bibliographers were examining the text with greater care did not alter the assumptions that bore upon interpretations of the text. Indeed, Wolfgang Fleischmann argues that Johnson's position on the unities is a preromantic argument. Insisting that René Wellek's assessment of Johnson's position on the unities leaves out of account the Bergsonian concept of time that is prefigured in romanticism, Fleischmann suggests that "in conflating long and short time in his argument against the unities Johnson is a precursor of romanticism but does not know it" (128-34). By contrast, P. R. Grover employs Johnson's remarks on *Hamlet* to exemplify a "narrow morality" that "violates the context of art" (157).

The next logical step was to suggest that Johnson, despite his opposition, prepared the way for the romantics. In the words of

Northrop Frye, although a reptilian product of the cold Age of Reason, Johnson nonetheless made way for the warm, mammalian romantics. In 1970 Murray Kreiger attempts to show how Johnson's *Preface* cleared the way for Coleridge. Krieger sees a tension in Johnson between the general, the "just representation of nature," and irreducible particulars. Johnson attempts to erect a system that mediates between these two extremes, but this "general system is art not nature, a fictional unity," and in that sense leads to the concept of "discordia concors," the position of Coleridge. So "archneoclassicist Samuel Johnson" anticipates Coleridge, the romantic (184-98). Even Johnson's supporters accepted this dichotomy and were therefore obliged to defend elements of the Age of Reason, such as common sense or Lockean reason. Charles Harrison focuses upon Johnson's "common sense." For Johnson, Shakespeare is not about poetry but about life, a view that for Harrison is a source of "sanity." In this way, Harrison explains why Johnson's position on the unities, unlike his moral disapproval, still engages us (1-10). John Middendorf explains how Johnson's method is based upon the philosophy of Locke. Johnson, according to Middendorf, believed that Shakespeare neglects sound in favor of sight. Locke reasons that "visual experiences" are at the root of life, not words. In the *Rambler* and the *Dictionary*, words for Johnson are "the vehicles by which ideas are conveyed to the understanding. ... Shakespeare's mind was rooted in the world of things." Johnson's commentary, accordingly, moves from "particular experiences of the play (the dramatic idea) to the common experiences (the general idea), from primitive to consequential meaning in Dictionary terms. ... Acting upon ... Shakespeare's seeing life in all its concreteness, Johnson in his notes offers the results of his own seeing" (251-70). The price of such arguments is the tacit admission that for Johnson the nonvisual and poetic were less immediate than the visual and nonpoetic .

In 1973 Arthur Sherbo examines the revisions of 1773, particularly in relation to the fourth and last revision of the *Dictionary*. Sherbo demonstrates the clear interrelationship of the two revisions and establishes that, contrary to the belief that Steevens did most of the work, Johnson was in charge and responsible for about 500 changes, 84 new notes, and final strictures for *The Tempest*, *A Midsummer Night's Dream*, and *The Merry Wives of Windsor* (21-35). In the same year the first full-length study of Johnson on Shakespeare appeared, R. D. Stock's *Samuel Johnson and Neoclassical Dramatic Theory: The Intellectual Context of the "Preface to Shakespeare."* As the title suggests, Stock regards the *Preface* as the important document; the *Notes* are only mentioned in passing in a miscellaneous way. Johnson is understood as the exemplar of his age, an era that Stock admits cannot be expected to withstand the onslaught of romanticism: "Thus, Johnson's judiciousness could hardly be expected to survive along with the 'reverential tone' which, Coleridge decreed, was the true test of Shakespearean criticism; nor is reason very compatible with the oracular rhapsodies of Carlyle" (196). Even the preface is now seen to be only of historic interest, a document relegated to the past not only by Coleridge but also by modern criticism.

In the quarter century since 1948, the scholarship on Johnson's edition has succeeded in demonstrating that Johnson took as great care over the notes as he did over the *Preface*, but the critics, still employing postromantic methods and assumptions, continued to neglect the notes. In the 1980s Johnson's Shakespeare criticism is again relegated to the orthodox neoclassical realm, that which is merely of historical interest, as opposed to the aspect of his criticism that remains pertinent for us. Some critics set out to remedy this situation. In 1982 John Needham places Johnson's Shakespeare criticism in the tradition of Coleridge, Eliot, and Leavis. But Needham does not explain why the tradition is composed of these three writers rather than Johnson himself and others, and it is noteworthy that the three critics selected share certain romantic preconceptions. On the other hand, G. F. Parker places certain of the notes in the context of a consistent mimetic theory based on the concept of general nature found in the *Preface*. But Parker does not distinguish Johnson's concept of general nature from that of his contemporaries and does not make clear why a mimetic theory is of interest to modern critics. Walter Jackson Bate demonstrates that Johnson completed the Shakespeare edition in the midst of a psychological crisis so severe that he thought at times that he might lose his sanity. Bate returns to Raleigh's assessment at the beginning of the century: "But what Raleigh goes on to add still remains true of all major Shakespearean scholars and editors in our time: in using the variorum editions, the practiced scholar soon falls into the habit, when he meets with an obscure page, of consulting Johnson's note before the others'" (397). In the 1980s the notes began to draw some critical attention, but the notion of a tradition, be it a mimetic theory or a concept of psychic nobility, does not explain the value of this material as "naked criticism."

In 1991 Edward Tomarken sets out to resolve this issue in *Samuel Johnson on Shakespeare: The Discipline of Criticism*. Tomarken examines the *Notes* to entire plays and argues that the "strictures" indicate that Johnson has an overall view of the play and that the *Preface*, written at the end of the project, serves as an introduction to interpretations of the dramas, not as a preface to miscellaneous notes. These interpretations are seen as great literary criticism because they connect the eighteenth and twentieth centuries. Johnson was a man of his age, but as a critic he pointed beyond his own time. Since Johnson was a greater practical critic than theoretician, his theoretical terminology was traditional in his own day, and outmoded in our own. Tomarken therefore attempts to convert Johnson's insights into modern terminology and arrive at a concept of literary criticism as a discipline that has an ethical goal, what he calls a "New Humanism." One important element of this approach is an alternative concept of dramatic empathy that includes reason and, unlike that of Coleridge, need not require total "delusion." "Johnson believes that interpretation is a moral imperative," and Tomarken argues by extension that "interpretation can open the way to alternatives to outmoded orthodoxies by explaining which fissures are important and by articulating their ideological innovative purport. Literary criticism will come into its own as a discipline only when it demonstrates that the singularity of literature resides in the way it contributes to the humanities, to the discovery and articulation of procedures that enable us to better endure and understand the human condition" (179).

The future of commentary on Johnson's edition of Shakespeare depends upon the recognition that Johnson's Shakespeare criticism helps us endure and understand the human condition. It is not adequate to explain this commentary as dated or merely in relation to ideas of historical interest. If Johnson's criticism of Shakespeare speaks to us, then we must find methods that serve to explain how and why. That perception is prior to and more important than our principles, theories, and ideologies, from neoclassical mimeticism to romantic empathy. And the problem of a reified romantic approach that denigrates Johnson's Shakespeare commentary can only be remedied by combining theory and practice, by devising a method that does justice to the insights in the notes. Johnson's Shakespeare edition itself is an excellent model for this procedure. The notes constitute the naked criticism or practice, and the preface is a series of generalizations based upon practice, a theory derived from the method of the edition. Johnson's Shakespeare criticism constitutes an exemplary document of criticism as a discipline. Like Johnson, we must build our theories in relation to insights and problems that arise from the practice of criticism and recognize that our practical perceptions are limited by our tacit and overt theoretical assumptions Only when theory and practice are understood as dialectically related, as mutually interactive, will we be able to hear the voice of Johnson on Shakespeare, the voice of the critic. For that task, we need to focus on the relationship between the notes and the *Preface* in order to understand how Johnson's Shakespearean principles and perceptions bear upon ours.

7: The Journey to the Western Islands of Scotland

THE HISTORY OF CRITICISM OF THE *JOURNEY* is peculiarly instructive. For the last quarter of the eighteenth century it was the
subject of a heated controversy: the issue was whether Johnson does
justice to the Western Islands of Scotland. Those who opposed Johnson also attacked him personally, since they claimed that the historical evidence is so obvious that the only explanation for overlooking
it is prejudice. This vituperative controversy focused upon historical
and psychological issues. But the debate ended by the beginning of
the nineteenth century, and for nearly a century almost nothing was
published on the *Journey*. The reason for this neglect is that the romantics and Victorians assumed that since the exclusive concern of
previous commentators was historical and psychological, the *Journey* has no import as literature. Indeed, the recent revival of interest
in the *Journey* began in 1960 with an essay that isolates themes as
part of an argument that the *Journey* is literature. But this position
set off a new debate, one that is ongoing. The question now is
whether the proposed literary structure can accommodate the historical concerns that preoccupied eighteenth-century critics. But why,
we may well ask, should there be a problem of literature including
references to history? After all, fictional works often include facts.
The problem is not that the *Journey* alludes to history but that it is
itself a historical event. Johnson makes clear that he is not construct-
ing an imaginative tour but recording the events and impressions of
an actual trip, and, most importantly, he concludes with the hope
that his account of his journey will contribute to the future of Highland culture. This recent controversy, in my view, cannot be resolved because the two sides employ mutually exclusive methods, in
Meyer Abrams's terms, the mirror versus the lamp. In fact, the problem stems from this very conception: it is more than coincidental
that the neglect of the *Journey* began with the rise of the lamp of
romanticism, the assumption that symbolic structures contain their
own source of light or inspiration, which is distinct from the reflection of history. I therefore believe that to understand the *Journey* we

need to seek an alternative to an approach based upon a dichotomy between literature and history and that we should begin by listening to Johnson, who demonstrates at the end of the *Journey* how a literary structure can become a historical event.

Few writers can boast of having articles written about their works before they are published. In January 1774, in the *London Magazine*, an article appeared designed to "whet" the appetite in preparation for Johnson's account of his journey: parts of this essay were reprinted later in the same year in the *Aberdeen Journal* and *Gentleman and Lady's Weekly Magazine*. It consists of an outline of Johnson's itinerary, his response to Scottish hospitality, his opposition to Knox, and disbelief in Ossian. This essay makes clear that Johnson's tour was anticipated, not merely as the basis of a book or even as the visitation of a famous writer, but, most important, as an event or what recent journalists call a happening. During this same year Robert Fergusson publishes a poem entitled "To Dr. Samuel Johnson: Food for a new Edition of his Dictionary." The poem parodies the language of the *Dictionary* by placing the lexicographer out of his London habitat. The following stanza helps us understand why Johnson's arrival receives such acclaim.

> To meminate thy name in after times,
> The mighty Mayor in each regalian town
> Shall consignate thy work to parchment fair
> In roll burgharian, and their tables all
> Shall fumigate with fumigation strong:
> SCOTLAND, from perpendicularian hills,
> Shall emigrate her fair MUTTONIAN store,
> Which late had there in pedestration walk'd,
> And o'er her airy heights perambuliz'd. (CH, 232)

The lexicographer is portrayed in a position of power because it is recognized that the English language is the foundation of English culture. Understandably, the Scottish people wonder how this English authority from the south will respond to their northern form of British culture. When understood as an event, Johnson's *Journey* is at once political, social, and literary.

The high expectations of the account of this most famous English writer of his day may help explain the polemical responses. In 1775 after publication of the *Journey*, Ralph Griffiths defends Johnson's *Journey* by comparing it to that of Thomas Pennant: "Mr. Pennant travels, chiefly, in the character of the naturalist and antiquary; Dr. Johnson in that of the moralist and observer of men and manners." Griffiths commends Johnson for his skepticism with regard to Ossian, "the northern Homer," and comically compliments Johnson on his careful, pious investigation of the local belief in the "second sight" (CH, 234-36). On the other hand, "Ixion," writing in the same year, cannot refrain from remarking on Johnson's "uninformed petulance ... for oats are the food of men in England." "I predicted early," Ixion continues, "that your Tour would be rather favourable to the people of this country, and I am glad to find it is so," but your "compliments are frigid and awkward and your style is unsuitable" (205-6). Another reviewer of the same year begins with a negative premise: "A man is not likely to be a very unprejudiced traveler through a country which he has held for forty years in contempt" and then replies to specific critical remarks in the *Journey*. For example, Johnson is disturbed at the conversion of a church into a greenhouse: "Let not him complain that an episcopalian chapel is turned into a green-house, who would not hesitate to convert a presbyterian kirk into a privy" (CH, 237-38).

Those reviewers who saw their main purpose as defending Scotland dispensed with the appearance of fair-mindedness. "Whackum," suggests the following "cure" for Johnson's inability to find enough old trees in Scotland: "Lets take a good old Scottish *birch* and lay it smartly to his breech" (256). "Philaletheois" accuses Johnson of traveling "with jaundice and spleen" (289). And James McIntyre composes Gaelic songs on the *Journey*: a sample stanza is translated as follows: "You are the brat in the midst of filth, The badger with its nose in his buttocks three quarters of a year. A sheep-tick that is called the leech. Foul is the wealth that you share, and if it were not that I do not like the name of satirist, I myself would earnestly desire to abuse you" (CH, 241). In the last entry for this year, Andrew Henderson sustains his vituperation for forty-eight pages. Johnson is portrayed as having preferred "idle and trifling amusements" to "solid investigation and search," thereby having missed the fact that the Scottish plains are "diversified with trees" and the evidence of the genuineness of Ossian manifest in his proper use of Erse. Finally, Johnson's assertion that "Scotchmen loved Scotland better than the truth is peevish and false" (6-46). The heat here indicates that for some Scottish critics a great deal more was at stake than literary merit.

Gradually, as the heat subsided somewhat, light was shed on what was at stake. In 1776, Miss Brace published some verses on the *Journey*: the tone can be made clear from a few couplets. "Paoli the second, to make people stare / Thro' Scotland once led a huge English bear; / And to laugh at his countrymen formed a plan / To make them caress this strange *beast* as a *man*" (272). In the same year Ewen Cameron finds Johnson's skepticism about the authenticity of Ossian as "groundless as it is invidious" and then goes on to assert that he has "established the authenticity of Ossian." Cameron surmises that Johnson's skepticism is bred of "contempt of our best men" and of "illiberal Manners and surly Disposition" (57-87). Johnson's physical size and ungainliness are emphasized in an attempt to explain why he is so indelicate with Ossian, who is seen as representative of Scottish art. In 1779 Donald McNicol defends Ossian in these same terms and attacks the *Journey* in a lengthy work that Boswell refers to as "a scurrilous volume, larger than Johnson's own, filled with malignant abuse" (2, 308). The last two sentences of this work characterize the nature of the attack: "Every line is marked with prejudice; and every sentence teems with the most illiberal invectives. If he has met with some correction, in the course of this examination, it is no more than he ought to have expected; unless he feels in his own mind, what his pride perhaps will not allow him to acknowledge, that misrepresentation and abuse merit no passion superior to contempt" (371). But by 1781 William Shaw is able to declare that "the defenders of that cause [Ossian] have not hitherto been able to produce an original, though some disingenuous attempts have been used ... [and] nothing but the original can persuade" (86). Nevertheless, in 1789 the *Journey* was again attacked. A. G. Sinclair declares that Johnson's "contemptible ideas" stem from the "motives of a bad heart," and that "the silly Doctor was either blind or very near-sighted" to have missed the "well-grown" woods of Scotland (88). The Scottish defensiveness about Ossian and the lack of trees are connected: Johnson makes clear in the *Journey* that trees are to be planted for posterity and that they, like genuine ancient Scottish literature, are aspects of the past that bear upon the present. Many Scottish reviewers felt that their culture was under attack. Although couched in terms of Ossian and trees, the real issue was whether this Englishman did justice to the native culture of what was then a remote part of Great Britain. Interestingly, Johnson did not respond directly to these critics, but he did face this issue at the end of the *Journey*

Hawkins is one of the first to recognize that this political issue was obscuring others equally important. Admitting that Johnson has not overcome his prejudice against Scotland, Hawkins explains:

his manner of describing them [the Hebrides] and the inhabitants, as also, his reception, is entertaining; but it is not enough particular to render it intelligible to a stranger. ... If any particular subject may be said to have engaged his attention, it must have been the manners of a people of whom he knew little but by report. ... That in this employment he has conducted himself with that impartiality which becomes a lover of truth, the natives of the kingdom deny; and, that he carried out of this country the temper of a man who hoped for an hospitable reception among strangers, few are so hardy as to assert. Accordingly, we find in his narrative an intermixture, not only of praise and blame, but of gratitude and invec-

tive. ... The volume which this tour gave birth to may properly be called a dissertation, for it has scarcely any facts, and
consists chiefly in propositions which he hunts down, and en-
livens with amusing disquisition. ... Yet the merit of this tract
is great; for, though I will admit that no one going his route
could derive from him direction or intelligence; though no
remembrance could be refreshed, nor remarks corroborated;
because his web was spun, not from objects that presented
themselves to his view, but from his own pre-existent ideas; I
am convinced that everybody must have regretted the omis-
sion, had he, for any reason, withheld so entertaining a series
of reflections. ... Had Johnson been more explicit in his acknowledgments of the hospitable and courteous treatment he
experienced from a people, who had reason to look on him
rather as a spy than a traveler ... he would have given a proof,
that he had, in some degree, overcome his prejudices against
them. ... Johnson's prejudices were too strong to permit him
to extend his philanthropy much beyond the limits of his native country, and the pale of his own church.

Hawkins concludes with an account of the correspondence between
Johnson and Ossian that leads the Englishman to provide "himself
with a weapon, both of the defensive and offensive kind, ... an oak
plant of a tremendous size" (214-17). Hawkins suggests that the
Journey should be appreciated as a moral, not a historical work: an
old-fashioned schoolmaster, Johnson wields a big stick that is often
used unfairly but from the best moral principles.

Boswell, often quick to defend his native land, is more charitable:

His "Journey to the Western Islands of Scotland" is a most
valuable performance. It abounds in extensive philosophical
views of society, and in ingenious sentiments and lively description. A considerable part of it, indeed, consists of specula-
tions, which many years before he saw the wild regions which
we visited together, probably had employed his attention,
though the actual sight of those scenes undoubtedly quick-
ened and augmented them. ... That he was to some degree of
excess a true-born Englishman, so as to have ever entertained
an undue prejudice against both the country and the people of
Scotland, must be allowed. But it was a prejudice of the head,
and not of the heart. He had no ill will to the Scotch; for, if he
had been conscious of that, he would never have thrown
himself into the bosom of their country, and trusted to the
protection of its remote inhabitants with a fearless confidence.
His remark upon the nakedness of the country, from its being
denuded of trees, was made after having traveled two hun-

dred miles along the eastern coast, where certainly trees are not to be found near the road. ... His disbelief of the authenticity of the poems ascribed to Ossian ... was confirmed in the course of his *Journey*. ... Johnson's grateful acknowledgments of kindnesses received in the course of this tour, completely refute the brutal reflections which have been thrown out against him, as if he had made an ungrateful return. (II, 300-303)

Boswell believes that Johnson's prejudice is superficial and that he gradually overcame it so that the *Journey* is significant as history. This difference between Boswell and Hawkins, the historical versus the moral reading of the *Journey*, will reemerge in the twentieth century when the question of the development of the narrator becomes an issue.

For nearly a century (from 1791 to 1890) only one entry in the standard bibliography—and that one is a brief note in 1870—was listed. The *Journey* was rescued from neglect by G. B. Hill, who in 1890 retraces *The Footsteps of Dr. Johnson*. As in so many other areas of Johnson scholarship, Hill begins serious study of the *Journey*. Combining the three accounts of the trip to Scotland Johnson's *Journey* Boswell's *Tour* and Johnson's letters to Mr. Thrale, Hill attempts to place before the reader the "Scotland which Johnson saw" because "of all history ... Johnson held [nothing] equal to the history of manners." Hill goes on in his introduction to point out that not all Scots were hostile to the *Journey*, but that his position on Ossian raised many hackles because Ossian was the pride of Scotland, ranked by Blair with Homer, and defended by McNicol even as a fraud. But, according to Hill, Johnson caused most irritation by his remarks on the lack of trees on the east coast of Scotland. Hill believes that part of the problem was bad weather, only three clear days during his two months in the Highlands (viii-30). Johnson's attitude toward Scotland had yet to be treated as a deliberate posture even though he regularly baits Boswell, as reported in the *Life*, in precisely the terms mentioned by Hill.

In 1899 George Whale assesses Johnson's notions about travel in general. Although Johnson condemns the "grand tour," he, according to Whale, is "no enemy to travel." On the contrary, he advises travel to widen one's experience and prefers a "man of the world to a scholar." His attitude toward the publication of an account of a journey is that it must contain "something by which [the] country may be benefited." Hence, his refusal to publish the diary of his trip to France, and for this same reason the journal of the Welsh tour, only comes to the public notice by way of Johnson's servant, Francis Barber. Still, having read many travel books, especially as a young man in his father's book shop, he is himself not suited to travel: he is physically incapable of being a good walker and suffers from an "insensibility to natural, or rather rural beauty" (259-70). Readers of the *Journey* will recall that Johnson often is less concerned about physical discomforts than Boswell and that the decision to write the *Journey* is described as occurring in a natural scene of rural beauty that is presented in some detail. But the nineteenth-century image of Johnson prevails over the facts of the narrative.

In 1921 Arthur McDowall compares Johnson's *Journey* to Dorothy Wordsworth's account of her travels. Unlike Dorothy Wordsworth, who regularly goes off alone to record "each detail sharply" of nature, Boswell and Johnson remain together, observing humanity not nature. While Dorothy Wordsworth loves the moor and its various sources of water, Johnson, we are informed, prefers "rationalism." Johnson describes a woman as he would a matchbook; Dorothy Wordsworth writes a lyric about her. McDowell concludes that Johnson's book "lives" in the quality of its prose, an "unadorned" prose that is appropriate to the austere scenery (271-78). In the same year Edward S. Roscoe compares Johnson's *Journey* to William Wordsworth's 1803 tour of the Highlands. Johnson wants to see a "strange social order"; Wordsworth, not curious for "positive knowledge," looks for "contentment upon wild shores." The scenery, Roscoe asserts, is "repulsive to Johnson." While Wordsworth is constantly "touching emotional chords," Johnson feels no "pathos," nothing below the surface. This distinction between the "intelligent" and the "reflective" is explained by the historical epoch: in Johnson's age appreciation of nature "scarcely existed" (690-95). The romantics not only supplied the touchstone for judgment but also the methodology of evaluation. The Wordsworths' accounts of their journeys serve as examples of how to travel and how to write about it, what to notice on the trip and what to communicate to the reader. Johnson's *Journey* is unlikely to be appreciated until it is recognized to be of a different kind than the romantic journal.

But in 1924 Catherine Maclean begins to consider the specifics of Johnson's text. She points out that Johnson's account is an attempt to prevent the destruction of the "old way of life" in the Highlands, a recognition that shows a "truly statesman-like consciousness." In his "deep sympathy" for the poor and for the old ways, Johnson is said to move "beyond the realm of prejudice." Maclean also notes that Johnson's "power of description ... sense of sublime in nature ... emotional note ... [are] rare in the literature of that century" (686-90). And by 1929 J. Lovat-Fraser, after remarking that Johnson's "utterance on Iona is so well known as not to need quoting," points out that Johnson is right that the death of Col, the leader of the island of the same name, doomed the island, since the population has dwindled from 1200 in Johnson's day to 400 (484-85). In 1939 James Ferguson notes that in 1775 William Nairne followed Johnson's advice and enjoyed the resulting prosperity (115). The distinctive qualities, both literary or generic and historical, were beginning to be noted. The *Journey* has a clear strategy with regard to Highland culture, and Johnson's presence was already having some effect upon the people of the land. But as isolated observations without a method that enabled them to become part of a new interpretation they pass over the land unseen and unheard, like, in the words of Eliot, "wind in dry grass."

In 1960 Jeffrey Hart is the first to argue that although the *Journey* has personal and cultural significance, it is a work of art or what he calls "history as art." Hart locates three major "themes" in the text: "the destruction of Pre-Reformation Christian culture," "the destruction of Highland culture," and "the rise of middle-class, progressive culture." Treating these themes simultaneously, Hart believes, Johnson superimposes "the present upon the past," generating ironic analogies, like that between the "'enlightened' commercial classes" and the "'Goths' who destroyed Rome." The result is, Hart maintains, a sort of prose tragedy: like Gibbon, Johnson "sought tragedy in history. Cultures, they saw, did sometimes die violently" (44-58). Donald Greene replies to Hart by questioning the centrality of these themes. First, Greene explains that he sees little irony or disapproval in Johnson's account of the commercial advances of modern Scotland, then he goes on to show that Johnson is not completely opposed to the Christian Reformation, and finally he asserts that the *Journey* is not wholly nostalgic about Highland culture (476-80). In 1963 R. K. Kaul enters the fray, explaining that he agrees with Greene that "commercial society" is not treated ironically by Johnson, but asserts that the position needs to be expanded to the notion of civilization. Kaul maintains that although Johnson understands the limitations of and the price paid for modern civilization, he prefers it on the whole to the more primitive past: "Johnson was fully aware of the imperfections of contemporary civilization. ... Sooner than exchange Fleet Street for the South Sea Islands or the Hebrides, he chose to put up with the imperfections" (341-50). At this point, Hart's tragic form is not questioned: the opposition suggests that his structure can accommodate a more refined formulation of Johnson's perceptions of Scottish history.

In the same year Michael Lasser emphasizes that the *Journey* gives indication that the Western Islands modify some of Johnson's presuppositions. Lasser begins by demonstrating that Johnson's anti-Scottish propensities have been exaggerated and that Johnson often adopts the expected negative view for humorous purposes. Nevertheless, some of Johnson's ideas are changed by his *Journey*. "Even though he dislikes the wilderness, he finds himself being drawn toward it," and what Boswell calls "romantick fancy" has "at least partially grasped Johnson." Lasser concludes that "these new forces [in the Highlands] affected ... the last of the great Renaissance men" (227-33). Lasser's discovery of the alteration in the narrator was sustained by later critics, but it was neglected until included within a coherent new reading of the *Journey*.

In 1964 J. D. Fleeman located in the Hyde collection two copies of the *Journey* issued before the cancels were published, providing proof for Allen Hazen's theory of the cancels in the first edition of the *Journey*. And, a year later, Lyle Kendall, Jr. provides evidence of why some copies of the *Journey* contain uncanceled pages (317-18). In the same year Mary Lascelles seeks to explain why Johnson did not make the many factual changes to the manuscript of the *Journey* that Boswell suggested to him. Reviewing the list of factual errors pointed out by Boswell and recorded by R. W. Chapman, Lascelles cites Johnson's retort, "'I deal, perhaps, more in notions than facts,'" and suggests that Johnson "assumed ... [that] he and Boswell were of one mind." Lascelles infers that the *Journey*, like *Rasselas*, "is a singular compound of narrative and argument" and that any interference with "facts" destroys the integrity of the work (155-69). The difference in emphasis between Lasser and Lascelles is a manifestation of the postromantic distinction between history and literature. The possibility that a historical element, the effect of the Highlands upon Johnson, is also a literary aspect, the developing narrator, remained neglected by this methodology.

In 1966 Arthur Sherbo points out that previous commentators have neglected the significance of travel genre in the *Journey*. The travel book, according to Sherbo, has for Johnson four principal requirements: "1) veracity, 2) reflection on events, places, and people, 3) avoidance of barren enumeration of details, and 4) setting up a standard of comparison between the reader's state and that of the country described." Johnson for Sherbo is "putting down, in a fashion more memorable than that ... of other writers of travel literature, the thoughts and reflections that spring almost instinctively to one's mind in certain locales. To look upon this as characteristic of one man is to misread Johnson's *Journey* and to misunderstand travel literature of the eighteenth century." Sherbo concludes that "nothing ... both during the *Journey* or after, bespeaks an experience clouded by a tragic vision of fallen cultures and cultures in the process of collapse. All the real evidence points to Johnson's *Journey* as a book written in a traditional mode—that of the travel book—by a man who brought much learning, much knowledge and experience, and a great desire to learn with him" (382-96). Objecting to Hart's "tragic" structure, Sherbo broadens the range of the disagreement: now not merely a factor within the tragedy, history undermines the very concept of tragedy.

In 1967 Clarence Tracy also opposes the tragic reading. Tracy characterizes the *Journey* in similarly neutral terms, as a "study of the influence of environment on human life," in order to suggest that Johnson is not a "romantic Tory," "a great defender of ancient institutions." For Tracy, Johnson's account should be seen as a sensitive, empirical investigation: "Fully apparent throughout is his realization that the truth about such concepts as the simple life and state of nature can be arrived at not through reason itself looking inward but only through empirical investigation" (1593-1606). In the same year Ann Schalit compares Johnson's and Boswell's accounts of their travels and concludes that the former is an example of "literature as product" and the latter of "literature as process": "The *Journey* possesses form and balance, and the reader can sense Johnson firmly in control of, but relatively untouched by, his material. Boswell's Journal, in contrast ... [offers] a composite portrait of both Boswell and Johnson as they lived and reacted to shared experience and each other" (10-17). The problem then with Sherbo's and Tracy's rejection of tragedy is that it leaves a well structured *Journey* without a form.

In 1968 T. K. Meier defends Hart's position against Sherbo by arguing that although the *Journey* is a travel book, as Sherbo insists, it is also a work of art and that the "bleak view of Scotland" that predominates is attributable to Hart's tragic thematic conception. In the same year, in another essay, Meier agrees with Kaul's suggested modification of one of Hart's themes: "Kaul makes the point that the decay of Highland culture was due in large part precisely to 'the failure of the Scots to develop commerce and industry' ... because the inability of local industry to provide jobs to the Highlanders forced them to emigrate, thus weakening their culture" (350). Meier implies that Hart's tragic structure can accommodate the more sophisticated historical information supplied by scholars.

In 1969 Francis Hart presents a new focal point for the position of Jeffrey Hart, while keeping in mind the misgivings of Sherbo and Greene and the defense by Meier. For Francis Hart "recent gladiators overlook what was the central Enlightenment problem of the book's genesis and situation: the intellectual or 'philosophic' activity of travel itself. ... The center of interest is the traveler." In particular, "the philosophic traveler is characteristically preoccupied with modes of apprehension, with the imaginative limits of descriptive language and the sources of error." For Johnson, according to Francis Hart, this concern with "the art of attention" is to be found throughout his writings, since it constitutes "the art of learning itself." Hence, Francis Hart argues, "the philosophic traveler [in the *Journey*] is displayed repeatedly in the self-conscious process of perfecting his ideas," and "Johnson's lifelong concern with the acts of perception and the fixing of 'distinct ideas' is typical of him and central to the meaning and motive of the *Journey to the Western Islands of*

Scotland" (679-95). By implication, Francis Hart is suggesting that both the formal and historical gladiators have lost sight of Johnson the philosophical traveler whose development needs to be contained in a historical or literary form. We recall that Lasser earlier noted Johnson's development but was unable at that time to relate it to formal considerations.

In the same year Thomas Jemielty calls attention to the fact that in the critical effort to treat the *Journey* as social history and anthropology, we neglect the "philosophical, moral and reflective" aspects of the narrative. Reminding us that Johnson does not merely give us an account of his *Journey* but also takes a position on the major issues concerning Scotland—Ossian, the second sight, emigration, the laws against the wearing of tartan—Jemielty argues: "if philosophical as traditionally defined denotes a study of causes and effects, and a generality of presentation, a particular method of argument, a willingness to hypothesize, and, as moral philosophy, a concern with what should be done and what should be avoided, then [Johnson] ... 'wrote as a philosopher'" (319-29). Isolating philosophical development, Jemielty reinforces Francis Hart's belief that the debate neglects Johnson as traveler.

In 1970 Richard Schwartz enters the critical controversy, announcing that he sides with Greene and Sherbo. Schwartz attempts to demonstrate that the *Journey* is a good place to begin to question the "images of Johnson inherited from Boswell and Macaulay—the sentimental portrait and the caricature." The *Journey* "is especially helpful in pointing up the dynamic nature of Johnson's thought, and reveals a Johnson quite different from the counterfeit images of popular tradition." Schwartz proceeds through the *Journey* to demonstrate how it reveals "overlooked facets of Johnson's intellectual temper. ... The empirical temperament, cautious with regard to received opinion, founding its knowledge on experience, and rising to synthesis or generalization only when possible, and then with qualification; the dynamic struggle for knowledge with full awareness of the difficulty of the search; the humility and consciousness of limitations" (292-303). Schwartz, while siding with Greene and Sherbo, is actually producing evidence in favor of the modification suggested by Francis Hart and Jemielty, that Johnson as traveler needs more scrutiny.

In the 1971 edition of the *Journey*, Mary Lascelles emphasizes that Johnson was impressed with the destructive impulses of "Knox's reformation" and feared that the process was continuing to manifest itself in the emigration problem. Johnson, she remarks, "had a shrewd eye for the perplexities of a community passing rapidly from a natural to a money economy." At the same time, Lascelles grants that this subject was interrupted by the trip and the thoughts it occasioned in Johnson's mind: "passages of reflective analysis appear as pauses in a process of discovery, occasions for taking stock of facts which we have been allowed to watch him gathering, opportunities for entertaining and assessing newly acquired ideas" (xx-xxvii). The process of travel and the product, the conclusions about Scotland, are now given equal weight, but we are left without an explanation of how these two elements are connected.

In 1972 Ralph Jenkins compares Johnson's *Journey* to Thomas Pennant's *Tour of Scotland and Voyage to the Hebrides* (1772). Jenkins admits that "Pennant was neither an artist nor a philosopher, and his books cannot compare to the *Journey* in style or depth of thought; but his descriptions of the topography, zoology, industry, husbandry, architecture, and antiquities of Scotland far surpass Johnson's in scope and accuracy." Jenkins advises that "if we should argue, as some recent critics have done, that the *Journey* is best read not as a travel book but as a work of art, we must still consider that its proportions and details were often dictated not by Johnson's desire to create 'an impression of Scotland,' but by his desire to avoid direct comparison with a man whom he admired as a writer and respected as rival" (445-62). In the same year Thomas Preston points out that although at one level the *Journey* "offers a straightforward sociological analysis of the Highlands ... at the same time this analysis evaluates what it describes, indirectly exhorting the Highlands to emerge from the 'barbarous' state to a level of culture that unites them with the community of 'civilized' nations." Preston suggests that by way of implicit cultural parallels, Johnson relates "the feudal Highlands to the heroic age of ancient Greece," assuming that the reader of his day would recognize that "Greece's cultural development [serves] as an archetypal pattern for all 'barbarous' nations—a pattern which the 'civilized' nations of Europe prided themselves on having already completed." Johnson, according to Preston, implies a similar development for the Highlands. "The cultural parallels Johnson draws between the feudal Highlands and the heroic age of Greece ultimately imply that the Highlands, like the 'civilized' nations of the day, can repeat the history of Grecian culture if they also undergo cultural development." In conclusion, Preston further generalizes the challenge: "It is a challenge directed to all 'barbarous' ... nations. Like Homer, Johnson is addressing himself to a specific people, but he is also addressing man in general" (445-62). In the early 1970s it became clear that Johnson intermingles historical and literary procedures that prevent identification of the *Journey* with either exclusively. But while the tragic form of the 1960s no longer seemed adequate, a viable alternative had yet to appear.

In 1974 Thomas Curley published an essay on the relationship between *Rasselas* and the *Journey* that was to form the basis for a chapter of his book, the first full-length study of Johnson's travel writings, *Samuel Johnson and the Age of Travel* (1976), a study which, in

the words of one reviewer, "effectively document[s] the popular appeal of travel and travel books as well as Johnson's own involve-
ment around the fringes with reviews, introductions, and pam-
phlets." "*Rasselas*," Curley explains, "was a splendid prelude to
Johnson's later career of restless travel and distinctly foreshadowed
the thematic concerns of his *Journey to the Western Islands of Scotland* (1775). ... The elegant travel book that resulted had combined
the moral artistry displayed in *Rasselas* and the conventions of
travel literature found in previous accounts of Scotland." The problem, Curley believes, that Johnson confronts in the *Journey* concerns
the emergence of the ancient culture in the modern world: "The old
religious, social and ethical values represented by the native life-
style strongly appealed to Johnson's conservative temperament.
Somehow the dilemma had to be reconciled by an economic program that would safeguard the Highland heritage while advancing
national prosperity." Curley reasons that "the travel book chronicles
one of the happiest experiences in Johnson's career when the process
of moral discovery in *Rasselas* became an actual experiment in eighteenth-century travel" (183-218). For Curley, *Rasselas* provides the
formal model for the *Journey*, but the question then arises as to the
difference between the fictional and factual journey.

In 1976 Curt Hartog presents a view of the *Journey* as a "Johnsonian psychomachia," involving an interaction between Johnson
and the Highlands. "Essentially, the narrative divides into three
parts: an initial response, usually couched in melancholy imagery
but occasionally illuminated by the light of hospitality and by distancing reflections; a long "essay" (Ostig on Skye) in which initial
impressions are analyzed, synthesized, ordered, and finally mastered
through the power of reason; a concluding section, in which perceptions and reflections are softened, revealing sympathy, even a
guarded optimism toward the island and mountain culture." Hartog
explains that the purpose of this psychological approach is "to try to
understand why the Highlands affected Johnson so strongly. ... Sympathy is created not only by the formal arrangement of the narrative,
but by intuitive recognition of a shared battle, an intuition enhanced
by Johnson's refighting it and winning it—again—in the process of
writing the *Journey* " (3-16). Psychological development provides a
further distinction between fictional and factual travel, since few
maintain that the characters in *Rasselas* have this degree of sophisti-
cation.

In 1977 George Savage sees Johnson's *Journey* as an odyssey.
"Johnson's descriptions of the condition of Scotland, though in
themselves significant, are, through his artistry, pressed beyond the
bounds of that country until Scotland becomes a metaphor for the
condition of isolated humanity everywhere." Typical of the *Journey*,
according to Savage, is Johnson obscuring "objective measurement

of distance and duration, drawing the reader into the subjectivity of this latter-day odyssey." Finally, Savage suggests, "where Odysseus finally attains Ithaca, our odyssey, Johnson implies, must be unending. One's whole life must be devoted to the effort of, as he writes of some Highlanders, 'hastening to mingle with the general community'" (493-501). We are thus reminded of the formal and literary qualities of the *Journey* but are left to wonder how such a structure can accommodate the historical dimension, particularly, as John Radner shows, that Johnson's odyssey and the effects of that trip upon him involve such historical issues as emigration and the planting of trees (144).

In 1980 Catherine Parke develops a position that forms part of her book, *Samuel Johnson and Biographical Thinking* (1991). In the latest version, Parke clarifies her position: the title of the chapter, "The Biography of a Nation," suggests how Johnson for Parke combines biography and history. "He [Johnson] would reduce neither thought nor action to the mere result of a finite and predictable series of previous events. The *Journey* gives evidence of how whatever a traveler takes with him may condition but need not limit or even necessarily predict what he will find, because no simple model of cause and effect is adequate to explain this drama. The *Journey* also gives evidence of how, more generally considered, thinking itself is in equal parts both ordinary and wonderful. The model for this paradoxical account of learning is his *Journey* into unknown territory" (129). Parke employs the notion of the biography of a nation to accommodate the formal and historical elements of the *Journey*, concluding with a balance between the personal and the national. Within the context of Parke's book, however, the significance of this procedure for Johnson is much clearer than it is in relation to the *Journey*.

In 1989 Edward Tomarken devotes a chapter of his book *Johnson, 'Rasselas,' and the Choice of Criticism* to the *Journey*. Tomarken attempts to demonstrate that the method of literary perspectivism, first realized in *Rasselas*, is applied for historical ends in the *Journey*. Beginning with the generic question, Tomarken claims that the *Journey* has been misunderstood for so long because it combines "autobiography and travel tale, journal and tour." Then Tomarken turns to Johnson's decision to write the *Journey*. "In placing the decision to write the *Journey* in the text, Johnson inscribes one literary process in another, [initiating] the attempt not to enclose the literary process but to open it to history." This gesture toward history is explained as follows: "In the end, *A Journey to the Western Islands of Scotland* goes beyond the bounds of historical discourse, whether biography and autobiography or journal, and literary discourse, whether travel tale or novel. Johnson inscribes both kinds of discourse, presentation of self and aesthetically structured travel tale, within history. In its conclusion, the *Journey* presents itself as a historical act, the implantation of a literary tree, that will, like the seedling, be subject to the natural and human forces of future events" (150-64). By this means, Tomarken attempts to combine historical and formal elements within a conception that also does justice to Johnson as philosophical traveler, particularly, at the end of the *Journey* when Johnson is seen as using his travel persona to offer his historical-formal structure to posterity. The result, Tomarken claims, is a new methodology, one that is an alternative to the postromantic dichotomy between history and literature. Johnson in the *Journey*, according to Tomarken, uses a literary device to enter history.

In Eithne Henson's *"The Fictions of Romantick Chivalry:" Samuel Johnson and Romance.* (1992), the concluding chapter, "The Spiritual Quixote," is devoted to the *Journey*. She sees the *Journey* as a combination of literary and historical elements: "The Scottish journey, in which Johnson combined the roles of impartial philosophical observer and quixotic adventurer, triumphantly vindicated a lifetime of romance reading. The claims of his medievalist friends were justified; the 'manners' of romance, in the widest historical sense, were verified; Johnson's understanding was 'enlarged,' while his imagination was 'impregnated' with uniquely satisfying material" (224). We see here the elements that have been accumulating in this survey: a formal structure that is flexible enough to account for the narrator's development, historical elements that are factual and imaginative or romantic. This balance constitutes an important achievement for criticism of the *Journey* and has taken over two centuries to emerge. But it is not clear what purpose is served by this equilibrium. It seems to me that the future of *Journey* criticism will have to consider why Johnson chose to juxtapose literary and historical conventions. The resolution of this issue will require a methodology that explains how literature moves into history, a procedure that involves not merely crossing the boundaries between the disciplines of literary criticism and history, but also the experience of literature as a historical event.

8: The *Lives of the Poets*

THE *LIVES OF THE POETS* CAUSES the most problems to critics, yet it is generally regarded as Johnson's greatest critical work. The key to the difficulty lies in the original title, *Prefaces. Biographical and Critical, to the Works of the English Poets.* During the nineteenth century it became customary to refer to the work as the *Lives of the Poets*, the title that is still used and found in the best scholarly edition, George Birckbeck Hill's rendition, first published in 1905. The abbreviated title clearly favors the biographical aspect, a consequence of the nineteenth-century belief that Johnson has a better understanding of the authors than of their writings. Yet a cursory look at any one of the *Lives* reveals that the writers' lives and works are always related. Why is this relationship neglected? It might at first glance appear that focusing on the life sections avoids Johnson's controversial pronouncements against the writings of Milton, Swift, or Gray. But, in fact, the biographical section is equally negative. The problem is more complex. Johnson's critical remarks stand in no obvious or ordinary relation to his biographical comments. In this respect, the life of Pope is exemplary. Johnson accuses Pope of unjustly attacking and satirizing many of his friends, yet he commends his poetry as great social satire. Similarly, Gray is scorned as a habitué of the ivory tower, but his "Elegy," a learned poem about unlearned people, is praised. Milton is described as a tyrannical father, but *Paradise Lost*, dictated by Milton to his daughters, is recognized as a great epic. These views only present a problem for those who know that Johnson does not separate art from the artist. Of course, Johnson recognizes that great art stands on its own, apart from the artist, particularly if it is to pass the test of posterity. But the title, *Prefaces, Biographical and Critical*, suggests a relationship between the two that has yet to be understood. The difficulty results, I believe, from neglect of the ethical obligations of the writer. Modern critics are content to let historians decide whether or not a writer lives up to his or her principles. Critics restrict themselves to elucidating literature. But Johnson believed that the relationship between the writer's conduct and his writings is just as important as the writings in themselves. This ethical judgment is a problem for us because we lack a method for deciding how the literary applies to the extraliterary, how writing relates to conduct.

In fact, the _Lives_ began with an ethical problem. In 1777, Edward Dilly wrote to James Boswell explaining the origin of the _Lives of the Poets_. An edition of English poetry that had recently appeared in Edinburgh was considered "an invasion of our [English] Literary Property, [thereby] inducing the London Booksellers to print an elegant and accurate edition of all the English poets of reputation from Chaucer to the present time." Three of the "most respectable" booksellers decided to approach Samuel Johnson, who agreed to take on the project for a mere 200 guineas. Edmund Malone remarked, in 1804, that Johnson could easily have asked 1,000 or 1,500 guineas since the booksellers "probably got five thousand guineas by this work in the course of twenty-five years" (CH, 250-51). In 1779 Johnson characterized the project as follows: "My purpose was only to have allotted to every Poet an Advertisement, like those which we find in the French Miscellanies, containing a few dates and general character; but I have been led beyond my intention, I hope, by the honest desire of giving useful pleasure" (CH, 252).

Later in 1779 four volumes appeared, followed two years later by the remaining six. Starting in 1779 and continuing in 1781, Edmund Cartwright was one of the first of the reviewers. Referring to this last phrase of Johnson's Advertisement, Cartwright remarks that he has assumed from it that Johnson's name had been used as a "lure" but is delightfully surprised to find that "this honest desire is very amply gratified. ... Dr. Johnson has long been without a rival. ... The present work is no way inferior to the best of his very celebrated productions of the same class." Cartwright summarizes the lives of Cowley and Waller with general approval, but has misgivings about the life of Milton. "The active part which Milton took in the public transactions of the time he lived in, will ever subject him to the misrepresentations of partiality or prejudice. In the biographical part of the preface before us, we have observed some passages not totally free from the influence of one of these principles." Johnson has recorded his "merriment" at Milton's hurrying home from abroad upon hearing of the "differences between the King and parliament" only to end up tutoring schoolboys. Cartwright finds little here to excite merriment in Milton's _"vapouring away his patriotism in a private boarding-school."_ Indeed, Cartwright points out that "through the whole of his narrative Dr. Johnson seems to have no great partiality for Milton as a man: as a poet, however, he is willing to allow him every merit he is entitled to." And although Johnson's "censures " on "Lycidas" "are severe," yet Cartwright believes they are "well-enforced." Of Johnson's commentary on _Paradise Lost_, Cartwright describes it as "executed with all the skill and penetration of Aristotle, and animated and embellished with all the fire of Longinus." Johnson's view of Gray is seen as "not only hostile, but malignant." Finally, in his general assessment, Cartwright emphasizes that although the *Lives* are full of "profound and original criticism" they must be approached with caution since Johnson's taste is "singular"—particularly in preferring Blackmore to Collins and Gray—and because he quickly passes over "beauties" while dwelling upon defects (CH, 253-70). Cartright discriminates between the lives of Milton and Gray. Johnson is seen as blind to the poetry of Gray; his disapproval of Milton's behavior does not, however, prevent him from appreciating *Paradise Lost*.

During this same period, an anonymous reviewer in the *Critical Review* explains the national function of the *Lives*: "As the general character of every polished nation depends in a great measure on its poetical productions, too much care cannot be taken, in works of this nature, to impress on foreigners a proper idea of their merit." Johnson has the unenviable task of making tedious and already known material—literary biography—interesting, and he has succeeded surprisingly well. Although Johnson is, according to the reviewer, known for his "pompous phraseology," "very little of this kind appears in the work before us." And while most such works suffer from being "nothing but panegyrics," Johnson errs, if at all, in the other direction. Even Johnson's severe treatment of Gray's odes is applauded because Johnson separates Gray from the ranks of Dryden and Pope and places him with "minor bards" (CH, 270-72). We note here the national nature of this project, an important factor in understanding the institutionalization of the *Lives* that took place in the next century. Also, it was seen early on that Johnson's style at this late stage in his career is plainer than in his earlier work and that he deliberately opposes the fashion of panegyric.

William Cowper's comments, during this same period, provide a contrast to those of the anonymous reviewer for the *Critical Review*. Cowper is not surprised at Johnson's treatment of Milton the man, since "a pensioner is not likely to spare a republican." Johnson's view of "Lycidas" is accepted to some extent, but the condemnation of "the childish prattlement of pastoral compositions" neglects "the sweetness of the numbers, the classical spirit of antiquity." In similar terms, Johnson is accused of having "no ear for poetical numbers" and therefore of missing the "music" of *Paradise Lost*. In 1782 Cowper records Johnson's insensitivity to Prior's love lyrics, remarking that most readers are enchanted by the "romantic turn" of what Johnson finds tedious. Cowper believes that "King Critic" feels obliged to justify his position as a critic by contradicting the generally held opinion. In 1784 Cowper gives the following general assessment of the *Lives*: "His uncommon share of good sense, and his forcible expression, secure to him that tribute from all his readers.

He has a penetrating insight into character, and a happy talent of correcting the popular opinion, upon all occasions where it is erroneous; and this he does with the boldness of a man who will think for himself" (CH, 273-76). It might appear that Cowper is inconsistent. But we need to remember that Cowper shared with Johnson an understanding of the distinction between the ethical and the critical: for Cowper, Johnson's moral point about the conduct of the poet may stand even if his view of the poetry is questionable.

Similarly, Francis Blackburne, siding with Milton's politics, has no quarrel with Johnson's view of the poetry. "Milton, in contending for those against the tyrant of the day and his abettors, was serious, energetic, and irrefragable. ... In the Doctor's system of government public liberty is the *free grace* of an hereditary monarch, and limited in kind and degree, by his gracious will and pleasure." In defense of Johnson's accusation that Milton is tyrannical with his daughters, Blackburne asserts that Milton "seems to have been of St. Paul's opinion"(CH, 278-83). In the same year, however, William Fitzthomas defends Gray in different terms. Beginning by admitting that Johnson's "excellent" prefaces are in general written with "the doctor's usual precision, vigour and clearness of style," Fitzthomas singles out the "Life of Gray" as "unfair." After commenting on the details of Johnson's analysis of the "Sister Odes," Fitzthomas summarizes: "the doctor's critical process with Gray differs considerably from that which he makes use of towards every other writer. He is with Gray more verbal, logical and minute. ... He is less observant of the versification and imagery." Finally Fitzthomas finds it difficult to believe that "considering the well-known taste and discernment of Dr. Johnson, he should really be so callous to that beautiful simplicity which runs through many of Gray's productions." He therefore speculates that Johnson was perhaps attempting to compensate for Gray's "unexampled reputation" and thus "over-acted his part" (CH, 284-92). In the eighteenth century critics expected to disagree with Johnson's moral and historical judgments, but they did not expect his position in any one of these areas to prejudice his critical judgment.

In 1782 after the second six volumes appeared, the *Annual Register* summarizes, "Perhaps no age or country has ever produced a species of criticism more perfect in its kind, or better calculated for general instruction, than the publication before us: for whether we consider it in a literary, philosophical, or a moral view, we are at a loss whether to admire most the author's variety and copiousness of learning, the soundness of his judgment, or the purity and excellence of his character as a man." Nevertheless, the reviewer suggests that the harsh view of Gray exemplifies a common kind of failing: "in combating opinions we suppose to be erroneous, we are extremely subject to fall ourselves into the opposite extreme" (CH, 293-

94). The explanation suggested for Johnson's blindness is over-compensation for idolatry of Gray.

From 1781-1782 Robert Potter contributed essays to the *Gentleman's Magazine* on the *Lives*, which were in 1789 incorporated into a larger study, *The Art of Criticism as Exemplified in Dr. Johnson's Lives of the Most Eminent English Poets*. Cowley is, according to Potter, "on the whole, pourtrayed with ingenuity and penetration" (4), while Dryden is presented with the "candor" of "genteel and just eulogism" (66). Addison is treated justly, but Swift's *Gulliver's Travels* is "of more merit than is here allowed it" (129). Gray and Lyttleton have "venom diffused throughout." In general, Potter characterizes the *Lives* as marked by "classical erudition, strong sense and accurate observation" but with "dry humour." In spite of the "strabiliousness" of the style, the *Lives* are, according to Potter, "very valuable general criticism" (181-91). While Potter assumes Johnson could have done justice to *Gulliver's Travels*, Thomas Sheridan contradicts Johnson on a number of details and accuses Johnson of "folly, falsehood, and cowardice" (586). And in 1786 Gilbert Wakefield offers an "antidote to the severity of Dr. Johnson's strictures on Gray" because those "structures, without some antidote, under the sanction of his respectable character, might operate with malignant influence upon the public taste, and become ultimately injurious to the cause of polite literature" (iii). Even the attacks upon the *Lives* recognize the power of Johnson as an authority, and those who defend Milton, Swift, and Gray accept Johnson's moral position but expect it not to distort his critical judgment.

In 1787 John Hawkins notes that the *Lives* "contain the soundest principles of criticism, and the most judicious examen of the effusions of poetic genius, that any country, not excepting France, has to shew." Nevertheless, Hawkins maintains that Johnson is "totally devoid" of the "poetic faculty" necessary to a critic, a deficiency Hawkins attributes to Johnson's poor eyesight. This defect, Hawkins argues, accounts for Johnson's "frigid commendation" of the descriptive passages in the writings of Thomson, Dryden, and Prior. Moreover, Johnson's preference for rhyme leads him into error about Milton's blank verse. Johnson's censure of Lyttleton and Gray has, according to Hawkins, lost him many friends: his "injury done ... to the memory of Gray, is resented by the whole university of Cambridge." "The character of Swift," Hawkins continues, "he has stigmatized with the brand of pride and selfishness ... [but] few can be offended at Johnson' account of this man." Hawkins concludes, "Upon the whole, it is a finely written, and an entertaining book, and is likely to be coeval with the memory of the best of the writers whom it celebrates" (CH, 303-6). The 1788 reviewer for the *Gentleman's Magazine* has a similar opinion. Although Johnson shows the "perfect censoriousness of his feelings" throughout many of the

Lives, "the eighteenth century has reason to be proud" of this achievement (301-3). Even those like Hawkins who question Johnson's critical abilities applaud the *Lives* as a national and moral achievement.

Boswell, on the other hand, has a higher estimate of Johnson as a critic. He reprints a letter in which Johnson remarks, "I know not that I have written any thing more generally commended than the Lives of the Poets" (4, 146) and points out that Johnson is attacked by "some violent Whigs" for his views on Milton, "by some Cambridge men of depreciating Gray" and by friends of Lyttleton (4, 63-64). Boswell realizes that often the response to the *Lives* involves issues other than literary or critical ones. For instance, in her letters written between 1789 and 1797, Anna Seward remarks how "despicable" is Johnson's "contempt of Gray's noble odes," "the sweet, the matchless 'Lycidas,'" and his opinion that no one ever wished to reread *Paradise Lost*. These acerbic judgments Seward attributes to Johnson's own disappointed expectations for "poet fame," an accusation that may have more applicability to Seward herself, also known as the Swan of Lichfield (CH, 311-12). However opinions varied, throughout the eighteenth century, Johnson was treated as an authority and his views of the English poets were, for the most part, revered and respected even by those who disagreed with him violently. Johnson was seen as a profound and independently minded critic who as a moralist applied the highest ethical principles to the writers and their works. This moral aspect was seen in the nineteenth and twentieth centuries as exemplifying an outmoded didacticism. But if didacticism is moral absolutism that ignores context, the eighteenth-century response to Johnson's judgments makes clear that the nature of the moral tenet and its applicability are rigorously debated, indicating that Johnson's ethical criticism cannot be dismissed as solely didactic. During the next century, Johnson became institutionalized; the *Lives* was taken to be a compendium of established opinion. It became customary for the romantic and Victorian critic to establish his or her originality by opposing a critical position from the *Lives of the Poets*.

Johnson's views on Milton were attacked early in the century from many perspectives. In 1809 a reviewer for the *Monthly Repository* took issue with what he considered to be Johnson's assumption that Milton was not a Christian since he belonged to neither the Church of England nor of Rome and practiced no visible form of worship. But, the reviewer retorts, Johnson could not know what "happened in Milton's closet" (433). Nine years later Thomas Holt White disagreed with Johnson's criticism of Milton because it was based on a "precise and pedantic principle" (31). In 1833 Joseph Ivimey attacks the life of Milton as a "misrepresentation and perversion of facts, for the purposes of caricaturing and distorting the features of a public man ... in a foul blot on English biography" (349). In 1855 "Sir Nathaniel" disagrees with "Samuel Johnson but must preserve his judgments," for he "has understanding but Coleridge tells us poetry requires more." This reviewer recommends the life of Milton as a "good essay on hate" (19-27). The romantic view was now in the ascendancy. Its assumption that a writer's private life was private and possibly wholly different from his public persona was completely at odds with Johnson's ethical assumption that the writer is answerable for the relationship between the conduct of his life and the principles of his or her writing.

The reason for the attention to Milton is made clear by Henry Reed, who, in 1857, declares that the circulation of the *Lives* is "injurious to the cause of imaginative poetry." Where, Reed asks, are Chaucer, Spenser, Shakespeare, and Sydney: all, except for Milton, have been replaced by "second rate rhymesters." Indeed, the *Lives* are said to be full of "false canons of criticism" due to an "utter absence of imagination," yet they acquired an authority in their day that none dared question. In particular, Reed estimates that Johnson's praise of *Paradise Lost* has been "extorted out of him" because he lacks sympathy for the highest poetic genius, the same reason that "Gray and Collins get short shrift" (2, 16-24). Milton is seen as the only major lyric poet included in the *Lives,* and the favorable views of *Paradise Lost* are dismissed as aberrations.

In 1859 Thomas De Quincey continues the onslaught. Samuel Johnson is "the worst enemy that Milton and his great cause have ever been called on to confront." After taking Johnson up on some biographical details, De Quincey counters Johnson's view that *Paradise Lost* is "wearisome" by asserting that it is so only for the "ignorant" (104-15). In 1874 John Symonds attacks what he takes to be Johnson's position on blank verse, arguing that blank verse is a continuous tradition in English literature from the Middle Ages, while the heroic couplet is a "French aberration." Johnson's views show the ignorance of the "last century," since Milton learned to use blank verse from the dramatists and merely extended its use to the epic (221-32). These attacks are so negative that one wonders why the nineteenth-century critics continued to bother reading Johnson. Matthew Arnold supplied one answer to this question.

In 1878 Arnold edited a selection of six of the *Lives* for use as a school text. He explains in the introduction that Johnson's "blame of genuine poets like Milton and Gray, his overpraise of artificial poets like Pope, are to be taken as the utterances of a man who worked for an age of prose." Nonetheless, Arnold insists that Johnson is valuable even on poetry for students as a *"point de repère* or fixed center," a convenient starting point (xii-xxv). If the nineteenth-century lyric poet typically adopted the pose of alienation, then Johnson represents the source of that alienation. For the romantics and Victorians, Johnson of the *Lives* is the man they love to hate, the father of criticism who nonetheless stifles poetic creativity. It remains for us a century later to try to discover what draws the nineteenth century to Johnson while avoiding their contradictory evaluation.

The Victorian attacks are not restricted to the life of Milton. In 1896 C. E. Vaughan introduces the metaphysical poets by pointing out that Johnson's views are based upon principles derived from *The Dunciad* and other writings of the age that insist upon "narrow and perverted principles." Johnson, "the hanging judge," condemns Milton, Cowley, and Gray for breaking Augustan rules; Coleridge retrieves them. Vaughan concludes: "Is it a harsh judgment to say that no critic so narrow, so mechanical, so hostile to originality as Johnson has ever achieved the dictatorship of English letters?" (lv-lxiii). In 1906 Lytton Strachey attempts to explain the preoccupation with Johnson. "No one needs an excuse for reopening the *Lives of the Poets*," Strachey begins, "the book is too delightful. ... After Boswell, it is the book that brings us nearer than any other to the mind of Dr. Johnson." Moreover, the very fact that the *Lives* continued "to be read, admired and edited, is in itself a high proof of the eminence of Johnson's intellect." The continued interest in and respect for the *Lives* is remarkable because Johnson's "entire point of view is patently out of date"; in fact, the work represents a "dead tradition" that lacks "sympathy" for poetry. Johnson "judges poets as criminals against the crown" without concern for what they are trying to do. Once Augustan rules were replaced by romantic interest in understanding the poet—a form of sympathy that Strachey admits may have gone too far—"Johnson was out." Johnson, Strachey concludes, is "blind" to Milton, Donne, and Gray, as well as insensitive to "vegetable nature," the focal point of romanticism (67-73). In place of an explanation of the preoccupation with Johnson, Strachey gives us another example of the phenomenon in the form of his own fascination with Johnson. He asserts that romanticism has gone too far in its reaction against the father of criticism, to use the phrase Johnson applies to Dryden, but in the absence of an alternative method of approach can only repeat the old refrain with the addition of an ironic tone.

In 1905 George Birkbeck Hill's long awaited edition of the *Lives* appeared. This three-volume edition altered the course of our history and is still the most authoritative scholarly edition. Hill's *Lives* is a sort of Variorum Johnson in that the notes not only explain the historical and critical allusions but document other relevant sections of the Johnson and Boswell canon. Only someone like Hill who immersed himself in this material for most of his adult life could have produced such a compendium, and even Hill did not live to see his edition of the *Lives* in print. Hill's effect is nowhere more apparent than in the comments of the next two critics.

In a 1908 article J. Churton Collins asserts that the *Lives* "was the most popular of [Johnson's] writings in his own generation, and it has been the most popular of his writings ever since." Although its "permanency is secured," the *Lives* has serious defects: "like Aristotle [the *Lives*] is deficient in imagination, in fancy, in aesthetic sensibility and sympathy ... [Johnson's] taste [is] dictated by the classics so he could not appreciate "'lyrics' or Gray's Pindarics." But for Collins the most serious fault is that of the "temper and age," one marked by "prejudice," "arrogance," and "obstinate indifference" to the "plasticity" of the mind. Turning to the specific *Lives*, Collins has the least praise for Savage: its style is "Johnson's worst" and Savage has subsequently been shown to have been a "blackguard and a callous impostor." Cowley is used as an example of Johnson's best style and Waller as the "most finished," even though the position it contains on religious poetry is "splendid sophistry." Milton, Collins believes, is the most "careful" of the *Lives*, for although "polemical with too much weight on the negative," Johnson understands, even if he does not feel, the appeal of *Paradise Lost*. Both the biographical and critical sections of Dryden are "excellent," while Prior is "inadequate and unjust." The life of Thomson is a "pleasant surprise" and Addison "is almost without a flaw." Pope is the most "brilliant" of the *Lives*, while the worst are of Collins and Gray, the latter of whom is treated as an "effeminate coxcomb" (72-88). Collins is one of the first to recognize that Johnson's critical judgment does not always follow his "prejudice," particularly in the life of Milton. Collins need only have glanced at Hill's edition of the life of Milton to see that the section on Johnson's judgment of *Paradise Lost* demonstrates that Johnson is aware of contemporary positive evaluations of the epic and that his own remarks are related to his views in his other writings. In 1915 J. B. Williams attempts to disprove Johnson's assumption that Milton was responsible for the publication of the heathen prayer that Charles I was accused of using for Christian purposes (431-40). It is not coincidental that Hill in his edition of the life of Milton included an appendix devoted to this question. In the past it would have been possible to have accused Johnson of political prejudice against Milton; now after Hill, it is necessary to document such accusations.

From 1922-1925 Arthur Nethercot investigated the background to the term *metaphysical*. First Nethercot demonstrates that Johnson did not invent the term: it had been used in the seventeenth century by important writers, including Dryden, Davenant, and Chesterfield. Then, in a second and longer essay, Nethercot argues that Johnson is the first to use the term *metaphysical* to identify a tradition that since then has become "generally accepted" (103). The implication is that although Johnson did not originate the term he originated the conception of the metaphysicals, a discovery that should give pause to those assuming that Johnson's object was merely to discredit the metaphysicals. But the nineteenth-century belief that Johnson and his age were incapable of responding to poetry remains dominant. In 1928 Robert Bridges asserts that Johnson is unable to understand "Lycidas" because of "his unpoetic mind" and that if Johnson had become as a "little child he might have liked 'Lycidas' very well" (69). In 1929 H. W. Garrod announces that he knows of no critic "save Johnson [who] has ever been at pains to depreciate Cowley." On the metaphysicals, Johnson is "acute," but it is eighteenth-century dogma to believe that all poetry must be comprised of clear ideas. Rather, Garrod believes, we "must admit all kinds of poetry" (119).

By the 1930s it was no longer possible to dismiss the critical sections as the biased opinion of one unable to appreciate poetry. The question became how are the biographical and critical sections related, an issue that posed insurmountable problems for existent methodologies. In 1931 John Mark Longaker considers the *Lives* in a full-length study of *English Biography in the Eighteenth Century*. "No work of the century in the province of biography aroused so much interest among readers and critics, and it is safe to say that no series of biographical accounts has been so frequently consulted and so commonly used for quotations by students of literature." Longaker points out that as early as 1738 Johnson "recognized biography as a literary form worthy of his efforts." For Longaker the life of Savage is on a "higher plane" than the others because Johnson "understood" Savage; Johnson may have erred with regard to some facts but on Savage's character "he did not err." But in the other lives, unlike Boswell's *Life*, the major contribution is critical not biographical. The life of Cowley is cited as typical in this regard. Dryden is particularly fine since, although "disjointed," a view emerges of a "definite literary personality." By contrast, on Milton the man, Johnson "sunk to the depths of personal antipathy," but on his writings he "rose to supreme heights of impartial and inspired appreciation." The life of Pope is more evenhanded: Johnson is, according to Longaker, Pope's advocate but not blind to weaknesses in Pope's art and character. Thomson is considered the "most engaging" of the briefer lives because of its sane and sympathetic view of Thomson's weaknesses (314-94). Longaker is one of the first to discriminate among the lives on the basis of whether the critical or biographical sections are more important, but the method and principles that underlie this distinction remain obscure. Similarly, in 1940 James Osborn comments on Johnson's life of Dryden. Although Johnson was the first to make Dryden the subject of a biography instead of a chronicle, the real contribution is the critical section: "focusing attention on intellectual character, Johnson made one of the most inspired contributions to the development of English biography." Although historically the life of Dryden is innovative in describing

Dryden's "mental qualities," the critical portion provides "the foundation of nearly all interpretations of Dryden's genres" (23-38). The precise nature of the distinction between the biographical and the critical remains unclear here because it was still common at this stage of criticism to intermingle discussion of life and work.

In 1946 George Carver, in a full-length study of biography, includes Johnson. The early biographies are labeled "hack" writing with the exception of Savage, which is seen as preparation for the *Lives of the Poets*. Carver points out that for Johnson biography was a passion, almost a form of self-indulgence, but because of Johnson's inherent didacticism "morality must ever underwrite the art that defies oblivion." The *Lives* are viewed as the "climax" of Johnson's career: the booksellers chose Johnson because of his "philosophy of life writing," which Carver explains is set forth in *Rambler* 60 and *Idler* 84. Although the *Lives* "omit special consideration of John Donne and damn the whole group, including Cowley, with the pejorative 'metaphysical' in accordance with neoclassical tradition, berate Milton for his politics, misunderstand Gray ... they set the accepted neoclassical standard and [pioneered] in the genre of critical biography." Johnson's contribution, Carver explains, is inherent in the "comparative simplicity of the style" and the "vigor of [his] critical opinions." The exceptional *Lives* are Pope, Cowley, Addison, and Thomson, but the best is Savage. The latter most completely conforms to Johnson's own precepts for biography: it is morally useful, places us in "parallel circumstances" to that of the subject of the life, leads "'the thoughts into domestic privacies,' and 'displays details of daily life.'" Even though Johnson's facts about Savage are inaccurate, the narrative brings the tragic figure to life (123-36). It is difficult from this description to understand how Johnson's "vigorous critical opinions" prevail in the face of his inherent didacticism, particularly when the highest compliments are reserved for the life of Savage, one of the least important poets and for whom therefore the critical comments are least significant. Carver applauds Johnson for advancing the art of biography by being forceful in both a historical and critical sense but questions the nature of his historical evidence and of his critical judgments.

During this period it was common both to admire and disagree with Johnson, an indication that changes in approach were not keeping up with alterations in judgment. In 1949 Harold Williams assesses Johnson's life of Swift. Questionable and tasteless accusations against Swift are the result, Williams speculates, of Johnson's being "out of sympathy with Swift." Nevertheless, Williams concedes that the life of Swift is not "careless or perfunctory" and Johnson has a number of "high compliments" for Swift (114-28). In the same year Allen Tate discusses Johnson's view of the metaphysicals. "When we feel disposed to dismiss Johnson's views on the Metaphysical po-

ets as prejudiced," Tate warns, "we ought to consider whether we are
not opposing one prejudice with another, of another kind between
which sensible compromise is difficult or even impossible." The
problem for Johnson, according to Tate, is that Donne, unlike Den-
ham, deviates from nature and is not "translatable." Also, Tate argues that Johnson's view that "religious contemplation is not a subject for poetry" is "nonsense." Johnson, Tate continues, faults the
Metaphysicals for being incapable of the sublime, by which he means
the grandeur of generality, a position based upon seventeenth-century rationalism. Although impressed by Johnson's consistency of
point of view, Tate points out that Johnson is seldom consistent or
precise "in his particular judgments and definitions ... a defect that
perhaps accounts negatively for his greatness as a critic: the perpetual
reformulation of his standards, with his eye on the poetry." Johnson's concept of "concordia discors" is a great insight, but there is
fundamental disagreement about how violent is the yoking together
of heterogeneous ideas. Johnson and his age favor the poetry of experience, while we are prejudiced in favor of "the great tradition of
verse [uniting] Shakespeare and Donne, including Milton and much
of Dryden, but [passing] over the eighteenth century." Tate thus concludes with the chasm separating Johnson, the exemplar of classi-
cism, from the moderns (488-506). Here the critical insights of a fine
poet are no less inconsistent than those ascribed to Johnson. If Johnson is seldom consistent, how can we discover a relation between his
perceptions and principles, and if Johnson is out of sympathy with
the metaphysicals how do we account for the great insight of
"concordia discors"?

    In 1950 William Keast also considers Johnson on the metaphysi-
cals. Keast points out that it is "widely acknowledged that modern
criticism of the seventeenth-century poets is heavily indebted to
[Johnson's] analysis of metaphysical wit—even if modern critics
spurn the inferences which Johnson draws." Johnson's questions,
Keast explains, are different from ours. He is concerned with the
"pleasure" of literature—with whether or not it engages our attention and interest, and his criticism is above all marked by judgment
and evaluation based upon nature, not art. Nevertheless, Keast concludes, "it does not seem likely that anyone not fanatic in his devo-
tion to Cleveland or Cowley will disagree with Johnson's verdict
that their poetry is on the whole without any genuine power to interest or move." Although Johnson has "no method," he "focuses
upon our attention a concern for the ultimate effects and values of
literature" (59-69). But the amount of attention given to the metaphysical poets during this period suggests that they did "interest and
move" some readers. The problem is that those who favored the
metaphysicals appropriated the terms and conceptions of Johnson
with little interest and understanding of how they were used by

Johnson. Thus, Kathleen Tillotson asserts that Matthew Arnold "never seems to have wavered in his admiration of Johnson as a critic," but the nature of this relationship remains unexamined (147). Johnson is accepted as the father of criticism for most subsequent practitioners of the art, but the nature of the family resemblance is veiled. Meanwhile, the accumulation of important specifics continued. E. A. Horsman corroborates Johnson's accusation that Dryden's vocabulary is made up of many pretentious Frenchified words, a practice typical of the Restoration (346-51). And Edward Hart examines Nichols as a source of Johnson's *Lives* to find that while Johnson derived many of his facts from Nichols, the styles of the two writers are markedly different (1088-1111).

In 1951 Helen Darbishire examines Johnson's *Life of Milton*. As "the greatest man of letters of the next generation," Johnson, Darbishire begins, "wrote a life of Milton and estimate of his poetry which aimed at drastic criticism," but he did not let his prejudice against the person blind him to the poetry. Johnson recognizes the sublimity of *Paradise Lost*, and Darbishire congratulates him for "rightly [drawing] attention to the awkward attachment of the allegory of Sin and Death to the main story." But Darbishire wonders if Johnson is right about the lack of human interest in *Paradise Lost*; rather she believes that Milton "brings Adam and Eve to life" but agrees with Johnson that the characteristic quality of *Paradise Lost* is sublimity (7-51). The record of Johnson's sensitive perceptions omits any reference to his principles. We are left to wonder how Johnson can so carefully discriminate among the parts of a poem that he considers lacking in human interest.

In 1952 James Allison summarizes the elements of Warton's "Essay on the Genius and Writings of Pope" that are a reply to Johnson's *Lives*. Warton argues that imitation, however derivative, gives pleasure to the reader, and contests Johnson's assessment of the relationship between imagination and good sense in Pope. He points out that Dryden, not Johnson, was the first to use the term *metaphysical*, opposes Johnson's description of Addison's style, defends Gray's "Bard," contradicts Johnson on "Lycidas," and criticizes the style of the *Rambler* (186-91). And Jean Hagstrum, in *Samuel Johnson's Literary Criticism*, turns to an element of the life of Pope not considered by Warton to exemplify that for Johnson "rhetorical beauty" takes precedence over other aesthetic functions. Johnson gives Pope "the qualities of invention, imagination, and good judgment, but he concludes [with] 'every grace of elegant expression'" (133-34). It is important to note that some of these issues where Johnson was opposed by or different from his contemporaries were considered by previous critics as instances of Johnson as representative of his age.

The miscellaneous criticism of the *Lives* even led to reexamination of Johnson's historical evidence, generally assumed in the past to be his greatest weakness. In 1952 John Moore and Maurice Johnson analyze the accuracy of the anecdote reported in the life of Swift about Dryden's negative assessment of Swift as a poet. Both come in the end to accept its authenticity, the former because Swift shows his dislike of Dryden and the latter because the animosity between the two writers is referred to in print elsewhere (1024-34; 1232-39). Where else in the history of criticism can we find two scholars tracing the accuracy of one anecdote, leaving unexplained the significance of their research? During this period Swift's poetry was being subjected to a reassessment: those championing the cause of Swift as a poet would have been delighted to have such an anecdote discredited. The Johnsonian ghost haunts Swiftians even though most believe that his life is unfair to the great satirist.

Some critics did move to the general level, but without methodological innovation the results are not consistent. In 1954 Benjamin Boyce compares Johnson's life of Pope to earlier eighteenth-century accounts of Pope and concludes that "Johnson's remarks on Pope were not uniformly superior to these previous critics." Johnson is at his best, according to Boyce, "on Pope's intellectual habits and character but even here he is not original." In fact, Boyce argues that Johnson "adjudicated" among his predecessors and for that reason the life of Pope contains little "naked criticism"(37-44). This assessment indicates a great deal more about the limitations of Boyce's approach than about the life of Pope. For if there is one judgment throughout our history that persists it is that the life of Pope is Johnson's greatest achievement in the *Lives*. Boyce's inability to explain that fact reveals the inadequacy of his methodology.

In fact, F. W. Hilles's 1959 analysis of the making of the life of Pope suggests an alternative position. Hilles demonstrates that Johnson collected materials from various sources, written and oral, read and reread Pope's writings, leaving notes on much of this material. Owen Ruffhead served as one of Johnson's main sources. Hilles explains: "For clarity's sake the alterations which Johnson made [to Ruffhead] may be classified in three groups. Much that Ruffhead wrote, Johnson omitted; much that Johnson included is not found in Ruffhead; and much that is in Ruffhead Johnson corrected." Although Hilles stresses the care and consideration Johnson devoted to Pope, he is careful not to exaggerate his point. "Professor Boyce's admirable study may give the unwary reader the impression that Johnson carefully reviewed all earlier comments on Pope's poetry. In fact, with minor exceptions such as allusions to the criticism of Lord Kames, Dennis, and Warburton, Johnson's critique is based on statements of only two of his predecessors ... Warton and Ruffhead." The stylistic changes are of the sort we would expect: "while writing,

Johnson worked as he said, 'with vigour, and haste.' The chief signs of haste in the manuscript are the many slips of the pen, omissions of words, and grammatical mistakes." Hilles also clarifies the role of John Nichols: "Nichols was one of the 'respectable' booksellers ... who sponsored the edition of the English poets. He was also sole printer of the first edition. With him Johnson corresponded on all matters of detail. To him he turned for information and advice. ... He was a careful proof-reader. The order to 'Revise' on the first page of each gathering is in his hand, and he queried many of Johnson's statements." Finally, Hilles characterizes the proofing procedure: "When reading proof, Johnson's concern, as has been said, was with matters of style. Most numerous among the corrections in proof are those that eliminate careless repetitions of the same word. Long sentences are broken up, and qualifying words drop out, *probably*, for example becoming *certainly*" (257-84). The commonly held belief that Johnson was cavalier about his sources, composed carelessly without taking time to revise, Hilles demonstrates, needs much qualification.

Focusing upon principles rather than perception, Warren Fleischauer defends Johnson's strictures on "Lycidas." Fleischauer argues that Johnson's disapproval of Milton's pastoral elegy stems from one of the "norms" of his criticism, his objection to the mingling of "mythology ... with 'most awful and sacred truths'" (255). Three years later, John Hardy suggests that Johnson's use of the term *metaphysical* might derive from Locke: "Nature was the Augustan touchstone for testing the quality of Poetry, and it was Johnson's central charge against the 'metaphysical poets' that they were not poets of Nature. But their 'unnaturalness' is originally the result of their being *metaphysical* (in the sense of 'school metaphysics')" (232-33). James Leicester assesses Johnson's life of Shenstone, pointing out that at the time Shenstone is nearly as popular as Gray, but that "Johnson chose to write a Life of Shenstone which for the most part ran counter to the accepted views of his contemporaries." Knowing little about Shenstone himself, Johnson, Leicester demonstrates, relies heavily on Treadway Nash's biography of Shenstone, first published in 1774. But Johnson's own attitude determines the choice and tone of the material. "The Leasowes was to [Johnson] not the best of all possible worlds. ... For him, at least, it represented a false view. Solitude drove him into company, inactivity tortured his soul, poverty was a bitter memory. In consequence he found more to pity than to praise in Shenstone" (189-222). In three very different ways each of these critics attempts to demonstrate that Johnson's criticism is not a form of good taste but firmly based upon principles. But they lose sight of the fact that Johnson often judges by his critical perceptions in spite of his principles.

In 1963 William Keast analyzes Johnson's *Lives* in relation to those of Cibber. In 1753, under Cibber's name, five volumes containing 202 biographies, ranging in time from Chaucer to John Banks (d. 1751), appeared in weekly installments of seventy-two pages each. Keast demonstrates that Robert Shiels, one of the amanuenses for the *Dictionary* and a friend of Johnson's, was a collaborator of Cibber's: "Shiels and Cibber quarreled; Shiels ... no doubt told his patron how he was being used. ... Johnson, loyal to his friends ... did what he could to insure that justice should be done to poor Shiels." Specifically, Johnson allowed Shiels to use portions of his own *Lives*, borrowings seen by placing the two lives side by side. Hence "when Johnson seems to have borrowed from the 1753 *Lives of the Poets* and when we can find no other source for the information there, we must consider it as antecedently probable that Johnson was Shiels's source" (89-101). But why Cibber borrowed from Johnson, what interpretive principles were possibly shared by the two critics, is not pursued.

In 1964 Tommy Watson compares Johnson and Hazlitt on the imagination in Milton. Making use of Raymond Havens's five Johnsonian uses of the term *imagination*, Watson observes that in at least two of these categories "Johnson ... had much in common with the Romantic view of that faculty." Also "another important aspect of the creative process ... the power of combining and rearranging into meaningful patterns individual images ... both Johnson and Hazlitt [attribute] to the imagination ... in their judgments of Milton." Watson reasons that "although it would be patently false and equally absurd to argue that Johnson was, at heart, a Romanticist in his theory of literature, it may justly be affirmed that there are in Johnson's evaluations elements which begin to look forward to a broader, more inclusive interpretation of the importance of the imagination in the creative process" (123-33). Two years later Richard Fogle compares Johnson and Coleridge on Milton. "What Samuel Johnson and Samuel Taylor Coleridge see in Milton is the same quiddity, but they differ greatly on its quality. Both strongly emphasize his tremendous egotism. To Johnson this is the besetting sin for which Milton must answer; for Coleridge, on the other hand, it is his vital principle, a Platonic idea that Milton both is and expresses." According to Fogle, both Johnson and Coleridge see the sublime as the defining characteristic of *Paradise Lost*, but for the older critic Milton's egocentrism is central to this characteristic, and for the younger one it is superfluous to it (26-32). What in the nineteenth century was seen as sheer discontinuity—Johnson versus Milton and Coleridge versus Johnson—was now understood as discontinuity in continuity. The advantage of being at a further remove from Johnson than were the romantics and Victorians brings into view a family resemblance that is obscured by the polemics of antagonism toward the father of criticism. Yet we note that Johnson is reevaluated because believed to be closer to the romantics; the reverse possibility, that the romantics are more like the eighteenth century, was not even a possibility.

One kind of alternative to romantic teleology proposed at the time is that Johnson's criticism relates not to the later romantics but to earlier critical ages. In 1967 John Hardy attempts to explain why Johnson makes no reference in his life of Pope to his friend Percival Stockdale, who defends Pope against Warton. "Perhaps [Johnson] felt that such a refutation would have given Warton's views undue prominence. He would never admit that Pope's reputation was in any way diminished" (54). In the same year Oliver Sigworth supplements Fleischauer's defense of Johnson on "Lycidas," arguing that Johnson's objection to "Lycidas" stems from his desire for "genuine passion in literature ... [that was] in conflict with the renaissance traditions which his education had affirmed." Standing at the crossroads between the Renaissance and modernism, Johnson turns upon the "literary precepts of his own education" and affirms "that literature should be the expression of 'life' and of the author's passion" (159-68). Victor Milne comments upon Sigworth's article, pointing out that he agrees in general with it but objects to the notion that Johnson forgets or deliberately varies from the concept of the Renaissance pastoral. "Johnson did not forget the conventions that extended back through the Renaissance to Theocritus." Instead, Milne maintains, Johnson "redefined an ancient form and casually anathematized one of its most prominent branches ... by applying the Renaissance canon of decorum with a thoroughgoing rigor that would have appalled Sir Philip Sidney" (300-301). Here we begin to see that the attempts to provide principles for Johnson's criticism result in contrary accounts of "norms," a reminder of the theoretical ramifications of Johnson's valuing perceptions over principles.

More concrete criticism serves to place the *Lives* in their historical context. In 1968 Vereen Bell provides for the life of Milton what Boyce had done for the life of Pope, a demonstration that Johnson is responding to various contemporaneous critical positions. In particular, Bell shows that Johnson was reacting to the popularity of Milton fostered by Addison, Dennis, Voltaire, and Newton. "It was because of Milton's rising popularity," Bell argues, "not despite it, that Johnson undertook to expose what he considered the most conspicuous defects of Milton's creative method. But hardheaded rationalist that he was and stubbornly attuned to the impeccable music of the heroic measure Johnson was clearly out of his element in judging Milton" (127-32). In the same year Wayne Warncke examines the life of Swift in relation to its predecessors, pointing out that no adequate explanation of the singularly negative tone of the life of Swift has been offered. In particular, Warncke asks, why does Johnson base his life of Swift on that of "Lord Orrery, who had suffered a series of biographical retorts to his often false and narrow description of Swift and whom Johnson himself had once termed feeble-minded"? Moreover, according to Warncke, Johnson was familiar with two other lives of Swift, one more favorable than Orrery's and another by Johnson's friend Hawkesworth that steers a middle course between the two, yet Johnson "goes beyond ... and away from" Hawkesworth. Warncke explains that "although Johnson's prejudice accounts for the fundamental antagonism shown Swift throughout the Life, the reason that Johnson allowed it free sway is clearly related to the precedence the moralist took over the biographer. ... The Life ... becomes ... an example of 'pride punished in his own person, and an example of terror to the pride of others'" (56-64). Both of these critics attempt to modify the harshness of Johnson's position by implying that Johnson is reacting to contemporaneous bardolatry, but then retreat from their own defense, unable to explain what they believe is critical blindness. Ultimately Johnson, as a great critic, is expected to rise above his personal predilections, as he so often does, and to vary from his critical norms.

In 1969 two essays on the life of Addison by James Battersby appear. In the first, Battersby distinguishes between structure and form in the life of Addison. The life of Swift, according to Battersby, is, like most of the lives, structurally divided into three parts—the biography, the character sketch and the literary commentary—but the formal elements that give cohesion to each of these sections and bind the whole together are qualitative not quantitative, formal not structural. "The unifying principle of the Addison is the determination and establishment of the essential man, of the essential genius of Addison as manifested in significant action." Battersby asserts that "the various sections of Johnson's 'Life' ... have a kind of self-certifying validity and reliability; the power of this combination of self-validating parts is precisely formal power" (28-41). In the second essay on the sources of the life of Addison, Battersby demonstrates with regard to the relation of Cibber's to Johnson's *Lives*, as Keast maintained earlier, that "the only reasonable conclusion which emerges is that when Johnson wrote his account of Addison he simply reclaimed what was legitimately his own" (522). Battersby's analyses rest on an assumption, the essence of Addison that remains unarticulated, leaving in doubt how that essence inhabits the structure of the life of Addison.

In a 1969 article, Paul Korshin points out that "there exists no thorough consideration of the intellectual and factual bases for Johnson's opinion of Swift." The biographical explanations, Korshin demonstrates, ignore Boswell's testimony that there is no basis for personal animosity between Johnson and Swift. Instead, Korshin advises, we need to understand the gradual development of Johnson's opinion of Swift as part of his intellectual development. Also, it is necessary, Korshin cautions, to keep the circumstances of composition in mind. The life of Swift was composed, Korshin recalls, just prior to the life of Pope: Johnson was behind in his schedule and thus uncharacteristically abbreviated the third section of Swift, the literary assessment, "probably [thinking] that he had nothing new to add to what he had said previously." It should also be kept in mind, Korshin adds, that Johnson's interest in Swift went back to the 1750s when he helped Hawkesworth with his life of Swift and was aware of the controversy surrounding Orrery's account. Turning to *Gulliver's Travels*, Korshin points out that Johnson himself in his early career imitated Swift's style of irony, but by the middle of his life abandoned it, "indicating that he no longer found it effective or that he was dissatisfied with his earlier assessment of Swift's talents." Moreover, recent scholarship suggests that Book 4 of *Gulliver'sTravels* was rejected on ethical grounds in Johnson's day: "Johnson ... either did not perceive or rejected as methodologically unsuitable the irony of Swift's debasement of human nature. Indeed, so great was eighteenth-century opposition to Part 4 that two of the rare contemporaries of Johnson who did comprehend what Swift was undertaking to show, his biographers Deane Swift and Thomas Sheridan, are very much on the defensive. ... The genesis of Johnson's literary opinion on Swift, then, is to be found in his basic disagreement with Swift's conceptions of humanity and rationality as expressed chiefly in *Gulliver's Travels*." Korshin concludes that "Johnson's attitude toward Swift, then, based as it is upon early revulsion to Swift's representation of human nature, shows something of his unwillingness to open his mind to Swift's obvious merits in the face of what he construed as a great offense to mankind, acquires further prejudices along the way, and reaches its culmination in the life of Swift with an unfair treatment which Johnson could neither help nor avoid" (464-78). Korshin implies a new variation on the relationship between Johnson's personal and critical precepts: although Johnson usually scrupulously separated the two, when a perception of moral corruption in one sphere is reinforced in the other, the result can be a distorted or one-sided life.

Lawrence Lipking devotes the concluding chapter of *The Ordering of the Arts in Eighteenth Century England* (1970) to the *Lives*. "Wherever the study of the ordering of the arts in eighteenth-century England may begin, in the end it leads to Samuel Johnson. It was Johnson who adapted the lessons of Renaissance criticism to present use, Johnson who dedicated Reynolds' *Discourses* and Burney's *History*, Johnson who taught the public to trust its common sense about the arts, Johnson who stood for the force of reason against which Walpole and the Wartons wove their spells. ... Johnson is our intermediary to the good sense of his age, and almost everyone agrees that the *Lives* represent the permanent value, the *ponere totum*, of eighteenth-century criticism." Lipking demonstrates that the *Lives* combines different genres: literary criticism, biography, prefaces to a definitive anthology, literary and intellectual history, moral and psychological observations, and a biographical encyclopedia. Moreover, the individual lives vary in type and length, from 311 words for Pomfret to 446 paragraphs for Pope. The main precedent for the *Lives*, according to Lipking, is Fontenelle's *Recueil*, but Johnson expands upon this model: "Formally speaking, the originality of the *Lives* consists in a new weight placed upon this central section [the character], which is both clearly distinct from the rest of the *Life* and flexibly employed for a variety of purposes." The immediate forerunner is Cibber's *Lives*, which by its "diffidence" differs markedly from "Johnson's weight of judgment."

Lipking treats separately the lives of Cowley, Milton, Dryden and Pope because each represents a different principle of order. In the life of Cowley, the mode and nature of his poetry take precedence over the poet: "The whole of the life of Cowley is informed by the search for intrinsic and unalterable value, and that is why it never relaxes its spirit of criticism." The life of Milton, according to Lipking, is the most controversial of the *Lives* because its ordering principle is unpleasant: "the very independence, impatience, and ardor for fame which makes a man impossible to live with or like may help make a poet great." Nevertheless, Lipking concedes that the "method of the life of Milton remains somewhat unconvincing. Here if anywhere we have a right to complain that ... the moral lessons of the life sometimes sound ... more strident than just." The life of Dryden, Lipking argues, shows Johnson's critical judgment to "better advantage." "Johnson's poetic taste had been weaned on Dryden, whom the *Dictionary* cited more often than any other poet but Shakespeare, and in writing this life he combined the natural pleasure of talking about Dryden with the incentive of doing him justice." Here Johnson alters his customary structure. "As the second section adds a description of character to the events of the poet's life, the fourth part supplements a review of the poet's works with an estimate of his specifically poetic character. ... Here literary biography blends with literary history." But finally the structure here "remains experimental. ... The paradigm of Johnson's mastery" is the life of Pope. The problem, according to Lipking, is methodological: "the life of Pope is pulled in different directions by its effort to adjudicate even those disputes to which it brings no new information, and to stretch its wisdom thin until it can cover both the man and the poet." But "where Johnson excels all other biographers is not in method but in his profound analysis of behavior, an analysis which unites the virtues of the novelist and the moralist." So the life of Pope may be an example of the best of the *Lives* but cannot serve as a "paradigm" of the method of the *Lives,* for "no one Life stands for Johnson's *Lives.*" Nevertheless, Lipking concludes, there is a unifying principle of the *Lives:* "The *Lives of the Poets* records the professional histories of men who have tried to do something worthy of a man's attention, and thus implies that a literary vocation may do much to fill the vacuity of human life. ... Thus a poetic vocation ... can lend grace to a life otherwise of small fortune, like that of Savage, and sometimes confer even a limited kind of secular redemption. ... Thus the *Lives of the Poets* consciously assumes the burden of summing up a century of English poetry, as well as the human talents and careers that lie behind the poetry" (405-62). Lipking explains that the *Lives,* even a single life, cannot be adequately described with reference to a system of critical principles or norms. The *Lives,* for Lipking, provide various forms of order to an entire culture and are perceived not as interpretations organized around a single theme but as unique tapestries with appropriately different designs. Lipking's recognition that the *Lives* represent the first important assessment of British literary culture is an important contribution, but it is not clear from his analysis how Johnson moves from the lives of the poets to the culture.

During this period two scholars attempt to account for elements of the lives that are most off-putting to present-day readers. Maxine Turnage urges that Johnson's "adverse criticism" of Spenser be attributed to his aversion to the pastoral, which he encounters regularly in his searching for examples of "archaic and obsolete words" when compiling the *Dictionary* (557-67). Jordan Richman attempts to defend Johnson's portrait of Swift the man against the charge of prejudice. In comparison to previous biographers of Swift, Richman maintains, Johnson "relentlessly pursues a central theme in relating the facts": we are all taught to reform our ways by fear and shame, but Swift heard "nothing but his own praises." Richman characterizes the life of Swift as "one of the more laudably realistic" views of Swift. "Johnson's respect for Swift may not always be evident but it is nevertheless implicitly if perhaps grudgingly granted in his life of Swift" (91-102). Again, the problem with basing a Johnsonian critical view on his prejudice or on his agreement with contemporary opinion is that Johnson as a critic regularly rises above his personal predilections and the commentators of his age.

Similarly, James Swearingen attempts to demonstrate that Johnson's life of Gray has been seen in overly negative terms: "the edge of the argument is not directed at the dead poet, but the growing cult of idolaters who made Gray the flawless measure of excellence in poetry." Swearingen distinguishes between "Johnson's comments on the life and character of Gray [which] are ... at least moderate, and perhaps ... even charitable" and those on the poetry, where "the standard of judgment is too limited to provide an estimate of Gray's work." But Johnson is shown in his analysis of Gray's poetry to be consistent to the "mimetic view of poetry." "The "Life of Gray" ... is [neither] a product of temperamental differences between the two men nor a biased discussion of poems that the critic could not understand." Swearingen asserts that Johnson remains true to his aesthetic principles: "to condone the popular enthusiasm for poetry like the Odes would be to contribute to the destruction of the ideal of reason in poetry and to turn back the progress of the imagination" (289-302). This defense—reminiscent of the earlier resort to "norms" to justify the attack on "Lydicas"—leaves out of account not only Johnson's habitual variance from his own 'norms' but also his admiration for Gray's "Elegy."

In 1978, Robert Folkenflik contests Wimsatt's assertion that Johnson's style remains essentially the same. "Wimsatt ... does not consider, evidently because of his belief in the consistency of Johnson's style, that the difference in genre might have led Johnson to the *choice* of a different style." Folkenflik suggests that "an examination of the theories of historical and biographical style which were prevalent in Johnson's day, of Johnson's criticism of style in biography, and finally of the expressive features of Johnson's biographies themselves leads to the conclusion that Johnson's biographies are different in style from his essays through conscious artistry" (175). But since Folkenflik ends with an examination of the life of Savage, a life that gives more emphasis to biography than the other lives, it is not clear how this plainer style is related to the more critical lives, such as Dryden and Pope.

In 1975 Frederick W. Hilles reconsiders Johnson's lines on Swift in *The Vanity of Human Wishes*. Hilles admits that Johnson's "heartlessness" is that of "bald truth." Turning then to the life of Swift, Hilles reminds us that Johnson makes reference to a plan that some time before 1755 he communicates to his friend Hawkesworth, who like Johnson relies not on "rumormongers but on the most authoritative information available to him." Hilles therefore detects "in Johnson's account of [Swift's] last years ... none of the bias that annoys Swift's defenders" (370-77). In the same year Howard Weinbrot demonstrates that Johnson, in the life of Milton, is probably influenced by John Clarke's *Essay on Study* concerning Satan's blasphemies and the materiality of angels (404-7). But those who regard Johnson the critic as greater than his contemporaries are still left to wonder how he can be so negative about the great works of Milton and Swift.

Also during the 1970s critics analyze the structure of the *Lives*. Paul Hanchock emphasizes that the *Lives* have a remarkably uniform structure: "No matter what the actual length of the *Life*, approximately the first half is 'life'; the middle eighth, 'character'; and the final three-eighths, 'works.'" This form, Hancock speculates,

Johnson may have found in Diogenes' *Lives*, particularly his *Life of Aristotle* (75-77). Colin Horne demonstrates how Johnson, in the life of Pope, adapts a method of Pope's, satirizing others by using the words originally designed for their enemies and applying them to the authors themselves: "clearly Johnson's adaptations of Pope, though lacking the crispness of Pope's decasyllabics, could generate their own trenchant wit and be used as effective means of retrospectively admonishing him" (313). Mark Booth analyzes the structure of the life of Roscommon as exemplary of Johnson's practice: "everywhere Johnson's judgments, on all different levels of subject, seem substantially independent of each other. They depend more upon remote and general principles than upon context." Booth concludes that "Johnson is engaged in reassessing received opinions and in exerting influence. His vigorous language urges to attention examples of what has merit and what does not, with reference to standing judgment." For Johnson's object is not to explicate or clarify; "the assumption at work is the educational power of the achieved example" (505-15). The formal configuration of the *Lives* is seen as general and vague enough to encompass great variation between and within the *Lives* themselves, but therefore offers little to explain their originality.

In *The Uses of Johnson's Criticism*, Leopold Damrosch, Jr., devotes nearly half of the text to the *Lives*, a chapter on the *Lives* in general and then one each on Dryden and Pope. In the general discussion, Damrosch points out that the *Lives* should be categorized not as "treatises on aesthetics," but as a "series of great works [that] sought to define the nature and limits of human achievement." Although these works have contemporary analogues, Damrosch continues, Johnson surpasses them all. For Damrosch, the greatness of the *Lives* rests "not upon criticism as a discipline ... but upon a broad conception of literary history as a branch of human history," for it is here that we "feel the presence of Johnson himself" (123-64). Moving on to Dryden, Damrosch emphasizes that it was recognized at the outset that it was written "*con amore*," that is, was in direct contact with Dryden's genius and the result is, again, not criticism "but an appreciation of Dryden's mind" (167-91). On Pope, Damrosch notes that it "has generally been regarded as the finest of the *Lives*" and explains that its special excellence consists in that "both poetry and poems are intimately related to character." He concludes that "Johnson hopes to show that Pope's limitations are the function of individual qualities of mind ... rather than of his art" (192-215). Damrosch is certainly right to point out that part of the greatness of the two greatest lives, those of Dryden and Pope, resides in Johnson's ability to be both with and at one remove from Dryden and Pope and that the result is not only literary criticism but also human history.

But precisely how Johnson achieves this double view and double conclusion requires fuller analysis.

In 1977 William McCarthy focuses on the account of "poets' careers." Since Johnson is concerned less with factual accuracy than with literary impression, McCarthy advises us to attend less to sources and "more to ... genre." Here the key, according to McCarthy, is the brief life that is "generically fascinated with the sheer frailty of the human enterprise" and "comes out of a Christian milieu in which man is continually being exhorted to see the skull beneath his skin." Thus the *Lives* is an ironic survey of the human condition and the life of Swift shows the satirist to have been "stripped of his humanity by his own very human determination to be better than 'merely human'" (503-17). This assessment leaves out of account the critical section, particularly the condemnation of *Gulliver's Travels*. Also, Johnson specifically asks that someone like Watt be included in the *Lives*, presumably not because he is a great poet but because he exemplifies a kind of piety that Johnson admires. Such positive examples point up the negative element of lives like that of Swift.

In the 1980s two critics use historical positions to explain the life of Milton. J. R. Brink sets out to modify the assumption that Johnson is deeply antagonistic to Milton as a person. Rather, Brink maintains, Johnson's life of Milton can be explained on the basis of Johnson's political and literary critical views. "Johnson ... was not only ... an objective scholar, but also as an eighteenth-century man of letters interested in supplying the public with useful instruction and correcting the tastes of his own age." More specifically, when Johnson comes to write the life of Milton, "he regarded the assignment," according to Brink, "in part as a charge to promote piety and in part as an opportunity to correct [the] ... sentimental tendencies in Milton criticism." These critical concerns are combined with political ones: "Milton's revolutionary politics developed out of his visionary idealism and his tendency to regard society as an aggregate of individuals rather like himself. Johnson, on the other hand, was a social realist, acquainted with people at every level of the social scale; his theories about government and the church were empirically based." Brink concludes "that when we recognize that Johnson set out not only to weigh Milton's weaknesses and strengths, but also to instruct his audience and promote piety, his final assessment of *Paradise Lost* becomes more significant" (493-503). Indeed, it does, but we still need to know whether that "final assessment" is a function of Johnson's critical acumen, or of his political and scholarly beliefs.

In 1984 Stephen Fix argues that previous critics who defend Johnson on the basis that he separates Milton the man from the poet have gone too far, almost making Johnson into a "new critic." Rather, Fix maintains, Johnson relates the life and writings of Milton: "the subtle purpose of the *Life of Milton* is to show how Milton's life allowed him to develop the kind of genius necessary to write a poem as great as *Paradise Lost*, but not to acquire the lesser talents necessary to succeed in the minor poems." Beginning with "Johnson's edgy estimate of Milton's literary genius ... Johnson, the perpetual moralist, found himself faced with the unnerving task of writing the life of a man whose works and days seemed to be separated from common humanity by a wide gulf and whose genius flourished not in spite of that separation, but because of it." Indeed, Fix admits that "Johnson regards Milton as a man who, like the geometricians, avoids the challenge of criticism." But for Johnson "the genius of Milton's art and the remoteness of his life are intertwined. ... However much Johnson may appreciate the strength of will and sallies of imagination that Milton's distance from common things allows, the example of this poet's icy reserve remains unnerving." Although "it would have been safer and easier for a man like Johnson to separate Milton's artistic accomplishments from his character and personality; and it would have been more comforting for such a critic to think—and make us think—that a work as great as *Paradise Lost* was the product of the same talents and habits that gave meaning and hope to Johnson's life ... he chose instead the richer and more troubling alternative" (244-64). Three years later Fix turns to the problem of "Lycidas" to argue that Johnson's remarks do not denigrate the elegy but suggest that the inordinate praise lavished upon it detracts from the greatness of *Paradise Lost*. But the historical position is less likely to be persuasive when it overlooks the possibility that Johnson in addition to being in history is also capable of making history. If his contemporaries are uncritical in their praise, that is not sufficient excuse for Johnson's characterizing one of our greatest pastoral elegies as "easy, vulgar and therefore disgusting," particularly when the generic hierarchy of the eighteenth century places any accomplishment in the realm of the pastoral well below that of the genre of *Paradise Lost*, the epic. Moreover while correctly reminding us that the modern separation of biography from criticism was alien to Johnson, Fix does not take into account that for Johnson the relationship between the two was often so complex that differences and even contradictions are regularly discovered. It could be suggested that the case for Johnson as a great critic in the *Lives* will be advanced by admitting that Johnson is wrong about "Lycidas" and that he was capable of making an error. If his great critical acumen permitted him to overcome his prejudice against blank verse and recognize the greatness of *Paradise Lost* and *The Seasons*, then his bias against pastoral and that of his contemporaries in favor of Milton can only serve as excuses for lesser critics than Johnson.

In 1987 David Wheeler edited a volume on the Johnsonian art of biography. Wheeler explains that because biography "holds a central place in Johnson's canon ... [and] it was Johnson's favorite genre ...

[it] provide[s] a particularly apt place to 'know' Johnson" (2). The range of the eight essays in this volume suggests a new interest in Johnson as biographer. The final essay, Michael Stuprich's assessment of the previous fifteen years criticism, lists fifty-five bibliographical entries. In addition to the essay on "Lycidas" mentioned above, the volume includes a consideration of Johnson's interest in Charles XII of Sweden, a reading of an early poem by Johnson and the difficulty of beginning, an account of how modern students in the classroom respond to the *Lives*, a conception of Johnson as a biographical thinker, an essay on the significance of the character of the author in and of the *Lives*, and a socioeconomic reading of the life of Savage. Even this cursory summary suggests that the *Lives* is seen to bear upon many aspects of present-day extraliterary problems.

In 1989 Edward Tomarken attempts to explain the relationship between the literary and the extraliterary in the life of Pope. In the last chapter of his book, *Johnson, 'Rasselas,' and the Choice of Criticism*, Tomarken notes that the biographical and critical sections of the life of Pope seem to contradict one another. "If Pope and his poetry are almost synonymous," Tomarken asks, "how can his successful poetry be used as evidence of his failure as a man?" Tomarken suggests in reply that "Pope's pride blinded him to the fact that literary understanding applies not merely to the poet but also to the man. ... Pope is severely criticized for not recognizing the boundaries of literature: writing, however accomplished, cannot disguise our limitations as human beings" (174-78). For Tomarken the relationship between the biographical and critical sections involves ethical considerations, the writer's responsibility to his readers, the relationship between moral language and decent conduct. These are issues, Tomarken addresses in the conclusions of both of his books, that require a new literary theory, an approach that he calls a "New Humanism."

Annette Wheeler Cafarelli, on the other hand, approaches Johnson's *Lives* as part of the "tradition of subjective sequencing of lives in which a sustained ideological program emerges ... as in the prologue to *The Canterbury Tales* or *A Mirror for Magistrates*" (5). In her conclusion, Cafarelli clarifies her position: "we must accustom ourselves to thinking of biographical narrative as a symbolic structure" (191). I am not certain that Johnson would accept this view of biography. But it should be pointed out in Cafarelli's defense that hers is a study of how Johnson's *Lives* influences romantic prose writers, and she demonstrates very clearly that "the Romantics paid Johnson the compliment of imitating him even as they anathematized him" (69). The difference between Tomarken and Cafarelli is methodological. In explaining how Johnson contributes to romantic biography, Cafarelli employs a postromantic concept of a symbolic system, in which biography is "like other literary genres." Tomarken argues that Johnson criticizes Pope for attempting to escape into a similar sort of literary system. The method that Tomarken develops enables biography to point beyond the literary to the extraliterary, a realm where for Johnson ethics takes precedence over all literary values. This distinction may help explain why the *Lives* has featured prominently in many studies of biography and literary criticism but the biographical method of the *Lives*—specifically, the complex relationship between the biographical and the critical sections—has not yet been the subject of a full-length study. Future critics will have to begin by understanding the reason for this gap. It seems that the problem is generic in nature. We have long since ceased to write critical/biographical works like the *Lives*: the two elements have been clearly separated for decades. Modern biographers often make reference to writings, and present-day critics may refer to an author's life, but one or the other clearly predominates, which is seldom the case in Johnson's *Lives*. I would speculate that this generic alteration is cultural in nature: we have ceased to take seriously in the way that Johnson and his contemporaries did, the ethical obligation of the writer to his society. For us the conduct of an author is a matter of interest to historians unless it bears upon our understanding of his or her writing. Johnson agrees with us that great writing should stand on its own apart from the author for purposes of posterity, but, unlike us, believes that criticism should also judge how the writer's conduct relates to his or her writings. We are therefore unlikely to have a successful attempt at a study of the *Lives of the Poets* until the distinctive nature of that genre is carefully analyzed.

Conclusion

EACH SECTION OF THIS STUDY ENDS with remarks about how considerations of Johnson's writings point beyond the literary realm to the extraliterary. The early biographies, particularly the life of Savage, lead to questions about eighteenth-century culture; *The Vanity of Human Wishes* suggests kinds of conduct that are less vain than others; *Irene* calls for relating style, action, and theater conventions to history; the *Rambler* arrives at ethical imperatives; *Rasselas* concludes with the role of the individual critic's choice in the history of criticism and theory; the Shakespeare criticism finally focuses upon shared concerns of the eighteenth and twentieth centuries; the *Journey* concludes with literature as historical event; *The Lives of the Poets* suggests the ethical consequences of neglecting genre. Johnson's writings push the literary critic beyond literary criticism into history, not as a discipline but as a realm of conduct.

This extraterritorial move causes a problem for modern criticism and explains why the two longest critical works of this greatest of British literary critics, the Shakespeare edition and *The Lives of the Poets*, have produced few full-length studies. Modern criticism relates the literary and extraliterary by way of ideology, but Johnson's ideology is the least interesting aspect of his thought. He regularly beats what Northrop Frye calls the "antique drum," and the message is as repetitive for him as it is tedious to us. We are all familiar with the pontifications from Boswell's *Life* which, detached from their proper context, range from didactic criticism to political dogma. However, Johnson is most alive for us, I believe, when he makes his extraterritorial gesture by way of ethical criticism, a move that is particularly prominent in the Shakespeare commentary and the *Lives*. Here he asks, why must Cordelia die and why are Pope's great satires derived from petty malevolence?

These ethical questions emerge when the critic confronts the generic decisions that inhere in Johnson's writings. Why does he embed his interpretations of the dramas in the *Notes to Shakespeare*, and why does he want his views to be a part of the reading process? Because Johnson believes that there is a close relationship between the procedure of literary understanding and the way we make moral decisions. Why does Johnson in the *Lives* insist equally upon the distinction and the relationship between the life and writing of an author? Because for Johnson ultimate human differences or the subject of biography, ideologies is the modern term, can be mediated and modified by means of critical insights, quotidian ethical choices. Pope and Savage are at opposite ideological poles, the one recognized as the greatest poet of his day and the other rejected by what he believes to be his family. Pope retreats into his prickly satires like a hedgehog, while Savage indulges his self-pity in mawkish poetry and dissipates charity. Johnson holds each responsible for not understanding the response elicited by his own conduct. This blindness of the author to the behavioral consequences of his writing amounts to the refusal to compromise or modify ideologies. In this respect, genre is a function not only of writing but also of living, the face we prepare to face another face.

Meeting Johnson on his own terms, confronting his generic choices, requires a new literary methodology, a "New Humanism." The generic approach is a critical handshake, a willingness to engage people and writings in the terms in which they present themselves. The goal is not some essential humanity inherent in us and in our humanistic endeavors: that was the premise of old humanism. Rather, the new humanism's generic handshake is an attempt at conversation, an admission that humanity, like all other notions, is historicized, subject to change, and ever open to reinterpretation. To essentialize humanity or genre is to reify a means by which we can come to understand one another and alter our world for the better. The generic approach is for me part of the ethical imperative of criticism, a way of relating writing to conduct, in the faith that better understanding of one another's radical of presentation in conversation and writing, in the literary and the extraliterary, can lead to improvement of our collective life, our civilization.

The history of criticism is a key element of the discipline of criticism that directs us to the ethical means of mediating between and modifying opposing ideologies. Accordingly, I have attempted to mediate between Johnson and his critics, suggesting that we critics need to grant authors' generic presentations in order to understand but not necessarily to agree with their ideologies. The process that takes place in between the beginning and the end of an analysis often results in the revising of positions and the better understanding of the opposition. In that sense, the history of criticism can play a part in improving the way we behave toward difference, whether that experience of opposition takes the form of racial, religious, sexual or gender discrimination in the street or an innovative interpretation of *Rasselas*. The history of criticism is then a study of difference, the very issue that at the moment divides nations and peoples, as well as state legislatures and universities.

Works Cited

B. "To the Author, etc." *General Advertiser* (18 February, 1749).

An Essay on Tragedy, and with a Critical Examine of Mahomet and Irene. London: R. Griffiths, 1749.

A Criticism on Mahomet and Irene, in a Letter to the Author. London: Reeve, 1749.

"To the Author of the Rambler. On Reading His Allegories," *Daily Advertiser* 24 (August 1750). Reprinted. *GM*, 20 (October 1750): 465.

Critical Review (April 1759): 372-75.

Gentleman's Magazine (April 1759): 184-86.

London Magazine (May 1759): 258-62.

[Owen Ruffhead]. *Monthly Review* (May 1759): 428-37.

Annual Register (December 1759): 477-98.

[Penny, Anne]. *Anningait and Ajutt; a Greenland Tale. Inscribed to Mr. Samuel Johnson, M.A. Taken from the IVth Volume of His Ramblers, Versified by a Lady.* London: R. & J. Dodsley, 1761.

Critical Review (December 1761): 481.

Critical Review (November 1765): 321-22.

Heath, Benjamin. *A Revisal of Shakespear's Text.* London: Johnston, 1765.

London Magazine 43 (January 1774): 26-27.

Gentleman and Lady's Weekly Magazine Edinburgh 26 (22 April, 11 May 1774).

Whackum. "A Cure for Dr. J—s--n [verse]." *Weekly Magazine* Edinburgh 27 (16 February 1775): 256.

Palmer, Samuel. Comment on Life of Cheynel, in edition of Edmund Calamy, *The Nonconformist's Memorial; Being an Account of the Ministers Who Were Ejected or Silenced after the Restoration.* Vol. 2. London, 1775, 467-68.

Ixion. "To Dr. Samuel Johnson, on His Tour through Scotland. "*Weekly Magazine* Edinburgh. 27 (9 February 1775).

Staffa. "Anecdote of the Last Hebridean Traveller." *St. James's Chronicle* No. 2191 (28 February 1775).

Cameron, Ewen. *The Fingal of Ossian, an Ancient Epic Poem in Six Books.* Warrington: William Byres, 1776.

Brace, Miss. "On Reading Dr. Johnson's Tour to the Western Islands of Scotland."*Weekly Magazine* (Edinburgh) 33 (22 August 1776): 272.

M'Nicol, Donald. *Remarks on Dr. Samuel Johnson's Journey to the Hebrides.* London: Cadell, 1779.

Shaw, William. *An Enquiry into the Authenticity of the Poems Ascribed to Ossian.* London: Murray, 1781.

Knox, Vicesimus. "No. XCIV. Cursory Thoughts on Biography,"In *Essays Moral and Literary.* Vol. 2. London: Dilly, 1782, 48-52.

"Anecdote of Literature," *European Magazine* I (January 1782): 24.

Ritson, Joseph. *Remarks, Critical and Illustrative, on the Text and Notes of the Last Edition of Shakespeare.* London: J. Johnson, 1783.

Sheridan, Thomas. "The Life of the Reverend Dr. Jonathan Swift" in Swift, *Works.* Vol. 1. London: Bathurst, 1784, 520-39.

Tyers, Thomas. *A Biographical Sketch of Dr. Samuel Johnson.* London, 1784.

Mason, John Monck. *Comments on the Last Edition of Shakespeare's Plays.* London: Dilly, 1785.

Wakefield, Gilbert, ed. *The Poems of Mr. Gray, with Notes.* London: Kearsley, 1786.

Hawkins, Sir John. *The Life of Samuel Johnson.* London: Buckland, 1787, 154-57.

Rasselas. Introduction. Dublin, 1787, 4-6.

Amerus. *Gentleman's Magazine* 58 (1788): 300-303.

Potter, Robert. "Remarks on Dr. Johnson's Lives of the Poets," *Gentleman's Magazine* 51 (October 1781): 46-67 (November). 506-10; (December): 561-64; 52 (January 1782): 24-26; (March): 116-18. Reprinted (expanded) as *The Art of Criticism as Exemplified in Dr. Johnson's Lives of the Most Eminent English Poets.* London: T. Hookham, 1789.

Sinclair, A. G. *The Critic Philosopher; or Truth Discovered* London: Strahan and Kearsley, 1789, 15-16, 86-91.

Knight, [Ellis] Cornelia. *Dinarbas: A Tale, Being a Continuation of Rasselas, Prince of Abyssinia.* London, 1790.

Boswell, James. *Boswell's Life of Johnson.* 6 Vols. London, 1791.

Murphy, Arthur. "An Essay on the Life and Genius of Samuel Johnson, LL.D." In *Johnsonian Miscellanies.* London, 1792.

Mudford, William. *A Critical Enquiry into the Moral Writings of Dr. Samuel Johnson.* London, 1802, 80-85.

Rasselas. Introduction. Dublin, 1803, 3-39.

Chalmers, Alexander. "Historical and Biographical Preface to the *Rambler.*" In his *The British Essayists.* London, 1803.

Aikin, John. *Letters to a Young Lady*. London: J. Johnson, 1804, 273-78.

More, Hannah. *Hints Towards Forming the Character of a Young Princess*. 2 Vols. London: Cadell and Davies, 1805.

Hunt, Leigh. *Rasselas*. In *Classic Tales Serious and Lively, with Critical Essays on the Merits and Reputations of the Authors*, London, 1807, 3, 1-13.

Brydges, Sir Samuel Egerton. "The Ruminator, No. 58. On the Reception Originally Given to Dr. Johnson's Rambler," In *Censura Literaria*. Vol. 10. London: Longman, 1809, 71-77.

Monthly Repository 4 (August 1809), 432-33.

Rasselas. Introduction. London, 1809, i-xx.

Drake, Nathan. *Essays, Biographical, Critical, and Historical*. Vol, 1 London: 1809, 111-488.

Barbauld, Anna Letitia. "Johnson. " In *British Novelists, with . . . Prefaces, Biographical and Critical*. Vol. 16. London: Rivington, 1810, i-viii.

Rasselas. Introduction. Edinburgh, 1812, v-xii.

Rasselas. Introduction. London, 1815, i-xx.

White, Thomas Holt. *A Review of Johnson's Criticism on the Style of Milton's English Prose; with strictures on the introduction of Latin idioms into the English language*. London: R. Hunter, 1818.

Hazlitt, William. *Lectures on the Comic Writers*. London, 1819, 102-3.

Rasselas. Ed. Sir Walter Scott. London, 1823. xl-xivi."Reflections upon the Moral and Biographical Writings of Dr. Johnson," *European Magazine*, 87 (April 1825): 320-29.

Macaulay, Thomas Babington. "Boswell's Life Of Johnson." In *The Six Chief Lives from Johnson's Lives of the Poets*, ed. M. Arnold. London: Macmillan, 1878, 21-22. [First appeared in *Edinburgh Review* 54 (1831): 1-38.]

Ivimey, Joseph. "Animadversions upon Dr. Johnson's Life of Milton."

In *John Milton, His Life and Times,.* London: Effingham Wilson, 1833, 349-82.

Whately, Elizabeth Pope. *The Second Part of Rasselas, Prince of Abyssinia.* London, 1835.

Rasselas. Introduction. London: Charles Till, 1838. iii-v.

Whitehead, Charles. *Richard Savage: A Romance of Real Life*. London: Richard Bentley, 1842.

Rasselas. Introduction. London, 1843. iii-viii.

Chambers, Robert. "Johnson and Savage." *Chambers' Journal* 7 (January 1847): 65-68.

Sir Nathaniel. "Literary Leaflets. No. XXVII. Johnson's *Lives of the Poets*," *New Monthly Magazine*, 2d ser. 103 (January 1855): 18-27.

Macaulay, Thomas Babington. "Samuel Johnson," *Encyclopaedia Britannica*, 8th ed., (1856): 12, 793-804.

Reed, Henry. "Burns, with notices of Johnson's Lives of the Poets," In *Lectures on the British Poets*. Vol. 2. Philadelphia: Parry and McMillan, (1857): 16-24.

"Richard Savage." *Dublin University Magazine* 51 (June 1858): 701-12.

Moy, Thomas, W. "Richard Savage." *Notes and Queries*, 2nd ser. 6 (6 November-4 December 1858): 361-65, 385-89, 425-28, 445-48.

De Quincey, Thomas. "Prefatory Memoranda" to "Life of Milton." In *The Logic of Political Economy and Other Papers*. Boston: Ticknor and Fields, 1859 (Vol. 21 of the first American collected ed. of De Quincey's *Works*; also in Vol. 11 of his Works, Edinburgh: J. Hogg, 1859.)

Rasselas. Introduction. Ed. Rev. William West. London, 1869, xiii-xlv.

Symonds, John Addington. "The Blank Verse of Milton," *Fortnightly Review*, n. s.., 16 (1 December 1874): 767-81.

Arnold, Matthew, Ed. *The Six Chief Lives of Johnson's "Lives of the Poets."* London: Macmillan, 1878.

Stephen, Leslie. *Samuel Johnson*. English Men of LettersSeries. London: Macmillan, 1878.

Rasselas. Ed. Alfred Milnes. Introduction. Oxford: Clarendon, 1879, v-xxxii.

"Johnson's *Rasselas*." *Bibliographer* 3 (May 1883): 173-75.

Hill, George Birkbeck. "On a Neglected Book" [*The Rambler*], *Macmillan's* 48 (September 1883): 414-23.

"The Story of 'Rasselas.'" *BookLore* 1 (December 1884): 5-11.

Rasselas. Ed. Henry Morley. London: Routledge, 1884, 5-8.

Morris, Mowbray. "The Terrific Diction." *Macmillan's* 54 (September 1886): 361-68.

Hill, George Birkbeck. *Footsteps of Dr. Johnson*. London: Sampson Low, 1890.

Raleigh, Walter A. "*Rasselas*." *The English Novel*. London: John Murray, 1894, 203-6.

Radford, George H. "Johnson's 'Irene,'" In *Shylock and Others*. London: Fisher Unwin, 1894.

Rasselas. Ed. Oliver F. Emerson. Introduction. New York: Holt, 1895, 18-53.

Vaughan, C. E. "Samuel Johnson," In *English Literary Criticism*, London: Blackie, 1896.

Emerson, Oliver F. "The Text of Johnson's *Rasselas*." *Anglia* 22 (December 1899): 499-509.

Whale, George. "Dr. Johnson as a Traveller." In *Johnson Club Papers*, edited by John Sargeaunt. London: Fisher Unwin, 1899.

Ryley, Madeleine Lucette. *Richard Savage. A Play*, performed in New York City (playbill only), February 1901.

Minchin, Harry C. "Dr. Johnson among the Poets." *Macmillan's Magazine* 85 (December 1901): 98-105.

Bowen, Edwin W. "The Essay in the Eighteenth Century." *Sewanee Review* X (January 1902): 12-27.

Smith, David Nichol. ed. *Eighteenth Century Essays on Shakespeare*.Glasgow: MacLehose, 1903.

"Ranger." "The English Essayists, II. Johnson and Goldsmith." *Bookman* (London) 28 (July 1905): 124-26.

Courthope, William J. *History of English Poetry*. London:Macmillan, 1905, Vol. 5.

Hill, George Birckbeck, Ed. *The Lives of the Poets*. 3 Vols. Oxford: Clarendon, 1905.

Rasselas. Ed. C. S. Fearenside. Introduction. London, 1906, vii-xx.

Warner, Beverley. *Famous Introductions to Shakespeare's Plays*. New York: Dodd, Mead, 1906, 110-70.

Strachey, Lytton. *Books and Characters*. London: Chatto and Windus, 1922. First printed in *Independent Review* 10 (July 1906).

Raleigh, Walter. *Samuel Johnson*. Leslie Stephen Lecture. Oxford: Clarendon, 1907.

Conant, Martha P. *The Oriental Tale in England in the Eighteenth Century*. New York: Columbia University Press, 1908, 140-54.

Collins, J. Churton. "Dr. Johnson's 'Lives of the Poets,'" *Quarterly Review*, 208 (January 1908): 72-97.

"Johnson's Poems" *Athenaeum* (4 September 1909): 259.

Makower, Stanley V. *Richard Savage: A Mystery in Biography*. London: Hutchinson, 1909.

Johnson, Charles F. *Shakespeare and His Critics*. Boston: Houghton Mifflin, 1909.

Lane, John. "Johnson's Poems" *Athenaeum*. 4272 (11 September 1909): 298-99.

Rasselas. Ed. A. J. F. Collins. Introduction. London: Cline, 1910, ix-xxix.

Raleigh, Walter A. *Six Essays on Johnson*. Oxford: Clarendon, 1910, 33.

Saintsbury, George. *The English Novel*. London: Dent. 1913, 34-35.

Howells, W. D. "Editor's Easy Chair." *Harper's* 131 (1915): 310-13.

Williams, J. B. "Dr. Johnson's Accusation against Milton." *British Review* 9 (1915): 431-40.

Wheatley, Henry B. "Shakespeare's Editors, 1603—to the Twentieth Century." *Transactions of the Bibliographical Society*, 16 (October 1915-March 1917): 164-66.

Dunn, Waldo H. *English Biography*. London: Dent, 1916, 102-29.

Goad, Caroline. "Samuel Johnson," In *Horace in the English Literature of the Eighteenth Century*. Yale Studies in English, 58. New Haven, Conn.: Yale University Press, 1918, 233-70.

Hudson, William Henry. *Johnson and Goldsmith and Their Poetry*, ed. Poetry and Life Series. London: George G. Harrap, 1918.

Walkley, Arthur B. "Johnson and the Theatre." *Fortnightly Review* 105 (April 1919): 578-87.

Thayer, William Roscoe. *The Art of Biography*, New York: Scribner, 1920, 84-100.

Markland, Russell. "Dr. Johnson and Shelley." *Notes and Queries*, 12th ser. 9 (1921): 368.

McDowall, Arthur. "Johnson and Wordsworth: A Contrast in Travel." *London Mercury*, 3 (1921): 269-78.

Roscoe, Edward Stanley. "Johnson and Wordsworth in the Highlands" *North American Review*, 214 (November 1921): 690-96.

Armstrong, T. Percy. "Emerson and Dr. Johnson." *Notes and Queries* 12th series 10 (4 March 1922): 167.

Nethercot, Arthur H. "The Term 'Metaphysical Poets' before Johnson." *Modern Language Notes* 37 (1922): 11-17.

Strachey, Lytton. "The Lives of the Poets." In *Books and Characters*, London: Chatto and Windus, 1922, 71-80.

Saintsbury, George. *A History of English Prosody*. Vol. 2, London: Macmillan, 1923, 460-63.

Houston, Percy H. *Doctor Johnson: A Study in 18th-Century Humanism.* Cambridge, Mass.: Harvard University Press, 1923.

Powell, Lawrence F. "*Rasselas.*" *Times Literary Supplement.* (22 February 1923): 124.

Maclean, Catherine M. "Dr. Johnson in the Highlands." *English Review* 39 (1924): 686-90.

Tinker, Chauncey B. "*Rasselas* in the New World." *Yale Review* 14 (October 1924): 95-107.

Quayle, Thomas. *Poetic Diction: A Study of Eighteenth Century Verse.* London: Methuen, 1924.

Christie, O. F. *Johnson the Essayist.* London: Grant Richards, 1924.

Walker, Hugh. *English Satire and Satirists* London: Dent, 1925, 229-31.

Nethercot, Arthur H. "The Reputation of the 'Metaphysical' Poets during the Age of Johnson and the 'Romantic' Revival." *Studies in Philology* 22 (January 1925): 81-132.

Belloc, Hilaire. "Mrs. Piozzi's *Rasselas.*" *Saturday Review of Literature.* 2 (August 1925): 37-38.

Powell, Lawrence F. "Johnson's Part in The Adventurer." *Review of English Studies.* 3 (October 1927): 42-29.

Palser, Ernest M. *A Commentary & Questionnaire on the History of Rasselas.* London: Pitman, 1927.

Roberts, Sydney Castle. "On the Death of Dr. Robert Levet: A Note on the Text." *Review of English Studies* 3 (1927): 442-45.

Nicolson, Harold. *The Development of English Biography*, London: Hogarth, 1927, 79-86.

Raysor, Thomas M. "The Downfall of the Three Unities." *Modern Language Notes*. 42 (1927): 1-9.

Brown, Joseph Epes. "Goldsmith and Johnson on Biography." *Modern Language Notes*. 42 (March 1927): 168-71.

Bridges, Robert S. *Collected Essays, Papers*. Vol. 3. London: OxfordUniversity Press, 1928, 59-70.

Maurois, André. *Aspects de la Biographie*. Based on his Clark Lectures, 1928. Paris: Au Sans Pareil, 1928, 81-85. (La Conciliabule des Trente.) Translated by S. C. Roberts as *Aspects of Biography*. Cambridge: Cambridge University Press: New York: Appleton, 1929.

Quiller-Couch, Sir Arthur. *Studies in Literature*, Cambridge: Cambridge University Press, 1929, 43-45.

Lovat-Fraser, J. A. "Ghosts in the Isle of Coll." *Contemporary Review*. 135 (April 1929): 478-85.

Garrod, H. W. *The Profession of Poetry*. Oxford: Clarendon, 1929, 110-30.

Smith, David Nichol. *Samuel Johnson's Irene*. Oxford: Clarendon, 1929.

London: A Poem and The Vanity of Human Wishes, with Introduction by T. S. Eliot. London: Etchells and Macdonald, 1930.

Longaker, John Mark. *English Biography in the Eighteenth Century*. Philadelphia: University of Pennsylvania Press, 1931, 314-406.

Robinson, Herbert S. *English Shakespearian Criticism in the Eighteenth Century*. New York: H. W. Wilson, 1932, 121-46.

Collins, Norman. *Facts of Fiction*. London: Gollancz, 1932, 82-84.

Baker, Ernest A. *The History of the English Novel*. London: H. F. & G. Witherby, 1934, 5, 55-76.

Evans, Bergen B. "Dr. Johnson's Theory of Biography" *Review of English Studies*. 10 (July 1934): 301-10.

Sutherland, James R. *The Medium of Poetry*. London: Hogarth, 1934, 86-87.

Lovett, David. "Shakespeare as a Poet of Realism in the Eighteenth Century. *ELH* 2 (1935): 267-89.

Clark, Arthur Melville. *Autobiography: Its Genesis and Phases*. Edinburgh: Oliver and Boyd, 1935, 10-15.

Lovett, David. "Shakespeare as a Poet of Realism in the Eighteenth Century." *ELH* 2 (1935): 267-89.

Murphy, Mallie J. "The Rambler, No. 191." *Publications of the Modern Language Association of America* 50 (1935): 926-28.

Jones, Gwyn. *Richard Savage*. London: Gollancz, 1935.

McAdam, Edward L., Jr. "A Johnson Pamphlet." *Times Literary Supplement* (14 March 1936): 228.

Hazen, Allen T. *Bulletin of the Institute of the History of Medicine*. 4 (June 1936): 455-65.

Britt, Albert. *The Great Biographers*. New York: Whittlesey House, [1936], 67-76.

Pratt, Willis Winslow. "Leigh Hunt and The Rambler." *University of Texas Studies in English.* 1938, 67-84.

Lindsay, Jack. *Life and Letters Today.* 22 (1939): 384-93.

Ferguson, James. "Worthy Nairn." *Cornhill Magazine,* 159 (1939): 101-15.

Bradford, Curtis B. "Johnson's Revision of The Rambler." *Review of English Studies* 15 (July 1939): 302-14.

Jenkins. Harold D. "Some Aspects of the Background of *Rasselas.*" In his *Studies in English in Honor of R. D. O'Leary and S. L. Whitcomb.* University of Kansas, 1940.

Leyburn, Ellen Douglass. "The Translations of the Mottoes and Quotations in the Rambler," *Review of English Studies* 16 (April 1940): 169-76.

Osborn, James M. *John Dryden: Some Biographical Facts and Problems.* New York: Columbia University Press, 1940, 22-38.

Johnson, Edgar. *A Treasury of Biography.* New York: Howell, Soskin, 1941, 148-201.

Cameron, Kenneth N. "A New Source for Shelley's *A Defence of Poetry.*" *Studies in Philology* 38 (1941): 629-44.

Smith, David Nichol and Edward L. McAdam, Jr. *The Poems of Samuel Johnson.* Oxford: Clarendon, 1941.

Smith. "Samuel Johnson's Poems," *Review of English Studies* (January 1943): 44-50.

McAdam. "Johnson's Lives of Sarpi, Blake, and Drake." *Publications of the Modern Language Association of America* 58 (June 1943): 466-76.

Krutch, Joseph Wood. *Samuel Johnson.* New York: Henry Holt, 1944, 174-84.

Bronson, Bertrand H. *Johnson and Boswell: Three Essays.* University of California Publications in English, 3, no. 9. 1944.

Dobrée, Bonamy. *English Essayists.* London: William Collins, 1946, 22-24.

Carver, George. *Alms for Oblivion.* Milwaukee: Bruce Publishing Co., 1946, 123-36.

Bronson, Bertrand H. "Personification Reconsidered." *ELH* 14 (1947): 163-77.

Brown, Wallace Cable. "Johnson as Poet." *Modern Language Quarterly* 8 (March 1947): 53-64.

Wimsatt, William K., Jr., *Philosophic Words.* New Haven, Conn.: Yale University Press, 1948.

Eastman, Arthur M. "Johnson's Shakespearean Labors in 1765." *Modern Language Notes* 63 (1948): 512-15.

Tate, Allen. "Johnson on the Metaphysicals." *Kenyon Review* 11 (Summer 1949): 379-94.

Williams, Harold. "Swift's Early Biographers." in *Pope and His Contemporaries,* eds. James L. Clifford and Louis A. Landa. Oxford: Clarendon, 1949, 114-28.

Keast, William R. "Johnson's Criticism of the Metaphysical Poets." *ELH* 17 (March 1950): 59-70.

Eastman, Arthur M. "The Texts From Which Johnson Printed His Shakespeare." *Journal of English and Germanic Philology* 49 (1950): 182-91.

Eastman. "Johnson's Shakespeare and the Laity." *Publications of the Modern Language Association of America* 65 (1950):1112-21.

Moore, John Robert. "Johnson as Poet." *Boston Public Library Quarterly* 2 (April 1950): 156-66.

Metzdorf, Robert F. "*The Second Sequel to Rasselas.*" *New Rambler* 16 (1950): 5-7.

Horsman, E. A. "Dryden's French Borrowings." *Review of English Studies* n. s. 1 (1950): 346-51.

Hart, Edward. "Some New Sources of Johnson's *Lives.*" *Publications of the Modern Language Association of America* 65 (1950): 1088-1111.

Tracy, Clarence R. "Democritus, Arise." *Yale Review* 39 (1950): 294-310.

Tillotson, Kathleen. "Arnold and Johnson." *Review of English Studies* n. s.., 1 (April 1950): 145-47.

Darbishire, Helen. *Milton's Paradise Lost.* London: Oxford University Press, 1951, 7ff.

Lascelles, Mary. "*Rasselas* Reconsidered." *Essays and Studies by Members of the English Association* , n. s.. 4 (1951): 37-52.

Sherbo, Arthur. "Dr. Johnson on *Macbeth*: 1745 and 1765." *Review of English Studies* n. s. 2 (1951): 40-47.

Kolb, Gwin J. "The Structure of *Rasselas.*" *Publications of the Modern Language Association* 66 (1951): 698-717.

Hagstrum, Jean. *Samuel Johnson's Literary Criticism.* Minneapolis: University of Minnesota Press, 1952.

Bloom, Edward A. "Symbolic Names in Johnson's Periodical Essays." *Modern Language Quarterly* 13 (1952): 333-53.

Johnson, Maurice. "A Literary Chestnut: Dryden's 'Cousin Swift.'" *Publications of the Modern Language Association* 67 (1952): 1024-34.

Davie, Donald. *Purity of Diction in English Verse.* London: Chatto and Windus, 1952, 82-90.

Jack, Ian. "'Tragical Satire': *The Vanity of Human Wishes.*" in *Augustan Satire.* Oxford: Clarendon, 1952, 135-45.

Leavis, F .R. *The Common Pursuit.* New York: New York University Press, 1952, 115.

Bloom, Edward A. "Symbolic Names in Johnson's Periodical Essays." *Modern Language Quarterly* 13 (1952): 333-52.

Moore, John Robert. "Conan Doyle, Tennyson, and *Rasselas.*" *Nineteenth Century Fiction* 7 (1952): 221-23.

Allison, James. "Joseph Warton''s Reply to Dr. Johnson's Lives." *Journal of English and Germanic Philology* 51 (1952): 186-91.

Johnson, Maurice. "A Literary Chestnut: Dryden's 'Cousin Swift,'" *Publications of the Modern Language Association,* 67 (1953): 1024-34.

Kolb, Gwin J. "The Use of Stoical Doctrines in *Rasselas*, Chapter XVIII." *Modern Language Notes* 58 (1953): 439-47.

Connelly, Cyril, ed. *Great English Short Novels*, New York: Dial, 1953.

Graham, W. H. "Dr. Johnson's *The Rambler.*" *Contemporary Review* 184 (July 1953): 50-53.

Schoff, Francis G. "Johnson on Juvenal." *Notes and Queries* (July 1953): 293-96.

Monaghan, T. J. "Johnson's Additions to His Shakespeare for the Edition of 1773." *Review of English Studies* n. s.. 4 (July 1953): 234-48.

Tracy, Clarence R. *The Artificial Bastard: A Biography of Richard Savage.* Toronto: University of Toronto Press, 1953.

Sherbo, Arthur. "The Mottoes to Idlers 88 and 101." *Johnsonian News Letter* 13 no. 4 (1953), 10-11.

Graham, W. H. "Dr. Johnson's The Rambler." *Contemporary Review* 184 (July 1953), 50-53.

Boyce, Benjamin. "Samuel Johnson's Criticism of Pope in the Life of Pope." *Review of English Studies* n. s. 5 (1954): 37-46.

Moore, John Robert. "*Rasselas* and the Early Travelers to Abyssinia." *Modern Language Quarterly* 15 (1954): 36-41.

Osgood, C. G. "Johnson and Macrobius." *Modern Language Notes* 59 (1954): 246.

Hovey, Richard B. "Dr. Samuel Johnson, Psychiatrist." *Modern Language Quarterly* 15 (1954): 321-35.

Sherbo, Arthur. "Two Notes on Johnson's Revisions." *Modern Language Review* 50 (1955): 311-15.

Bate, Walter Jackson. *The Achievement of Samuel Johnson.* New York: Oxford University Press, 1955.

Chapin, Chester F. *Personification in Eighteenth-Century English Poetry.* New York: Columbia University Press, 1955.

Whitley, Alvin. "The Comedy of *Rasselas.*" *ELH* 23 (1956): 48-70.

Sherbo, Arthur. "Johnson and a Note by Warburton." *Johnsonian Newsletter* 16 (1956): 11-12.

Watson, Melvin R. *Magazine Serials and the Essay Tradition, 1746-1820.* Louisiana State University Studies, Humanities Series, No. 6. Baton Rouge: Louisiana State University Press, 1956.

Boyce, Benjamin. "Johnson's Life of Savage and Its Literary Background." *Studies in Philology* 53 (October 1956): 576-98.

Wagley, Mary F. and Philip F. "Comments on Samuel Johnson's Biography of Sir Thomas Browne." *Bulletin of the History of Medicine* 31 (July-August 1957): 318-26.

Tucker, Susie I., and Henry Gifford. "Johnson's On the Death of Dr. Robert Levet." *Explicator* 15 (1957): 9.

Tucker and Gifford. "Johnson's Latin Poetry." *Neophilologus* 16 (July, 1957): 215-21.

Garraty, John A. *The Nature of Biography.* New York: Knopf, 1957.

Kenney, William. "Johnson's *Rasselas* After Two Centuries." *Boston University Studies in English* 3 (Summer 1957): 88-96.

Bronson, Bertrand. *Samuel Johnson: Poems and Selected Prose.* New York: Holt, Rinehart and Winston, 1958, xv-xvi.

Hilles, Frederick W. "The Making of The Life of Pope." In *New Light on Dr. Johnson: Essays on the Occasion of His 250th Birthday* edited by Frederick W. Hilles. New Haven, Conn.: Yale University Press, 1959, 257-84.

Morgan, H. A. "Johnson's Life of Savage." *Contemporary Review* 195 (January, 1959): 38-41.

Lombardo, Agostino. "The lmportance of lmlac." *Cairo Studies in English* (1959): 31-49.

Butt, John. "Pope and Johnson in Their Handling of the Imitation." *New Rambler,* 1959, 3-14.

Kenney, William. "*Rasselas* and the Theme of Diversification." *Philological Quarterly* 38 (1959): 84-89.

Sherburn, George. "Rasselas Returns—to What?" *Philological Quarterly* 38 (1959): 383-84.

Tillotson, Geoffrey. "Time in *Rasselas.*" in *Bicentenary Essays on Rasselas* edited by Magdi Wahba. Supplement to *Cairo Studies in English.* 1959, 97-103.

Lascelles, Mary. "Johnson and Juvenal." in *New Light on Dr. Johnson* edited by Frederick D. Hilles. 1959, 35-55.

Ricks, Christopher. "Notes on Swift and Johnson." *Review of English Studies* n. s.. 11(1960): 412-13.

Hart, Jeffrey. "Johnson's *A Journey to the Western Islands*: History as Art," *Essays in Criticism* 10 (1960): 44-59.

Greene, Donald J. "Johnsonian Critics," *Essays in Criticism* 10 (1960): 476-80.

Adler, Jacob H. "Johnson's 'He That Imagine This.'" *Shakespeare Quarterly* 11 (1960): 225-28.

Elder, A. T. "Irony and Humour in the *Rambler.*" *University of Toronto Quarterly* 30 (1960): 57-71.

Knieger, Bernard. "The Moral Essays of Dr. Samuel Johnson."*Personalist* 42 (Summer 1961): 361-6.

Aden, John M. "*Rasselas* and *The Vanity of Human Wishes.*" *Criticism* 3 (Fall 1961): 295-303.

Voitle, Robert. *Samuel Johnson the Moralist.* Cambridge, Mass.: Harvard University Press 1961. 37-46.

Eddy, Donald D. "Samuel Johnson's Editions of Shakespeare (1765)."*Publications of the Bibliographical Society of America* 56 (4th quarter, 1962): 428-44.

Fleischauer, Warren. "Johnson, Lycidas, and the Norms of Criticism." in *Johnsonian Studies,* Cairo,1962, 235-56.

Grange, Kathleen M. "Dr. Samuel Johnson's Account of a Schizophrenic Illness in *Rasselas* (1759)." *Medical History* 6 (1962): 162-69.

Leicester, James H. "Johnson's Life of Shenstone: Some Observations on the Sources." in *Johnsonian Studies*, edited by Magda Wahba. Cairo, U. A. R.: Privately printed, 1962, 189-222.

Fleeman, J. D. "Some Proofs of Johnson's *Lives of the Poets.*"*Library* 17 (1962): 213-30.

Leyburn, Ellen Douglass. "Two Allegorical Treatments of Man: *Rasselas* and *La Peste.*" *Criticism* 4 (1962): 197-209.

Mayo, Robert D. *The English Novel in the Magazines, 1740-1815.* Evanston, Ill.: Northwestern University Press, 1962, 93-117.

Keast, W. R. "Johnson and Cibber's Lives of the Poets, 1753." in *Restoration and Eighteenth-Century Literature*, edited by Carroll Camden. Chicago: University of Chicago Press for Rice University, 1963, 89-101.

Lockhart, Donald M. "'The Fourth Son of the Mighty Emperor': The Ethiopian Background of Johnson's *Rasselas.*" *Publications of the Modern Language Association*, 78 (1963): 516-28.

Kaul, R. K. "*A Journey to the Western Isles* Reconsidered." *Essays in Criticism* 13 (1963): 341-50.

Lasser, Michael L. "Johnson in Scotland: New Life amid the 'Ruins of Iona.'" *Midwest Quarterly* 4 (1963): 227-34.

Buckley, Vincent. "Johnson: The Common Condition of Man." *Melbourne Critical Review* (1963): 16-30.

Watson, Tommy G. "Johnson and Hazlitt on the Imagination in Milton." *Southern Quarterly* 2 (January 1964): 123-33.

Leicester, James H. "Dr. Johnson and Isaac Watts." *New Rambler* 1964, 122-36.

Siegel, Paul N. *His Infinite Variety: Major Shakespearean Criticism Since Johnson.* New York: J. B. Lippincott, 1964.

Fleeman, J. D. "Johnson's 'Journey' (1775) and Its Cancels." *Publications of the Bibliographical Society of America* 58 (1964): 232-38.

Hilles, F. W,. "*Rasselas*, an 'Uninstructive Tale.'" *Johnson, Boswell and Their Circle: Essays Presented to Lawrence Fitzroy Powell.* Edited by Mary M. Lascelles, James L. Clifford, J. D. Fleeman, and John P. Hardy. Oxford: Clarendon Press, 1965, 111-21.

Kendall, Lyle H., Jr. "A Note on Johnson's Journey (1775)." *Publications of the Bibliographical Society of America*, 59 (1965): 317-18.

Altick, Richard D. "Johnson and Boswell." In *Lives and Letters: A History of Literary Biography in England and America.* New York: Knopf, 1965, 4-74.

Lascelles, Mary. "Notions and Facts: Johnson and Boswell on Their Travels." In *Johnson, Boswell and their Circle: Essays Presented to Lawrence Fitzroy Powell*, edited by Mary M. Lascelles, James L. Clifford, J. D. Fleeman. Oxford: Clarendon, 1965, 215-29.

Abbott, John L. "Dr. Johnson, Fontenelle, Le Clerc, and Six 'French' Lives." *Modern Philology* 58 (1965): 121-27.

Hardy, John. "Johnson and Raphael's Counsel to Adam." In *Johnson, Boswell, and their Circle*, Oxford 1965, 122-36.

Waingrow, Marshall. "The Mighty Moral of Irene." In *From Sensibility to Romanticism*, edited by Frederick Hilles and Harold Bloom. New York: Oxford University Press,1965, 79-92.

Elder, A. T. "Thematic Patterning and Development in Johnson's Essays." *Studies in Philology* 57 (1965): 610-32.

Rhodes, Rodman D. "Idler No. 24 and Johnson's Epistemology." *Modern Philology* 64 (August 1966): 10-21.

Fogle, Richard H. "Johnson and Coleridge on Milton." *Bucknell Review* 14 (March 1966): 26-32.

Kallich, Martin. "Samuel Johnson's Principles of Criticism and Imlac's 'Dissertation upon Poetry.'" *Journal of Aesthetics and Art Criticism* 25 (1966): 71-82.

Butt, John. *Biography in the Hands of Walton, Johnson, and Boswell*. Ewing Lectures, 1962. Los Angeles: University of California Press, 1966.

Sherbo, Arthur. "Johnson's Intent in the Journey to the Western Islands of Scotland." *Essays in Criticism* 16 (1966): 382-97.

Fleischmann, Wolfgang Bernard. "Shakespeare, Johnson, and the Dramatic 'Unities of Time and Place.'" *Studies in Philology* 4 (1967): 128-34.

Tracy, Clarence. "Johnson's Journey to the Western Islands of Scotland: A Reconsideration." *Studies on Voltaire and the Eighteenth Century* (Institut et Musée Voltaire, Geneva) 58 (1967): 1593-1606.

Tillotson, Geoffrey. "Imlac and the Business of a Poet." In *Studies in Criticism and Aesthetics, 1660-1800: Essays in Honor of Samuel Holt Monk*. Edited by Howard Anderson and John S. Shea, Minneapolis: University of Minnesota Press, 1967, 296- 314.

Schalit, Ann E. "Literature as Product and Process: Two Differing Accounts of the Same Trip." *Serif* 4 (1967): 10-17.

Jones, Emrys. "The Artistic Form of *Rasselas*." *Review of English Studies* n. s. 18 (1967): 387-401.

Grover, P. R. "The Ghost of Dr. Johnson: L. C. Knights and D. A. Traversi on *Hamlet*," *Essays in Criticism* 17 (1967): 143-57.

Alkon, Paul. *Samuel Johnson and Moral Discipline*. Evanston, Ill.: Northwestern University Press, 1967.

Sachs, Arieh. *Passionate Intelligence: Imagination and Reason in The Works of Samuel Johnson*. Baltimore: Johns Hopkins Press, 1967.

Clifford, James L. "How Much Should a Biographer Tell? Some Eighteenth-Century Views." In *Essays in Eighteenth-Century Biography*, edited by Philip B. Daghlian. Bloomington: Indiana University Press, 1968, 67-95.

Hardy, John. "Stockdale's Defence of Pope." *Review of English Studies* n. s. 18 (1967): 49-54.

Sigworth, Oliver F. "Johnson's *Lycidas*: The End of Renaissance Criticism." *Eighteenth-Century Studies* 1 (1967): 159-8.

Greene, Donald J. "The Uses of Autobiography in the Eighteenth Century." in *Essays in Eighteenth-Century Biography*, edited by Philip B. Daghlian. Bloomington: Indiana University Press, 1968, 43-66.

Corder, Jim W. "Ethical Argument and Rambler No. 154." *Quarterly Journal of Speech 54* (1968): 352-56.

Wiles, R. M. "The Contemporary Distribution of Johnson's *Rambler.*" *Eighteenth-Century Studies*, 2 (1968): 155-71.

Warncke, Wayne. "Samuel Johnson on Swift: The Life of Swift and Johnson's Predecessors in Swiftian Biography." *Journal of British Studies* 7 (1968): 56-64.

Bernard, F. V. "A Possible Source for Johnson's Life of the King of Prussia." *Philological Quarterly* 47 (1968): 206-15.

Meier, Thomas K. "Johnson on Scotland." *Essays in Criticism*, 18 (1968): 349-52.

Bell, Vereen M. "Johnson's Milton Criticism in Context." *English Studies*, 49 (1968): 127-32.

Wimsatt, W. K. "In Praise of *Rasselas*: Four Notes (Converging)." In *Imagined Worlds: Essays on Some English Novels and Novelists in Honor of John Butt*, edited by Maynard Mack and Ian Gregor. London: Methuen, 1968, 111-36.

Milne, Victor. Reply to Sigworth "Johnson's *Lycidas.*" *Eighteenth-Century Studies* 2 (1969): 300-302.

Hardy, John. *Rasselas*. Introduction. New York: Oxford University Press, 1968, viii-xxiv.

Bullough, Geoffrey. "Johnson the Essayist" *New Rambler* 1968, 16-33.

Kelley, Robert E. "Studies in Eighteenth-Century Autobiography." In *Essays in Eighteenth-Century Biography*, edited byPhilip B. Daglian, Bloomington: Indiana University Press, 1968, 102-8.

Wolper, Roy S. "Johnson's Neglected Muse: The Drama." In *Studies in the Eighteenth Century: Papers Presented at the David Nichol Smith Memorial Seminar, Canberra* 1966, Edited by R. F. Brissenden, Canberra: Australian National University Press, 1968, 109-17.

Korshin, Paul J. "Johnson and Swift: A Study in the Genesis of Literary Opinion." *Philological Quarterly* 48 (1969): 464-78.

Weinbrot, Howard D. *The Formal Strain: Studies in Augustan Imitation and Satire*. Chicago: University of Chicago Press, 1969.

Battersby, James L. "Patterns of Significant Action in the 'Life of Addison.'" *Genre* 2 (March 1969): 28-42.

Milne, Victor. *Eighteeenth-Century Studies* 2 (1969), 300-302.

Sigworth, Oliver. *Eighteenth-Century Studies* 2 (1969), 300-302.

Battersby, James L. "Johnson and Shiels: Biographers of Addison." *Studies in English Literature* (Rice University), 9 (1969): 522-37.

Preston, Thomas R. "The Biblical Context of Johnson's *Rasselas.*" *Publications of the Modern Language Association* 84 (1969): 274-81.

Hart, Francis R. "Johnson as Philosophic Traveler: The Perfecting of an Idea." *ELH* 36 (1969): 679-95.

Jemielity, Thomas. "'More in Notions than Facts': Samuel Johnson's Journey to the Western Islands." *Dalhousie Review* 49 (1969): 319-30.

Lipking, Lawrence. "The Lives of the Poets." In Lipking, *The Ordering of the Arts in Eighteenth-Century England*. Princeton, N. J.: Princeton University Press, 1970, 405-62.

Turnage, Maxine. "Samuel Johnson's Criticism of the Works of Edmund Spenser." *Studies in English Literature* 10 (1970): 557-67.

Krieger, Murray. "Fiction, Nature, and Literary Kinds in Johnson's Criticism of Shakespeare." *Eighteenth-Century Studies* 4 (1970): 184-98.

Lascelles, Mary. "*Rasselas*: A Rejoinder." *Review of English Studies*, 21 (1970): 49-56.

Greene, Donald. *Samuel Johnson*. New York: Twayne, 1970.

O'Flaherty, Patrick. "Dr. Johnson as Equivocator: The Meaning of *Rasselas*." *Modern Language Quarterly* 31 (1970): 195-208.

Schwartz, Richard B. "Johnson's Journey." *Journal of English and Germanic Philology* 69 (1970): 292-303.

Bloom, Edward A., and Lillian D. Bloom. "Johnson's 'Mournful Narrative': The Rhetoric of 'London.' " In *Eighteenth-Century Studies in Honor of Donald F. Hyde*, edited by W. H. Bond. New York: Grolier Club, 1970, 107-44.

Budick, Sanford. "The Demythological Mode in Augustan Verse." *ELH* 37 (1970): 389-414.

Kupersmith, William. "Declamatory Grandeur: Johnson on Juvenal." *Arion* 9 (1970): 52-72.

O'Flaherty, Patrick. "The Rambler's Rebuff to Juvenal: Johnson's Pessimism Reconsidered." *English Studies* 51 (1970): 517-27.

Selden, Raman. "Dr. Johnson and Juvenal: A Problem in Critical Method." *Comparative Literature* 22 (1970): 289-302.

Weinbrot, Howard D. "Samuel Johnson's 'Short Song of Congratulation' and the Accompanying Letter to Mrs. Thrale: The Huntington Library Manuscripts." *Huntington Library Quarterly* 34 (1970): 79-80.

Woodman, T. M. "An Echo of Parnell in Johnson's 'London," *Notes and Queries* 17 (1970): 300.

Bate, Walter Jackson. "Johnson and Satire Manqué." In *Eighteenth-Century Studies in Honor of Donald F. Hyde* edited by W. H. Bond. New York Grolier Club, 1970, 145-60.

Langford, Thomas. "'Vanity of Vanities, All is Vanity.'" *Christianity and Literature* 20 (1970): 10-13.

O'Flaherty, Patrick. "The Rambler's Rebuff to Juvenal: Johnson's Pessimism Reconsidered." *English Studies* 51 (1970): 517-27.

Rewa, Michael. "Aspects of Rhetoric in Johnson's 'Professedly Serious' Rambler Essays." *Quarterly Journal of Speech* 56 (1970): 75-84.

Weinbrot, Howard. "The Reader, the General and the Particular." *Eighteenth-Century Studies* 5 (Fall 1971): 80-96.

Greene, Donald. *Samuel Johnson.* New York: Twayne, 1970.

Maxwell, J. C. "Quotation in Johnson's Letters." *Notes and Queries* 18 (1971): 346.

Middendorf, John H. "Ideas vs. Words: Johnson, Locke, and the Edition of Shakespeare," In *English Writers of the Eighteenth Century* edited by John H. Middendorf. New York: Columbia University Press, 1971, 249-72.

Harrison, Charles T. "Common Sense as Approach." *Sewanee Review* 79 (Winter 1971): 1-10.

Richman, Jordan. "Subjectivity in the Art of Eighteenth Century Biography: Johnson's Portrait of Swift." *Enlightenment Essays* 2 (1971), 91-102.

Schwartz, Richard B. *Samuel Johnson and the New Science.* Madison: University of Wisconsin Press, 1971, 155-56.

Pagliaro, Harold E. "Structural Patterns of Control in *Rasselas.*" In *English Writers of the Eighteenth Century* edited by John H. Middendorf. New York: Columbia University Press, 1971, 208-29.

Johnson, Samuel. *A Journey to the Western Islands of Scotland* edited by Mary Lascelles. New Haven and London: Yale University Press, 1971. (Vol. 9 of the Yale Johnson Edition.)

Fussell, Paul. *Samuel Johnson and the Life of Writing.* New York: Harcourt Brace Jovanovich, 1971, 216-48.

Moody, A. D. "The Creative Critic: Johnson's Revisions of *London* and *The Vanity of Human Wishes,*" *Review of English Studies* 22 (1971), 137-50.

Jenkins, Ralph E. "'And I travelled after him': Johnson and Pennant in Scotland,"

Studies in Language and Literature 14 (1972): 445-62.

Preston, Thomas R. "Homeric Allusion in A Journey to the Western Islands of Scotland." *Eighteenth-Century Studies* 5 (1972): 545-58.

Damrosch, Leopold, Jr. *Samuel Johnson and the Tragic Sense.* Princeton, N. J.: Princeton University Press, 1972, 152-53.

Swearingen, James E. "Johnson's 'Life of Gray.'" *Texas Studies in Language and Literature* 14 (1972): 283-302.

Boyd, D. V. "Vanity and Vacuity: A Reading of Johnson's Verse Satires." *ELH* 39 (1972): 387-403.

Mell, Donald C. "Johnson's Moral Elegiacs: Theme and Structure in 'On the Death of Robert Levet.'" *Genre* 5 (1972): 293-306.

White, Ian. "The Vanity of Human Wishes." *Cambridge Quarterly* 6 (1973): 115-25.

Wilson, Gayle Edward. "Poet and Moralist: Dr. Johnson's Elegiac Art and 'On the Death of Dr. Robert Levet.'" *Enlightenment Essays* 4 (1973): 29-38.

White, Ian. "On *Rasselas.*" *Cambridge Quarterly* 6 (1973): 6-31.

McIntosh, Carey. *The Choice of Life: Samuel Johnson and the World of Fiction*. New Haven: Yale University Press, 1973.

Fleeman, J. D. ed. *Early Biographical Writings of Dr. Johnson*. Westmead, Hampshire: Gregg International, 1973.

Damrosch, Leopold, Jr. "Johnson's Manner of Proceeding in the Rambler." *ELH* 40 (1973): 70-89.

Sherbo, Arthur. "1773: The Year of Revision." *Eighteenth-Century Studies* 7 (1973): 18-39.

Stock, R. D. *Samuel Johnson and Neoclassical Dramatic Theory: The Intellectual Context of the Preface to Shakespeare*. Lincoln: University of Nebraska Press, 1973.

Schwartz, Richard B. "Johnson's 'Mr. Rambler' and the Periodical Tradition." *Genre* 7 (1974): 196-204.

Curley, Thomas M. "Philosophic Art and Travel in the Highlands: Johnson's *A Journey to the Western Islands of Scotland.*"*Exploration* 2 (1974): 8-23.

Clayton, Philip T. "Samuel Johnson's *Irene*: 'An Elaborate Curiosity.'" *Tennessee Studies in Literature* 19 (1974): 121-35.

Holtz, William. "We Didn't Mind His Saying So: Homage to Joseph Wood Krutch: Tragedy and the Ecological Imperative." *American Scholar* (1974): 267-79.

Alkon, Paul K. "The Intention and Reception of Johnson's Life of Savage." *Modern Philology* 72 (1974), 139-50.

Dussinger, John A. "Johnson's Life of Savage: The Displacement of Authority." In his *The Discourse of the Mind in Eighteenth-Century Fiction*. The Hague: Mouton, 1974, 127-47.

Griffin, Dustin. "Johnson's Funeral Writings." *ELH* 41 (1974): 192-211.

Batten, Charles L., Jr. "Samuel Johnson's Sources for 'The Life of Roscommon.'" *Modern Philology* 72 (1974): 185-89.

Reynolds, Richard R. "Johnson's Life of Boerhaave in Perspective." *Yearbook of English Studies* 5 (1975): 115-29.

Donaldson, Ian. "The Satirist's London." *Essays in Criticism* 25 (1975): 101-22.

Horne, Colin J. "Johnson's Corrections of Lines 137-38 of *The Vanity of Human Wishes*." *Publications of the Bibliographical Society of America* 69 (1975): 552-60.

Kupersmith, William. "'More like an Orator than a Philosopher': Rhetorical Structure in *The Vanity of Human Wishes*." *Studies in Philology* 72 (1975), 454-72.

McGlynn, Paul D. "Rhetoric as Metaphor in The Vanity of Human Wishes." *Studies in English Literature* 15 (1975): 473-82.

O'Flaherty, Patrick A. "The Art of Johnson's *London*." In *A Festschrift for Edgar Ronald Seary: Essays in English Language and Literature presented by Colleagues and Former Students*, edited by A. A. Macdonald, P. A. O'Flaherty, and G. M. Story. St. John's Memorial University of Newfoundland, 1975, 77-89.

Hilles, Frederick W. "Dr. Johnson on Swift's Last Years: Some Misconceptions and Distortions." *Philological Quarterly* 54 (1975): 370-79.

Wasserman, Earl R. "Johnson's *Rasselas*: Implicit Contexts." *Journal of English and Germanic Philology* 74 (1975): 1 -25.

Phelps, Gilbert. Introduction. *Rasselas*. Edinburgh: Folio Society, 1975.

Mell, Donald C. *A Poetics of the Augustan Elegy: Studies of Poems by Dryden, Pope, Prior, Swift, Gray, and Johnson.* Amsterdam: Rodopi N. V., 1975, 77-89.

Lipking, Lawrence. "Learning to Read Johnson: *The Vision of Theodore* and *The Vanity of Human Wishes.*" *ELH* 43 (1976): 517-37.

Sherbo, Arthur. "Johnson's 'Falling Houses.'" *Essays in Criticism* 26 (1976): 376-78.

Hartog, Curt. "Johnson's Journey and the Theatre of Mind." *Enlightenment Essays* 7 (Spring 1976): 3-16.

Damrosch, Leopold, Jr. *The Uses of Johnson's Criticism.* Charlottesville: University Press of Virginia, 1976.

Booth, Mark W. "Johnson's Critical Judgments in *The Lives of the Poets.*" *Studies in English Literature* 16 (1976): 505- 15.

Weinbrot, Howard. "John Clarke's *Essay on Study* and Samuel Johnson on *Paradise Lost.*" *Modern Philology* 72 (1975): 404-07.

Hanchock, Paul. "The Structure of Johnson's Lives: A Possible Source." *Modern Philology* 74 (1976): 75-77.

Horne, Colin J. "The Biter Bit: Johnson's Strictures on Pope." *Review of English Studies* 27 (1976): 310-13.

Weinbrot, Howard D. "Johnson's London and Juvenal's Third Satire: The Country as 'Ironic' Norm." *Modern Philology* 73 (1976): 56-65.

Curley, Thomas M. "Johnson and the Geographical Revolution: *A Journey to the Western Islands of Scotland,*" *Studies in Burke and His Time* 17 (1976): 180-98.

Gray, James. "Mahomet and Irene: More Tragedy Than Triumph, Part I." *Humanities Association Review* 27 (1976): 421-40.

Curley, Thomas M. *Samuel Johnson and the Age of Travel.* Athens: University of Georgia Press, 1976. Reviewed by Joel J. Gold, *Journal of English and Germanic Philology* 76 (1977): 557-59.

Savage, George H. "'Roving Among the Hebrides': The Odyssey of Samuel Johnson." *Studies in English Literature* 17 (1977): 493-501.

McCarthy, William. "The Moral Art of Johnson's Lives." *Studies in English Literature* 17 (1977): 503-17.

Sitter, John E. "To *The Vanity of Human Wishes* through the 1740s." *Studies in Philology* 74 (1977): 445-64.

Walker, Robert G. *Eighteenth Century Arguments for Immortality and Johnson's Rasselas.* Victoria, B.C.: University of Victoria, 1977.

Vesterman, William. *The Stylistic Life of Samuel Johnson.* New Brunswick, N.J.: Rutgers University Press, 1977, 69-104.

Knight, Charles A. "The Writer as Hero in Johnson's Periodical Essays." *Papers in Language and Literature* 13 (1977): 238-50.

Murphy, Mary C. "A Computer-Assisted Study of the Sight and Sound Image Pattern in Samuel Johnson's *The Vanity of Human Wishes*," *Linguistics* 203 (1978): 5-27.

Koper, Peter T. "Samuel Johnson's Rhetorical Stance in *The Rambler*." *Style* 12 (1978): 23-34.

O'Flaherty, Patrick. "Towards an Understanding of Johnson's *Rambler*." *Studies in English Literature* 18 (1978): 523-36.

Selden, Raman. "The 18th-Century Juvenal: Dr. Johnson and Churchill." In his *English Verse Satire, 1590-1765*. London and Boston: Allen and Unwin, 1978, 153-75.

Bate, Walter Jackson. *Samuel Johnson*. London: Chatto and Windus, 1977, 336-39.

Davidson, Virginia Spencer. "Johnson's *Life of Savage*: The Transformation of a Genre," In *Studies in Biography*. edited by Daniel Aaron. *Harvard English Studies* Vol. 8. Cambridge, Mass.: Harvard University Press, 1978, 57-72.

Folkenflik, Robert. *Samuel Johnson, Biographer*. Ithaca, N. Y.: Cornell University Press, 1978.

Woodruff, James F. "The Allusions in Johnson's *Idler* No. 40." *Modern Philology* 76 (1979): 380-89.

Burke, John J., Jr. "Excellence in Biography: *Rambler* No. 60 and Johnson's Early Biographies." *South Atlantic Bulletin* 44 (1979): 14-34.

Edinger, William C. "The Background of *Adventurer* 95: Johnson, Voltaire, Dubos." *Modern Philology* 78 (1980): 14-37.

Parke, Catherine N. "Love, Accuracy, and the Power of an Object: Finding the Conclusion in *A Journey to the Western Islands*." *Biography* 3 (1980): 105-20.

Vance, John A. "Edward III or Edward, the Black Prince: Esoteric Symbolism in Thomson, Pope, and Johnson." *English Language Notes* 17 (1980): 256-59.

Ellis, Frank H. "Johnson and Savage: Two Failed Tragedies and a Failed Tragic Hero." *English Language Notes* 17 (1980): 256-59.

Weinbrot, Howard D. "No 'Mock Debate': Questions andAnswers in *The Vanity of Human Wishes*." *Modern Language Quarterly* 1980, 248-67.

Wendorf, Richard. "The Making of Johnson's 'Life of Collins.'" *Publications of the Bibliographical Society of America* 74 (1980): 95-115.

Brink, J. R. "Johnson and Milton." *Studies in English Literature* 20 (1980): 493-50.

Ehrenpreis, Irvin. "*Rasselas* and Some Meanings of 'Structure' in Literary Criticism." *Novel* 14 (1981): 101-17.

Finch, Geoffrey J. "Johnson's 'Sincerity' in London." *Papers in Language and Literature* 17 (1981): 353-62.

Orr, Leonard. "The Structural and Thematic Importance of the Astronomer in *Rasselas.*" *Recovering Literature* 9 (1981): 15-21.

Weinsheimer, Joel. "'London' and the Fundamental Problem of Hermeneutics." *Critical Inquiry* 9 (1982): 303-22.

McKenzie, Alan T. "Logic and Lexicography: The Concern with Distribution and Extent in Johnson's *Rambler.*" *Eighteenth-Century Life* 23 (1982): 49-63.

Kaminski, Thomas. "Was Savage 'Thales'?: Johnson's London and Biographical Speculation." *Bulletin of Research in the Humanities* 85 (1982): 322-35.

Needham, John. "Complexity and the Doctrine of Propriety in Johnson's Shakespeare Criticism" In *The Completest Mode: I. A. Richards and the Continuity of English Literary Criticism.* Edinburgh: Edinburgh University Press, 1982, 120-34.

Cohen, Michael M. "Johnson's Tragedy of Human Wishes." *English Studies* 63 (1982): 410-17.

Olson, Robert C. "Samuel Johnson's Metamorphosis of Ovid." *Comparative Literature Studies* 19 (1982): 11-20.

Radner, John B. "The Significance of Johnson's Changing Views of the Hebrides." In *The Unknown Samuel Johnson,* edited by John J. Burke, Jr. and Donald Kay. Madison: University of Wisconsin Press, 1983, 131-49.

Pierce, Charles E. *The Religious Life of Samuel Johnson.* London: Athlone Press, 1983.

Cullum, Graham. "Dr. Johnson and Human Wishing." *Neophilologus* 67 (1983): 305-19.

Bronson, Bertrand H. "Johnson, Travelling Companion, in Fancy and Fact." In *Johnson and His Age,* edited by James Engell. Cambridge: Harvard University Press, 1984, 163-87.

Fix, Stephen. "Distant Genius: Johnson and the Art of Milton's *Life.*" *Modern Philology* 81 (1984): 244-64.

Liu, Alan. "Toward a Theory of Common Sense: Beckford's *Vathek* and Johnson's *Rasselas.*" *Texas Studies Language and Literature* 26 (1984): 183-217.

Trowbridge, Hoyt. "The Language of Reasoned Rhetoric in *The Rambler.* " In *Greene Centennial Essays: Essays Presented to Donald Greene,* edited by Paul J. Korshin and Robert R. Allen. Charlottesville: University Press of Virginia, 1984, 200-216.

Kolb, Gwin J. "The Early Reception of *Rasselas.*" In *Greene Centennial Studies.* ed. Paul Korshin and R. R. Allen. Charlottesville: Univ. of Virginia Press, 1984, 217-49.

White, James Boyd. *When Words Lose Their Meaning: Constitutions and Reconstructions of Language, Character,and Community.* Chicago and London: University of Chicago Press, 1984.

Chapin, Chester. "Johnson's Intentions in *The Vanity of Human Wishes.*" *Eighteenth-Century Studies* 18 (1984): 72-75.

Jemielity, Thomas. *"The Vanity of Human Wishes*: Satire Foiled or Achieved?" *Essays in Literature* 11 (1984): 35-48.

Ricks, Christopher. "Samuel Johnson: Dead Metaphors and 'Impending Death.'" In his *The Force of Poetry*. Oxford: Clarendon Press, 1984, 80-88.

Kniskern, William F. "Satire and the 'Tragic Quartet' in *The Vanity of Human Wishes*." *Studies in English Literature* 25 (1985): 633-49.

Perkins, David. "Johnson and Modern Poetry." *Harvard Library Bulletin* 33 (1985): 303-12.

Stock, R. D. "Johnson Ecclesiastes." *Christianity and Literature* 34 (1985), 15-24.

Schwalm, David E. "Johnson's *Life of Savage*: Biography as Argument." *Biography* 8 (1985): 130-44.

Riley, Michael D. "Johnson's Proper Irony in *London* and T*he Vanity of Human Wishes*." *Renascence* 37 (1985): 108-30.

Grundy, Isobel. *Samuel Johnson and the Scale of Greatness*. Leicester: Leicester University Press, 1986.

Jemielity, Thomas. "Samuel Johnson, *The Vanity of Human Wishes* and Biographical Criticism." *Studies in Eighteenth-Century Culture* 15 (1986): 227-39.

Epstein, William H. "Patronizing the Biographical Subject: Johnson's Savage and Pastoral Power." In *Johnson After Two Hundred Years*, edited by Paul J. Korshin. Philadelphia: University of Pennsylvania Press, 1986, 141-57.

Brack, O. M., Jr. "The Gentleman's Magazine, Concealed Printing, and the Texts of Samuel Johnson's *Lives of Admiral Robert Blake and Sir Francis Drake*." *Studies in Bibliography* 40 (1987): 140-46.

Greene, Donald. "Samuel Johnson, Psychobiographer: *The Life of Richard Savage*." In *The Biographer's Art*, edited by Jeffrey Meyers. London: Macmillan, 1987.

Wheeler, David, ed. *"Domestick Privacies"*: *Samuel Johnson and the Art of Biography*. Lexington: University Press of Kentucky, 1987.

Temmer, Mark J. *Samuel Johnson and Three Infidels: Rousseau, Voltaire, Diderot*. Athens: The University of Georgia Press, 1988.

Maner, Martin. *The Philosophic Biographer*. Athens: The University of Georgia Press, 1988,

Parker, G. F. *Johnson's Shakespeare* Oxford: Clarendon, 1989.

Tomarken, Edward. *Johnson, 'Rasselas,' and the Choice of Criticism*. Lexington: University Press of Kentucky, 1989.

Davis, Philip. *In Mind of Johnson: A Study of Johnson's "The Rambler."* Athens: The University of Georgia Press, 1989.

Gill, R. B. "The Enlightened Occultist: Beckford's Presence in *Vathek*." In *Vathek and the Escape from Time: Bicentenary Revaluations*. Edited by Kenneth Graham. New York: AMS, 1990, 131-43.

Campbell, Charles L. "Image and Symbol in *Rasselas*: Narrative Form and 'The Flux of Life'" *Eighteenth-Century Studies* 1990, 263-77.

O'Shaughnessy, Toni. "Fiction as Truth." *Studies in English Literature* 30 (1990): 487-501.

Cafarelli, Annette Wheeler. *Prose in the Age of Poets: Romanticism and Biographical Narrative from Johnson to De Quincey.* Philadelphia: Pennsylvania University Press, 1990.

Braverman, Richard. "The Narrative Architecture of *Rasselas*,: *American Journal of Architecture* 1990, 91-111.

Hudson, Nicholas. "'Open' and 'Enclosed' Readings of *Rasselas*," *Eighteenth-Century Life* 31 (1990): 47-67.

Parke, Catherine N. *Samuel Johnson and Biographical Thinking.* Columbia: University of Missouri Press, 1991.

Tomarken, Edward. *Samuel Johnson on Shakespeare: The Discipline of Criticism.* Athens: The University of Georgia Press, 1991.

Henson, Eithne. *"The Fictions of Romantick Chivalry": Samuel Johnson and Romance.* Rutherford: Fairleigh Dickinson Press, 1992.

Gross, Gloria Sybil. *This Invisible Riot of the Mind: Samuel Johnson's Psychological Theory.* Philadelphia: University of Pennsylvania Press, 1992.

Lynn, Steven. *Samuel Johnson After Deconstruction: Rhetoric and The Rambler.* Carbondale, Illinois: Southern Illinois University Press, 1992.

INDEX

Johnson in the *Life* of Milton probably influenced by John Clarke's *Essay on Study*, 140

Weinsheimer, Joel, 168
uses *London* to question E. D. Hirsch's distinction between meaning and significance, 34

West, William, 152
Rasselas contains religious optimism, 68

"Whackum," 149
a "cure" for Johnson's inability to find enough old trees in Scotland, 106

Whale, George, 152
assesses Johnson's notions about travel in general, 109

Whately, Elizabeth Pope, 151
continuation of *Rasselas*, 67

Wheatley, Henry, 153
the first to point out that Johnson's Shakespeare is "practically the founder of the Variorum editions," 98

Wheeler, David, 168
edited a volume on the Johnsonian art of biography, 143

White, Ian, 164
argues that *Rasselas* can be seen to have as its final goal education, 85
distinguishing between the *Vanity* and *Rasselas*, 29

White, James Boyd, 168
on the *Rambler*, 58
first to suggest in concrete terms how the rhetoric of Johnson's

periodicals points to new ends, 60

White, Thomas Holt, 151
disagreed with Johnson's criticism of Milton, 124

Whitehead, Charles, 7, 151
alters the narrative to first person, 12

Whitley, Alvin:
modifies the comic view of *Rasselas*, 76

Wiles, R. M., 162
original distribution of the *Rambler*, 53

William Shaw, William:
defenders of Ossian not able to produce an original, 107

Williams, Harold, 156
assesses Johnson's *Life* of Swift, 129

Williams, J. B., 153
attempts to disprove Johnson's assumption that Milton was responsible for the publication of a heathen prayer, 127

Wilson Gayle, 164
points to the epideictic elements of "On the Death of Dr. Robert Levet," 30

Wimsatt, William, Jr., 156, 162
the prose of Johnson's maturity, 51
doubts as to the significance of structure in *Rasselas*, 80

Wolper, Roy, 162
demonstrates that Johnson understood and appreciated the theater of his day, 41

Woodruff, James, 55-56, 167